CW00539262

Memento

Within a short space of time, the film Memento has already been hailed as a modern classic. Memorably narrated in reverse, from the perspective of Leonard Shelby, the film's central character, it follows Leonard's chaotic and visceral quest to discover the identity of his wife's killer and avenge her murder, despite his inability to form new long-term memories.

This is the first book to explore and address the myriad philosophical questions raised by the film, concerning personal identity, free will, memory, knowledge, and action. It also explores problems in aesthetics raised by the film through its narrative structure, ontology, and genre. Beginning with a helpful introduction that places the film in context and maps out its complex structure, specially commissioned chapters examine the following topics:

- Memory, emotion, and self-consciousness
- Agency, free will, and responsibility
- Personal identity
- Narrative and popular cinema
- Film genre such as neo-noir
- Memento and multimedia.

Including annotated further reading at the end of each chapter, Memento is essential reading for students interested in philosophy and film studies.

Contributors: Noël Carroll, Richard Hanley, Andrew Kania, Deborah Knight and George McKnight, Joseph Levine, Raymond Martin, Michael McKenna, and John Sutton.

Andrew Kania is Assistant Professor of Philosophy at Trinity University, San Antonio. His principle research is in the philosophy of music, film, and literature and he is the co-editor (with Theodore Gracyk) of the forthcoming Routledge Companion to Philosophy and Music.

Philosophers on Film

> The true significance of film for philosophy, and of philosophy for film, cannot be established in abstract or general terms. It can only be measured in and through individual philosophers' attempts to account for their experience of specific films. This series promises to provide a productive context for that indispensable enterprise.
>
> Stephen Mulhall, Fellow and Reader in Philosophy,
> New College, Oxford

In recent years, the use of film in teaching and doing philosophy has moved to center stage. Film is increasingly used to introduce key topics and problems in philosophy, from ethics and aesthetics to epistemology, metaphysics, and philosophy of mind. It is also acknowledged that some films raise important philosophical questions of their own. Yet until now, dependable resources for teachers and students of philosophy using film have remained very limited. *Philosophers on Film* answers this growing need and is the first series of its kind.

Each volume assembles a team of international contributors to explore a single film in depth, making the series ideal for classroom use. Beginning with an introduction by the editor, each specially commissioned chapter will discuss a key aspect of the film in question. Additional features include a biography of the director and suggestions for further reading.

Philosophers on Film is an ideal series for students studying philosophy and film, aesthetics, and ethics and anyone interested in the philosophical dimensions of cinema.

Available:

- *Talk to Her*, edited by A. W. Eaton
- *The Thin Red Line*, edited by David Davies
- *Eternal Sunshine of the Spotless Mind*, edited by Christopher Grau

Forthcoming:

- *Blade Runner*, edited by Amy Coplan
- *Fight Club*, edited by Thomas E. Wartenberg
- *Vertigo*, edited by Katalin Makkai

Memento

Edited by

Andrew Kania

Routledge
Taylor & Francis Group

LONDON AND NEW YORK

This edition published 2009
by Routledge
2 Park Square, Milton Park, Abingdon, Oxon OX14 4RN

Simultaneously published in the USA and Canada
by Routledge
270 Madison Ave, New York, NY 10016

Routledge is an imprint of the Taylor & Francis Group, an informa business

Typeset in Joanna by
Florence Production Ltd, Stoodleigh, Devon
Printed and bound in Great Britain by
CPI Antony Rowe, Chippenham, Wiltshire

British Library Cataloguing in Publication Data
A catalogue record for this book is available from the British Library

Library of Congress Cataloging in Publication Data
Memento/edited by Andrew Kania.
     p. cm.—(Philosophers on film)
    Includes bibliographical references and index.
  1. Memento (Motion picture).   2. Philosophy in motion pictures.
  3. Memory in motion pictures.   4. Identity (Psychology) in motion
pictures.   5. Motion pictures—Aesthetics.   I. Kania, Andrew.
PN1997.M4344M46 2009
791.43'72—dc22   2008053198

ISBN10: 0–415–77473–X (hbk)
ISBN10: 0–415–77474–8 (pbk)
ISBN10: 0–203–87659–8 (ebk)

ISBN13: 978–0–415–77473–4 (hbk)
ISBN13: 978–0–415–77474–1 (pbk)
ISBN13: 978–0–203–87659–6 (ebk)

Contents

Illustrations

Contributor biographies

Noël Carroll is a Distinguished Professor at the Graduate Center of the City University of New York. His most recent books are *The Philosophy of Motion Pictures* and *On Criticism*. Presently he is writing a book on humor for Oxford University Press.

Richard Hanley is Associate Professor in Philosophy at the University of Delaware. He specializes in metaphysics, philosophy of language, ethics, and philosophy and popular culture. He is the author of *The Metaphysics of Star Trek*, the main author of *Philosophy and South Park: Bigger, Longer, and More Penetrating*, and has published several articles on science fictions.

Andrew Kania is Assistant Professor of Philosophy at Trinity University in San Antonio. His principle research is in the philosophy of music, film, and literature. He recently won the inaugural Essay Prize of the British Society of Aesthetics, and is currently co-editing *The Routledge Companion to Philosophy and Music* with Theodore Gracyk.

Deborah Knight is Associate Professor of Philosophy at Queen's University, Kingston, Canada. Her main research area is the philosophy of art, with emphases on literature and film. Recent publications include chapters in *Philosophy of Film and Moving Pictures* (eds Noël Carroll and Jinhee Choi), the *Oxford Handbook of Aesthetics* (ed. Jerrold Levinson), *Dark Thoughts:*

Philosophical Reflections on Cinematic Horror (eds Stephen J. Schneider and Jay Shaw), and *Literary Philosophers? Borges, Calvino, Eco* (ed. Jorge Gracia *et al.*).

Joseph Levine received his BA in philosophy from UCLA in 1975, and his Ph.D. in philosophy from Harvard University in 1981. He has taught at North Carolina State University, The Ohio State University, and moved recently to the University of Massachusetts at Amherst. He is the author of *Purple Haze: The Puzzle of Consciousness*, which was published by Oxford University Press in 2001, and many articles on the philosophy of mind dealing with the problems of consciousness and intentionality.

Raymond Martin (Ph.D. Rochester, 1968) is Dwane W. Crichton Professor of Philosophy and Chair of the Department, Union College, Schenectady, New York. He is also Professor and Distinguished Scholar Teacher Emeritus, University of Maryland, College Park. His books, some co-authored or co-edited, include: *The Rise and Fall of Soul and Self*, Columbia University Press, 2006; *Personal Identity*, Blackwell, 2003; *Naturalization of the Soul*, Routledge, 2000; *Self-Concern*, Cambridge University Press, 1998; *Self and Identity*, Macmillan, 1991; and *The Past Within Us*, Princeton University Press, 1989.

Michael McKenna received his Ph.D. from University of Virginia in 1993. He is currently professor of philosophy at Florida State University. Previously he held a tenured position at Ithaca College, and has taught as a visitor at Bryn Mawr College and University of Colorado, Boulder. He has published various articles mostly on the topics of free will and moral responsibility.

George McKnight has recently retired from the Film Studies Program of the School for Studies in Art and Culture at Carleton University. He has edited *Agent of Challenge and Defiance: The Films of Ken Loach*, and has published articles on British cinema. With Deborah Knight, he has co-authored papers on *American Psycho*, *The Matrix*, Hitchcock's use of suspense, and detective narratives.

John Sutton is research professor in MACCS, the Macquarie Centre for Cognitive Science at Macquarie University in Sydney, where he was previously Head of the Department of Philosophy. He has been a visiting fellow at UCLA, Edinburgh, UCSD, and Warwick. He is co-editor of *Descartes' Natural Philosophy* and of the new interdisciplinary journal *Memory Studies*, and author of *Philosophy and Memory Traces: Descartes to Connectionism* and of recent articles on memory, distributed cognition, and dreaming. His current research addresses shared memory and social memory, and embodied skills and kinesthetic memory. He co-hosted a community radio program, Ghost in the Machine, on Eastside Radio in Sydney from 2001 to 2005, and he plays for Macquarie University Cricket Club.

Acknowledgements

"Oh, gee, thanks."

—Leonard to Teddy (A, 1:45:37)

I FIRST SAW MEMENTO in Washington, D.C., in the spring of
2001. I saw it again a couple of weeks later, in a state of somewhat
altered consciousness, with Jerry Levinson and the other students in his
aesthetics seminar. I was hooked. In trying to solve the narrative puzzles
the film presents I was led to the film's promotional website, and began
to ponder an ontological puzzle about Memento: Is it really just a film, or is
the website material part of the work of art that goes under the name
Memento? I was soon bending the ears of whoever would listen to help me
think about this and other issues connected with Memento. I would like to
thank some of those people here, though I am bound to leave some out,
to whom I apologize.

First, I should thank all my students at the University of Maryland,
College Park, and Trinity University for the invigorating discussions
they have had with me about the film. They provided me with opportunities to see the film again and again, and helped me look at it with
fresh eyes.

In 2005, Tom Wartenberg gave me the opportunity to put my
thoughts about the ontology of Memento into a serious form by inviting

me to participate in the Seventh Annual Comparative Literature Conference at the University of South Carolina, "Thinking on the Boundaries: The Availability of Philosophy in Film and Literature." Paisley Livingston and Carl Plantinga then kindly invited me to contribute a chapter on Memento to the Routledge Companion to Philosophy and Film, which led to Tony Bruce's invitation to submit a proposal for a volume on Memento in Routledge's series Philosophers on Film—the volume that you now hold in your hands. Both Tony and Adam Johnson have been wonderful to work with, and I thank them both for all their prompt replies to my many emails and their helpful advice.

I would like to thank Mark Conard, Amy Coplan, Gregory Currie, Berys Gaut, Paisley Livingston, Thaddeus Metz, Bradley Rives, Allen Stairs, and Matthew Talbert, who all provided helpful and detailed comments on drafts of various parts of the book.

I have had nothing but support from my colleagues at Trinity, both in the philosophy department and beyond. I should make special mention of Paul Myers, who watched the film closely with me, and Curtis Brown who gave generously of his time in helping with the line drawings and stills. Rob Chapman provided excellent technical support in preparing the stills. The Writers' Bloc—Rubén Dupertuis, Nicolle Hirschfeld, Denise Pope, and Harry Wallace—helped keep me on task. The Office of Academic Affairs awarded me a summer stipend that helped me to bring the book together. I am also grateful to Shirley Durst, who proofread much of the book.

I thank Julie Post for putting up with more conversation about a single film than anyone but a film scholar should have to. Not only is my work much better for those discussions, but this book would not be here were it not for her.

Finally, thanks to the contributing authors, whose book this really is.

A.K.
San Antonio, Texas
October, 2008

Note on the director

BORN IN LONDON in 1970, **Christopher Nolan** was fascinated with film from an early age, making short films with toy figures and his family's Super 8 camera. The son of American and English parents, his formative years in Chicago saw him experimenting in the medium with future director and producer Roko Belic. After returning to England, Nolan studied English Literature at University College London, where he made 16mm films with the college film society.

His first success as a young film-maker came in 1989 when *Tarantella* (1989) was featured on the PBS production *Image Union*, a showcase for independent films. A second short, *Larceny* (1996), was screened at the 1996 Cambridge Film Festival. *Doodlebug* (1997) eventually gained wide distribution in 2003 when it appeared on the *Cinema 16* DVD compilation of short films by British directors. Nolan's feature-length directorial debut, *Following* (1998), tells the story of a would-be writer seduced and set up by a con-man and his femme-fatale partner in crime. The film is also an experiment in the non-linear narrative structures that Nolan would employ to great effect in *Memento* and *The Prestige*.

Memento (2000), Nolan's first commercial film, quickly became a cult classic and a critical success, with Nolan's screenplay nominated for an Oscar and a Golden Globe. The film is structured around the fractured consciousness of its protagonist, Leonard Shelby, who claims to have been robbed of the ability to form new long-term memories by the assailants who broke into his house and raped and murdered his wife. The central narrative is presented in reverse chronological order, putting the audience into Leonard's epistemic shoes.

Nolan followed *Memento* with *Insomnia* (2002), a remake of Norwegian Erik Skjoldbjærg's 1997 film. He was then contracted by Warner Bros to revitalize the Batman franchise, directing *Batman Begins* (2005) and *The Dark Knight* (2008), the highest-grossing film in an opening weekend, and the fourth highest-grossing film of all time.

Between the first two installments of his Batman sequence, Nolan made *The Prestige* (2006). This film returns to the thematic concerns and intricate narrative structure of *Following* and *Memento*, telling the story of rival nineteenth-century magicians each willing to sacrifice anything to become the greatest illusionist in the world.

Throughout his feature films, from *Following* to *The Dark Knight*, Nolan has been centrally concerned with the nature of the self, and how it can be warped and fragmented both from the outside, by other people, and— under pressure from desire and obsession—from within.

Andrew Kania

INTRODUCTION

"Great story. Gets better every time you tell it."
— Teddy (A, 1:42:24)

TO SAY THAT MEMENTO (2000) IS thought-provoking would be, at best, an understatement. One of the main reasons for this neonoir's popular success is that audiences were hooked by the very puzzles that make the film a challenging one. These puzzles occur at various levels. There is the initial question of what exactly the structure of the film is and, once this is solved, the much more difficult task of extracting the story—what actually happens in the film, and the chronological order of the fictional events—from the fragmented plot. At the same time, however, the film quite explicitly raises philosophical questions such as what makes us who we are, both at any given moment in time and across time, with an emphasis on the role of memory.

One of the things that elevates *Memento* above other films that raise such issues is the interrelation of these puzzles. If you have a different view of memory from the person next to you, it might affect your view of the plausibility of the various interpretations of the events presented in the film. Depending on how you think one's past informs one's present responsibility for one's actions, you may find Leonard more or less blameworthy for his bloody deeds. Thus, as with our understanding of the world itself, the typical viewer's understanding of Memento is constantly changing: figuring out that one of the characters is lying in a particular scene might lead to certain details in other scenes becoming more salient, which might lead to another interpretive breakthrough, and so on.

In this volume, a number of leading philosophers address a variety of the philosophical puzzles Memento raises. I don't think any of them would claim to have found the definitive answer to the puzzles they address, but I'm certain that anyone intrigued by these puzzles will benefit from the clarity with which these philosophers set out their own thoughts about them.

Memento

Memento is the story of Leonard Shelby, a former investigator for an insurance company, who is on a quest to avenge his wife's murder. At some unspecified time before the main period covered by the film (a mere 48 hours), Leonard and Catherine Shelby's house was broken into. Catherine was raped and apparently killed, and Leonard suffered a blow to the head. However, Leonard believes, contrary to the official police report, that two people were involved in "the incident," one of whom, known only as "John G," escaped the scene of the crime without a trace. It is John G whom Leonard plans to find and kill in revenge for his wife's rape and murder. He is aided, or at least accompanied, in this task by John Edward "Teddy" Gammell—a cop, or former cop, whose motives are unclear. What is clear, at least by the end of the film, is that neither Teddy, whom we see Leonard kill in the first scene of the film, nor Jimmy Grantz, whom we see Leonard kill in the last scene, is actually the John G he seeks.

Jimmy is a drug dealer Teddy is double-crossing. Teddy has framed him as Leonard's John G in order to get him out of the way, leaving Teddy to pick up the $200,000 Jimmy has brought to what he thinks is a drug deal. Unfortunately for Teddy, in the wake of killing Jimmy, Leonard uncovers Teddy's ruse, and not only takes Jimmy's car for his own, along with the cash in the trunk, but sets himself up to kill Teddy as John G. The main action of the film shows Leonard slowly hunting Teddy down, along the way enlisting the aid of Natalie, Jimmy's girlfriend, and in turn helping her to get rid of Dodd, who is waiting for the drugs Jimmy was supposed to buy on his behalf.

If you have not seen Memento, none of this will make much sense, since I have withheld one key piece of information: The injury Leonard sustained during the incident left him with an impaired memory. As Leonard describes it, the condition he suffers from is "anterograde amnesia." This means that although his memory functions perfectly well with respect to events that occurred before the incident, he is unable to form new long-term memories. (This condition is confusingly glossed as "short-term memory loss" throughout the film. In fact, Leonard's short-term memory works perfectly well.)

Writer-director Christopher Nolan's stroke of genius was to elevate Leonard's condition to the structural principle of the film. Like Gaspar Noë's Irreversible (2002), another revenger's tragedy, Memento contains a series of scenes, shot in color, that are presented in reverse chronological order. In Noë's film, this narrative structure, like the title, suggests a kind of determinism. But in Memento, the same structure serves the very different purpose of putting us in Leonard's epistemic shoes. That is, just like Leonard, we do not know what events led up to those we witness at any given moment in the film. This, together with the film's focus on Leonard's point of view, plays a large part in our identification with Leonard.[1] Of course, unlike Leonard, we often know what will occur after the events we are viewing, and we can retain this information in memory (at least some of it!) in order to piece the story together by the end of the film.

However, Memento's structure is more complex than that of Irreversible, for it contains another sequence of scenes, shot in black and white, that are presented in normal chronological order, interleaved with the color scenes. All the black and white scenes occur, in the story's fictional world, before any of the color scenes. So, numbering the black and white scenes 1–21, and the color scenes B–V, we can represent the film's action, as it occurs chronologically in the fictional world, as in Figure 0.1 (Klein 2001):

Figure 0.1 The structure of Memento's story

If we bend this chronology in the middle, folding it back on itself (Figure 0.2) . . .

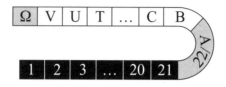

Figure 0.2 The generation of Memento's plot by a hairpin turn in the plot

. . . we can see why Nolan describes the structure of Memento as a "hairpin" (quoted in Mottram 2002: 33). The chronology of the film itself can thus be represented as in Figure 0.3:

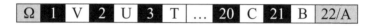

Figure 0.3 The structure of Memento's plot

An additional layer of complexity is provided by flashbacks. Within the black and white scenes, these are usually to the story of Sammy Jankis (Stephen Tobolowsky), the subject of Leonard's first serious insurance investigation, who apparently suffered from a condition very like Leonard's, and whose wife (Harriet Sansom Harris) apparently also met with a tragic fate. The color flashbacks usually represent Leonard's memories of his wife.

The two scenes I have not yet described, Ω and 22/A, are perhaps the most cunning in the film. 22/A is the hairpin scene, where the two chronological series in the film—forwards and backwards, monochrome and color—come together. Scene 22 begins in Leonard's motel room, where all of the black and white scenes have occurred, but follows Leonard as he leaves the room to go and kill Jimmy. Leonard takes a Polaroid of Jimmy, as he usually does when encountering a new person, though in this case he does so after killing Jimmy, presumably as a memento of having achieved his vengeance. As the Polaroid develops, in a close-up, color fades into not only the photograph but the whole shot, so subtly that many viewers miss the transition.[2] Scene A continues in color until the film ends, with the inexorable logic of its narrative structure, at the tattoo parlor where Leonard arrives at the beginning of the previous color scene (B).

The scene I label "Ω" is a color scene—the first scene in the film, but the last in the chronology of the fiction. It records Teddy's death at the hands of Leonard. But it does so in a more literally backward fashion than the reversed narrative of the other color scenes in the film. As the image in a fresh Polaroid slowly *fades away*, blood oozes *up* the wall, until Teddy's broken glasses tremble before flying onto his face, and Leonard's gun leaps into his hand, the fatal bullet sucked back into its barrel, pulling Teddy's brains back into his screaming skull. For the shooting of this scene, Nolan used a "reverse mag": Basically, the film was loaded into the camera backwards, so that when it was processed and projected, the events it recorded would appear to be temporally reversed. The one exception was the shot where the shell casing begins to move on the ground (0:02:28). Because this shot was such a tight close-up, it had to filmed "forwards," with Christopher Nolan on his hands and knees just outside the frame, blowing on the casing.[3] Interestingly, the soundtrack of this scene consists of "forwards" sounds, that is, unlike the images, the soundtrack has not been reversed. As Nolan puts it: "We can't hear backwards sounds. I wanted people to watch it as a physical sequence. If you reverse the sound, the physicality is gone. I wanted a realistic physical scene that happens to be chronologically reversed" (Nolan, quoted in Mottram 2002: 133).

Due to *Memento*'s structural complexity, we have adopted the convention throughout this book of referring to scenes by means of the labels given above, the time elapsed, or both. I have also supplied, after this introduction, tables summarizing the action of the individual scenes, arranged in both the order in which they occur in the film, and their chronological order within the fictional world. Both tables are keyed to the two major DVD editions of the film for ease of reference.

The DVD editions of the film add another layer of complexity. They contain (as "extras") the fictional material that first appeared on the official *Memento* website (still available at www.otnemem.com). This material derives from the time between the incident and the main action of the film—a period arguably not represented in the film—and includes newspaper clippings about Leonard's crimes, censored excerpts from Leonard's medical file, and notes Leonard has written to himself. If taken into account, this material arguably has significant impact on one's interpretation of the film, as I discuss in my chapter in this volume.

The Limited Edition (LE) DVD of Memento makes considering the possibility that Leonard has spent time in a mental institution since the incident unavoidable. Its organizing conceit is that it is Leonard's file from a mental institution he has presumably spent time in since the incident. Not only is the box designed to look this way, but the DVD menus are little puzzles in themselves. In order to access the film, or any of the sub-menus on the disc, you must select the right word or image from a large array, including several dead ends. Selecting the right item presents you with more apparent psychological tests, and the way you complete some of them has an effect on what you end up accessing, while others are irrelevant. This can be very frustrating, especially since there are some worthwhile special features, such as a version of Memento re-edited to follow the chronology of the fictional world, that is, according to the first diagram above. (Fortunately for us, Douglas Bailey has created a printable guide to navigating this DVD, available at http://world.std.com/~trystero/Memento_LE.html.) Watching the re-edited version of the film is, if nothing else, a very informative lesson in narrative theory. What you might think is a simplified version of the film is almost as difficult to follow as the original, not to mention that the pacing is very clunky, since, of course, the individual scenes were created with the actual structure of the film in mind. (For more on the narrative lessons to be learnt from Memento, see Noël Carroll's essay in this volume.)

I should also mention some apparent complexity at the other end of production. The penultimate opening credit claims that Memento is "based on the short story by [Christopher's brother] Jonathan Nolan" (0:01:47), and in an interview included on the regular edition DVD, Christopher says that Jonathan's story is "back-story" for the film. In fact, though, Jonathan Nolan had the original idea, and Christopher and Jonathan then worked on their projects relatively independently, as is evident from the huge differences between the resulting works.[4]

Film and philosophy

It has become *de rigueur* when discussing the philosophical interest of a film to address the relationship between philosophy and film. In particular, there is heated debate over whether or not, or the extent to which, film can "do philosophy," and the supposedly concomitant value of such work as the book you are now reading. Thus many such books or articles begin with an *apologia* explaining how it is that film can do philosophy, and by extension the (at least potential) value of the work defended.[5] I will avoid such a defense, since it seems to me that even the sceptics about film's ability to do philosophy claim nothing that would require such a defense. For example, the most that even Bruce Russell (2000) claims about texts on filmic philosophy, as opposed to the films themselves (and he is arguably the greatest sceptic about film's philosophical potential) is that what philosophical value such texts have is to be attributed to their authors, rather than to the film or its maker. The champions of philosophy through film, by contrast, claim that the philosophical value of such texts is to be attributed, at least in part, to the films from which their insights have been gleaned, or to those films' creators. What does not seem to be in dispute is the potential value of texts about philosophy through film. Thus such texts seem to require no apology, and it is such texts that constitute this volume.

Memento and philosophy

At the end of each color scene in *Memento*, we see something we have seen before—Natalie banging the lid of the dumpster behind the bar, or Teddy shouting "Lenny!"—that links the scene to its predecessor. (Its predecessor in the film, that is; its *successor* from a point of view within the fictional world). Nolan calls these moments of overlap "loops," noting that the different context of each repeated event leads us to see it differently.[6] The essays in this volume loop back over several issues in a similar fashion; each time the same topic is covered, the different context in which it is addressed sheds new light on the subject. The volume opens with Michael McKenna's essay on the extent to which Leonard can be considered a moral agent, responsible for the actions he commits in the course of the film. In order to consider that question, McKenna finds he must address issues of scepticism, knowledge of the self and others, the limits of the human mind, personal identity, and the role that truth and narrative play in giving our lives meaning. Thus his essay also serves well as an introduction to several others in the volume, which take up different threads in the tapestry of questions McKenna sees *Memento* as raising.

The next three essays consider different aspects of memory—arguably the central concept *Memento* addresses. Joseph Levine discusses the way memory works epistemologically, that is, with respect to giving us knowledge. He argues that the "architectural approach" to the philosophy of mind (according to which the mind consists of a central processing unit connected to a number of modules dedicated to specific tasks and isolated from one another) can explain why Leonard's system fails better than its main contenders, including the "extended-mind hypothesis" (according to which Leonard's mementos are simply part of his mind). John Sutton examines in detail the many different kinds of interrelated processes that we lump together under the single label "memory." He argues not only that *Memento* is a remarkably detailed illustration of some of these overlapping processes, showing us things about memory we don't usually notice, but that we can in turn use theories of memory to uncover aspects of the film otherwise easily missed. Raymond Martin, like Leonard throughout the film, considers the role memory plays in giving our lives meaning. Although Martin shows that memory has great instrumental and intrinsic value for us, he argues that even someone like Leonard can live a meaningful life, since there are many other things that contribute to a life's meaning, which can compensate to some extent for even such terrible losses as Leonard's.

Although, within Nolan's oeuvre, memory is a theme unique, or at least uniquely central, to *Memento*, there are other issues in which the film-maker has an abiding interest. *Memento* is the second film in what I see as an informal trilogy beginning with Nolan's first feature, *Following* (1998), and concluding with *The Prestige* (2006). All three films employ a fractured narrative structure, and all three take the nature of the self as a central theme. For instance, in both *Following* and *The Prestige* we encounter protagonists who let themselves be shaped by their perverse relationships with others, such as the protagonist's idolization of the slimy Cobb in *Following*. In *The Prestige*, each magician's desire to be the supreme illusionist motivates Angier's obsession with Borden, the Borden brothers' bizarre relationships to each other, and their perverse relationships with those dear to them. *Memento* is the most elegantly structured of these three films, and is the most successful in integrating the narrative structure with the "content" of the film, both at the level of the story (where it mirrors Leonard's condition), and the deeper levels of meaning in the film (for example, in raising the question of the extent to which we are all like

Leonard). But, as in the other two films, we see the protagonist being shaped by others. Leonard's beliefs, desires, and actions are diverted by Teddy, Natalie, and, most shockingly, Leonard himself.

Richard Hanley's essay grapples with an even more fundamental question about Leonard's personal identity: the question of whether Leonard's very self is compromised by his condition. Although we refer to "Leonard" throughout the film, is there really a single person whom that name picks out? Or is there rather only a series of "partial persons" who resemble each other in various ways? Hanley argues that Leonard is a single person according to any of the major theories of personal identity, but that thinking about cases like Leonard's can lead us to decide between these theories. Hanley ends by considering some cases of more radical personal reversal than that represented in Memento.

Noël Carroll looks closely at the reversed narrative structure that reflects Leonard's psychological fragmentation, and asks what other work it might be doing in the film. Carroll's answer is that Memento's structure teaches us not only about the human self, but also, reflexively, about the nature of narrative itself. More specifically, by employing a narrative structure that no viewer can comprehend "transparently," that is, without explicitly thinking about it, Nolan forces us to consider how it is that we understand not only films with confusing structures, but any narrative film. As Carroll notes, this concern with narrative is clear in Nolan's preceding film, Following, the very title of which is a double entendre referring to both the protagonist's voyeuristic activities and the audience's attempts to piece the film together. It is also evident in The Prestige, where parallels are implicitly drawn between the desire that draws us towards the deceptions of both magic and narrative film as entertainments.

The last two essays in the book follow Carroll's lead in considering Memento not only for its fictional and thematic content, but from the outside, as it were, as a work of art.[7] Deborah Knight and George McKnight consider Memento as a contemporary film noir, or "neo-noir." Their consideration of the ways in which Memento reconsiders various noir tropes is fascinating in itself, but Knight and McKnight argue further that it is precisely these aesthetic features of the film that lead to both (i) the narrative and thematic questions raised by the film, and (ii) some of the constraints on how we might go about answering them.[8]

In the final essay in this volume, my own, I consider the nature of the viewer's detective work in attempting to uncover the truth of what happens in *Memento*. Many viewers are led to the suggestive material that originally appeared on the promotional website for the film, and has been reproduced on DVD editions of it. I consider the status of this material, asking whether it should be considered a legitimate part of *Memento* for interpretive purposes. I conclude that because of the mainstream-film tradition in which Nolan was working, and the lack of any clear indication that *Memento* is a hybrid work, this material should not be considered part of the work. *Memento* is in fact the ordinary kind of thing that most people take it to be—a film—although it is an extraordinary instance of its kind.

Notes

1   By "Leonard's point of view" here, I do not just mean first-person camera angles, presenting things as Leonard would see them, which are in fact not used too often. I mean a general approach that includes all sorts of techniques for keeping Leonard center-stage in the audience's mind. Two such devices Nolan mentions in his commentary on the DVD are the tendency of the camera (i) to look over Leonard's shoulder, particularly as he enters a new environment, and (ii) to be closer to Leonard than to other characters in general, even in classically symmetrical devices such as shot/reverse-shot dialogue scenes. Thus Leonard often quite literally looms larger than the other characters in the film.

2   The transition is also prepared for by a number of color flashbacks within (black and white) scene 22.

     One of the most interesting themes in Nolan's commentary track on the Limited Edition DVD is his discussion of how, as the film progresses, the tone of the black and white scenes (that are initially very cool and objective, almost documentary) and the color scenes (initially more subjective) converges on the climactic scene in which the two sequences come together (22/A). Not only does this contribute to the seamless transition in the middle of the scene, it also adds to the sense of climax. One thing Nolan does not explicitly comment on is how the emotional tone is carefully modulated through the film across the black-and-white and color scenes, so that, for instance, tension is kept high across the scenes of Natalie's deception of Leonard and his "taking care of" Dodd (scenes G and F) by making the intervening black and white scenes (16 and 17) also high tension (in this case due to Leonard's discovery of his tattoo advising "NEVER ANSWER THE PHONE").

3   As it happened, in the confusion, the film was loaded backwards for this shot, too. "That was the height of complexity in terms of the film: an optical to make a backwards running shot forwards, and the forwards shot is a simulation of a backwards shot"! (Nolan, quoted in Mottram 2002: 133)

4 Jonathan's story, "Memento Mori," was originally published in Esquire magazine, and is available online: www.esquire.com/fiction/fiction/ memento-mori-0301?click=main_sr. It is also reprinted (with some changes) in Mottram (2002: 183–95). The relation between the idea, short story, and film, is discussed in Mottram (2002: 158–75) and Nolan (2001: 233–4).

5 Michael McKenna and Noël Carroll each provide a brief apologia of this sort in their essays in this volume. Richard Hanley voices a more sceptical view.

6 In fact, Nolan's attitude to these loops is slightly puzzling. For one thing, he explains why these loops are not in fact literal repetitions, why he introduced slight differences between them, by appealing to the importance of context to interpretation. But, of course, if context affects interpretation, he need not introduce such differences. Perhaps he means, rather, that he intends us to notice these differences and then wonder whether they are objective differences in the film or subjective impressions brought about by the different context. Also, these looped events are usually trivial markers, not items subject to interpretive dispute. But presumably Nolan intended them to prompt audiences to think more carefully about the objective status of more important events in the film.

7 Carroll's essay is actually a bridge between the earlier essays and these last two in this respect, since he argues that part of Memento's content is a substantive thesis about narrative art.

8 I assure you that "Knight and McKnight" are the authors' real names, despite how perfect those names would look in gold leaf on the door of a noir detective agency!

References

Klein, A. (2001) "Everything You Wanted to Know about Memento," online. Available at: http://archive.salon.com/ent/movies/feature/2001/06/28/ memento_analysis/index.html (accessed 15 October 2008).

Mottram, J. (2002) The Making of Memento, London: Faber and Faber.

Nolan, C. (2001) Memento and Following, London: Faber and Faber.

Russell, B. (2000) "The Philosophical Limits of Film," reprinted in N. Carroll and J. Choi (eds) (2006) Philosophy of Film and Motion Pictures, Malden, MA: Blackwell, pp. 387–90.

Further reading

Gaut, B. (1999) "Identification and Emotion in Narrative Film," reprinted in N. Carroll and J. Choi (eds) (2006) Philosophy of Film and Motion Pictures, Malden, MA: Blackwell, pp. 260–70. (A consideration of what it means to "identify" with a cinematic character, and some of the means by which such identification is elicited.)

Kania, A. (2008) "*Memento*," in P. Livingston and C. Plantinga (eds) *The Routledge Companion to Philosophy and Film*, London: Routledge, pp. 650–60. (A short overview of the philosophical interest of *Memento*.)

Wartenberg, T. (2007) *Thinking on Screen: Film as Philosophy*, London: Routledge. (A defense of the idea that film can "do philosophy," including several case studies.)

Scene tables

THROUGHOUT THE BOOK, we have adopted the convention of referring to scenes by means of the labels given below, the time elapsed in hours:minutes:seconds, or both (e.g. V, 0:03:10). All times given are approximate, and based on the American Limited Edition DVD. The times on the regular DVD often differ by a few seconds, and on discs that use different formats (e.g., those released for the British market), the differences may be greater.

Plot (scenes listed in the order in which they occur in the film)

Scene	DVD Chapter (Regular/ LE)	Time	Story
	1/1	0:00	[Opening credits, which continue over scene Ω.]
Ω	1/1	0:43	Leonard shoots Teddy and takes a Polaroid of Teddy's body.
1	2/2	2:33	FIRST SCENE OF DAY ONE: Loenard, in his room at the Discount Inn, describes the expreience of waking up in a hotel room with his condition.
V	2/2	2:57	Teddy arrives at the Discount Inn. He and Leonard drive to the derelict building. Leonard shoots Teddy.
2	3/3	6:24	Leonard begins explaining his condition, his system, and Sammy Jankis's story.

Plot (scenes listed in the order in which they occur in the film)

Scene	DVD Chapter (Regular/ LE)	Time	Story
U	3/3	7:00	Leonard writes "KILL HIM" on Teddy's Polaroid. He goes down to the lobby, discusses his condition with Burt, and pays for his room. Teddy arrives.
3	3/3	10:12	*Leonard continues explaining his system and begins shaving his thigh. The phone rings, and Leonard answers.*
T	4/4	11:05	In the bathroom, Leonard sees his "remember Sammy Jankis" tattoo. He returns to the Discount Inn and, examining his evidence, infers that Teddy is John G. He calls Teddy, who says he'll come over. He writes "HE IS THE ONE/KILL HIM" on Teddy's Polaroid.
4	5/4	16:11	*On the phone, Leonard continues to explain Sammy's story, comparing it to his own.*
S	5/4	16:57	Leonard meets Natalie at a restaurant. She gives him a copy of Teddy's driver's license and registration. They discuss the point of Leonard's quest for a revenge he won't remember. Natalie gives Leonard directions to a derelict building as a place for Leonard to take John G. Leonard goes to the bathroom and sees his "remember Sammy Jankis" tattoo.
5	6/5	22:16	*Leonard continues explaining Sammy's story, including his role in it.*
R	6/5	22:54	As Leonard leaves Natalie's place, Teddy is waiting for him. Leonard and Teddy discuss the unreliability of memory over lunch. Leonard returns to the Discount Inn and discovers he's been checked in to two rooms. He discovers his note from Natalie and goes to meet her at a restaurant.
6	6/5	26.43	*Leonard continues explaining Sammy's story, including Leonard's first visit to the Jankis household and his suspicion that Sammy recognizes him.*
Q	7/6	28:28	FIRST SCENE OF DAY THREE: Leonard wakes up at Natalie's. She offers to find out about John G's license plate. They arrange to meet later in the day. When Leonard leaves, Teddy is waiting for him.
7	7/6	31:41	*Leonard continues explaining Sammy's story, including the distinction between "short-term memory" and "conditioning," and the tests Leonard orders.*
P	7/6	32:33	Leonard goes to Natalie's place to ask about Dodd. She explains and they discuss knowledge and memory. Natalie discovers Leonard's tattoos and explains her recent loss of Jimmy. They go to bed and Leonard muses about his loss.
8	8/7	39:24	*Leonard explains that the tests showed Sammy's problem to be "psychological" rather than "physical." He says that, unlike Sammy, he can learn by "conditioning."*

Plot (scenes listed in the order in which they occur in the film)

Scene	DVD Chapter (Regular/ LE	Time	Story
O	8/7	40:11	In Dodd's room, Leonard dreams of the incident. Teddy arrives and they decide to run Dodd out of town. Leonard goes to Natalie's place to ask about Dodd.
9	8/7	45:00	*As he begins to prepare his tattooing tools, Leonard tells the story of Sammy's desperate wife asking him his opinion of Sammy's condition.*
N	8/7	46:01	Finding himself in a bathroom, Leonard takes a shower. Dodd arrives and they struggle. Leonard knocks Dodd out, ties him up, puts him in the closet, and calls Teddy.
10	9/8	48:53	*In response to something Teddy says on the phone Leonard asks to be called back, and hangs up.*
M	9/8	49:21	Leonard escapes from Dodd and goes to Dodd's room at the Mountcrest Inn to surprise him, hiding in the bathroom.
11	9/8	52:02	*Leonard prepares to tattoo "FACT 5: ACCESS TO DRUGS" on his thigh.*
L	9/8	52:15	FIRST SCENE OF DAY TWO: At dawn, Leonard stamps out his fire and leaves. Dodd discovers him driving around and pulls him over. Leonard escapes and Dodd begins to chase him.
12	10/9	53:31	*Leonard continues his preparations. The phone rings; he picks up.*
K	10/9	53:43	Leonard leaves the Discount Inn with his wife's things. He drives to a deserted industrial spot and burns them, musing on how he "can't remember to forget" her. (There is an extended flashback of their discussing her re-reading a book.)
13	10/9	56:35	*On the phone, Teddy says something connecting John G with drugs, as Leonard tattoos Fact 5. Leonard checks the police file. He explains why the police aren't looking for John G.*
J	10/9	57:27	Leonard wakes up, discovers the escort in the bathroom, and leaves the Discount Inn with his wife's things.
14	10/9	59:27	*On the phone, Teddy suggests that John G is a drug dealer. Leonard changes Fact 5 to "DRUG DEALER."*
I	10/9	1:00:07	Leonard sets up his stuff at the Discount Inn (in a new room, unbeknownst to him) and orders an escort to re-enact the night of the incident.
15	11/10	1:02:37	*Leonard continues to tattoo and talk. He recounts telling Sammy's wife that he believes "Sammy should be physically capable of making new memories," as he begins to itch a bandage on his arm.*
H	12/10	1:04:53	Teddy is waiting for Leonard in the Jaguar. He tells Leonard not to trust Natalie, explaining how she helps Jimmy deal drugs. He suggests Leonard check in to the Discount Inn.

Plot (scenes listed in the order in which they occur in the film)

Scene	DVD Chapter (Regular/ LE)	Time	Story
16	12/10	1:09:18	*Leonard uncovers his "NEVER ANSWER THE PHONE" tattoo. He asks "Who is this?" Teddy hangs up.*
G	13/11	1:09:52	Natalie returns to a frantic Leonard at her place, claiming Dodd beat her up, and convinces Leonard to run him out of town. When he leaves her house, Teddy is waiting for him in the Jaguar.
17	13/11	1:12:55	*The phone rings. Leonard picks up, immediately hangs up, then calls the front desk to ask Burt to hold his calls.*
F	13/11	1:13:20	Natalie returns to Leonard, who is waiting at her place. She says Dodd is after her, thinking she's got the $200,000. She hides all the pens in the room and riles Leonard up, insulting him and his wife and saying she's going to use him. Leonard hits her. She leaves and Leonard frantically tries to find a pen to write a note before he forgets, but fails. She immediately returns, claiming Dodd beat her up.
18	14/12	1:17:13	*Leonard listens through the wall with a glass. Burt comes up, saying that a cop keeps calling. Leonard refuses to take the call.*
E	14/12	1:17:47	Natalie takes Leonard back to her place. He tells her his memories of the incident. She offers him her place for a couple of days. He takes her photograph and she returns to the bar. As Leonard settles down to watch TV, he sees his Sammy Jankis tattoo, and has a brief memory of flicking a needle. Natalie returns, claiming someone has "come already."
19	15/12	1:21:39	*The phone rings, then stops, then an envelope is pushed under the door. In the envelope is a Polaroid showing Leonard covered in blood, smiling and pointing to the empty space on his chest.*
D	15/12	1:22:25	Natalie serves Leonard a beer. He tells her that his last memory is of his wife dying. She gets him a fresh beer.
20	15/12	1:23:12	*Leonard takes the call and asks why the person keeps calling him, saying you shouldn't believe someone with his condition.*
C	15/12	1:23:35	Leonard goes into Ferdy's Bar. Natalie knows of him but has never met him, and tries to discover who he and Teddy are and what has happened to Jimmy. She tests his condition by serving him a polluted beer.
21	16/13	1:26:27	*Leonard says the truth of his condition is that "you don't know anything," especially why you feel the way you do. He recounts the story of the "final exam" Sammy's wife set for Sammy and her death from an insulin overdose. (There is a flash of Leonard in Sammy's seat in the mental institution.) Leonard explains that he now knows that people with his and Sammy's condition fake recognition.*

Plot (scenes listed in the order in which they occur in the film)

Scene	DVD Chapter (Regular/ LE)	Time	Story
B	16/13	1:30:03	Leonard gets Fact 6 tattooed on his thigh. Teddy finds him, gives him his old clothes, and urges him to get out of town, claiming he's a snitch and that a bad cop has been calling Leonard up. Leonard sees his note not to believe Teddy, and a coaster with a note to come by Ferdy's Bar, so he escapes out a back window. Arriving at the bar, Natalie recognizes the Jaguar, but plays it cool.
22	17/14	1:33:52	*On the phone with Teddy, Leonard discusses the plan to get Jimmy. He packs up his stuff and meets Teddy in the lobby. He takes Teddy's picture in the car-park and Teddy tells him to write "Teddy," since he's undercover. Teddy gives Leonard directions to the derelict building and tells him to "make him beg."*
			Leonard arrives at the scene, taking a tire iron into the building. (In what follows, there are five color flashbacks of Leonard's wife.) Jimmy arrives, calling for Teddy. He recognizes Leonard as the "memory man." Leonard knocks him to the ground, makes him strip, and chokes him to death. He takes a Polaroid and begins to change into Jimmy's clothes. . . . (As the Polaroid develops, the shot fades into color, making the transition to scene A.)
A	17/14	1:39:42	. . . Leonard finishes changing and drags Jimmy down to the basement. He thinks he hears Jimmy say "Sammy." Teddy arrives. Leonard worries he has killed the wrong guy and pretends he doesn't know Teddy. Teddy plays along, but Leonard confronts him about who Jimmy is. Teddy says a number of things, including that the story of Sammy Jankis is really about Leonard, and that Leonard has already killed John G. (There are contradictory flashbacks about Leonard's wife being diabetic.)
			Leonard throws Teddy's keys into some long grass to buy some time. He writes "DON'T BELIEVE HIS LIES" on Teddy's Polaroid, burns the Polaroids of himself and Jimmy, and writes a note for another tattoo: "FACT 6: CAR LICENSE SG13 7IU." He takes a Polaroid of Jimmy's Jaguar, tosses his gun into the trunk on top of the cash for the drug deal, and takes the car. As he drives to a tattoo parlor, he muses on having to believe in a mind-independent world. (There are a few shots of his wife touching an "I'VE DONE IT" tattoo on his chest.)
	19/16	1:50:18– 1:53:19	[Closing credits.]

Story (scenes listed in the order in which they occur in the fictional world)

Scene	DVD Chapter (Regular/ LE)	Time	Story
1	2/2	2:33	FIRST SCENE OF DAY ONE: Leonard, in his room at the Discount Inn, describes the experience of waking up in a hotel room with is condition.
2	3/3	6:24	Leonard begins explaining his condition, his system, and Sammy Jankis's story.
3	3/3	10:12	Leonard continues explaining his system and begins shaving his thigh. The phone rings, and Leonard answers.
4	5/4	16:11	On the phone, Leonard continues to explain Sammy's story, comparing it to his own.
5	6/5	22:16	Leonard continues explaining Sammy's story, including his role in it.
6	6/5	26.43	Leonard continues explaining Sammy's story, including Leonard's first visit to the Jankis household and his suspicion that Sammy recognizes him.
7	7/6	31:41	Leonard continues explaining Sammy's story, including the distinction between "short-term memory" and "conditioning," and the tests Leonard orders.
8	8/7	39:24	Leonard explains that the tests showed Sammy's problem to be "psychological" rather than "physical." He says that, unlike Sammy, he can learn by "conditioning."
9	8/7	45:00	As he begins to prepare his tattooing tools, Leonard tells the story of Sammy's desperate wife asking him his opinion of Sammy's condition.
10	9/8	48:53	In response to something Teddy says on the phone Leonard asks to be called back, and hangs up.
11	9/8	52:02	Leonard prepares to tattoo "FACT 5: ACCESS TO DRUGS" on his thigh.
12	10/9	53:31	Leonard continues his preparations. The phone rings; he picks up.
13	10/9	56:35	On the phone, Teddy says something connecting John G with drugs, as Leonard tattoos Fact 5. Leonard checks the police file. He explains why the police aren't looking for John G.
14	10/9	59:27	On the phone, Teddy suggests that John G is a drug dealer. Leonard changes Fact 5 to "DRUG DEALER."
15	11/10	1:02:37	Leonard continues to tattoo and talk. He recounts telling Sammy's wife that he believes "Sammy should be physically capable of making new memories," as he begins to itch a bandage on his arm.
16	12/10	1:09:18	Leonard uncovers his "NEVER ANSWER THE PHONE" tattoo. He asks "Who is this?" Teddy hangs up.

Story (scenes listed in the order in which they occur in the fictional world)

Scene	DVD Chapter (Regular/ LE)	Time	Story
17	13/11	1:12:55	The phone rings. Leonard picks up, immediately hangs up, then calls the front desk to ask Burt to hold his calls.
18	14/12	1:17:13	Leonard listens through the wall with a glass. Burt comes up, saying that a cop keeps calling. Leonard refuses to take the call.
19	15/12	1:21:39	The phone rings, then stops, then an envelope is pushed under the door. In the envelope is a Polaroid showing Leonard covered in blood, smiling and pointing to the empty space on his chest.
20	15/12	1:23:12	Leonard takes the call and asks why the person keeps calling him, saying you shouldn't believe someone with his condition.
21	16/13	1:26:27	Leonard says the truth of his condition is that "you don't know anything," especially why you feel the way you do. He recounts the story of the "final exam" Sammy's wife set for Sammy and her death from an insulin overdose. (There is a flash of Leonard in Sammy's seat in the mental institution.) Leonard explains that he now knows that people with his and Sammy's condition fake recognition.
22	17/14	1:33:52	On the phone with Teddy, Leonard discusses the plan to get Jimmy. He packs up his stuff and meets Teddy in the lobby. He takes Teddy's picture in the car-park and Teddy tells him to write "Teddy," since he's undercover. Teddy gives Leonard directions to the derelict building and tells him to "make him beg." Leonard arrives at the scene, taking a tire iron into the building. (In what follows, there are five color flashbacks of Leonard's wife.) Jimmy arrives, calling for Teddy. He recognizes Leonard as the "memory man." Leonard knocks him to the ground, makes him strip, and chokes him to death. He takes a Polaroid and begins to change into Jimmy's clothes. . . . (As the Polaroid develops, the shot fades into color, making the transition to scene A.)

(Approximate total time of black and white scenes: 24:34)

A	17/14	1:39:42	. . . Leonard finishes changing and drags Jimmy down to the basement. He thinks he hears Jimmy say "Sammy." Teddy arrives. Leonard worries he has killed the wrong guy and pretends he doesn't know Teddy. Teddy plays along, but Leonard confronts him about who Jimmy is. Teddy says a number of things, including that the story of Sammy Jankis is really about Leonard, and that Leonard has already killed John G. (There are contradictory flashbacks about Leonard's wife being diabetic.) Leonard throws Teddy's keys into some long grass to buy some time. He writes "DON'T

Story (scenes listed in the order in which they occur in the fictional world)

Scene	DVD Chapter (Regular/ LE)	Time	Story
			BELIEVE HIS LIES" on Teddy's Polaroid, burns the Polaroids of himself and Jimmy, and writes a note for another tattoo: "FACT 6: CAR LICENSE SG13 7IU." He takes a Polaroid of Jimmy's Jaguar, tosses his gun into the trunk on top of the cash for the drug deal, and takes the car. As he drives to a tattoo parlor, he muses on having to believe in a mind-independent world. (There are a few shots of his wife touching an "I'VE DONE IT" tattoo on his chest.)
B	16/13	1:30:03	Leonard gets Fact 6 tattooed on his thigh. Teddy finds him, gives him his old clothes, and urges him to get out of town, claiming he's a snitch and that a bad cop has been calling Leonard up. Leonard sees his note not to believe Teddy, and a coaster with a note to come by Ferdy's Bar, so he escapes out a back window. Arriving at the bar, Natalie recognizes the Jaguar, but plays it cool.
C	15/12	1:23:35	Leonard goes into Ferdy's Bar. Natalie knows of him but has never met him, and tries to discover who he and Teddy are and what has happened to Jimmy. She tests his condition by serving him a polluted beer.
D	15/12	1:22:25	Natalie serves Leonard a beer. He tells her that his last memory is of his wife dying. She gets him a fresh beer.
E	14/12	1:17:47	Natalie takes Leonard back to her place. He tells her his memories of the incident. She offers him her place for a couple of days. He takes her photograph and she returns to the bar. As Leonard settles down to watch TV, he sees his Sammy Jankis tattoo, and has a brief memory of flicking a needle. Natalie returns, claiming someone has "come already."
F	13/11	1:13:20	Natalie returns to Leonard, who is waiting at her place. She says Dodd is after her, thinking she's got the $200,000. She hides all the pens in the room and riles Leonard up, insulting him and his wife and saying she's going to use him. Leonard hits her. She leaves and Leonard frantically tries to find a pen to write a note before he forgets, but fails. She immediately returns, claiming Dodd beat her up.
G	13/11	1:09:52	Natalie returns to a frantic Leonard at her place, claiming Dodd beat her up, and convinces Leonard

Story (scenes listed in the order in which they occur in the fictional world)

Scene	DVD Chapter (Regular/LE)	Time	Story
			to run him out of town. When he leaves her house, Teddy is waiting for him in the Jaguar.
H	12/10	1:04:53	Teddy is waiting for Leonard in the Jaguar. He tells Leonard not to trust Natalie, explaining how she helps Jimmy deal drugs. He suggests Leonard check in to the Discount Inn.
I	10/9	1:00:07	Leonard sets up his stuff at the Discount Inn (in a new room, unbeknownst to him) and orders an escort to re-enact the night of the incident.
J	10/9	57:27	Leonard wakes up, discovers the escort in the bathroom, and leaves the Discount Inn with his wife's things.
K	10/9	53:43	Leonard leaves the Discount Inn with his wife's things. He drives to a deserted industrial spot and burns them, musing on how he "can't remember to forget" her. (There is an extended flashback of their discussing her re-reading a book.)
L	9/8	52:15	FIRST SCENE OF DAY TWO: At dawn, Leonard stamps out his fire and leaves. Dodd discovers him driving around and pulls him over. Leonard escapes and Dodd begins to chase him.
M	9/8	49:21	Leonard escapes from Dodd and goes to Dodd's room at the Mountcrest Inn to surprise him, hiding in the bathroom.
N	8/7	46:01	Finding himself in a bathroom, Leonard takes a shower. Dodd arrives and they struggle. Leonard knocks Dodd out, ties him up, puts him in the closet, and calls Teddy.
O	8/7	40:11	In Dodd's room, Leonard dreams of the incident. Teddy arrives and they decide to run Dodd out of town. Leonard goes to Natalie's place to ask about Dodd.
P	7/6	32:33	Leonard goes to Natalie's place to ask about Dodd. She explains and they discuss knowledge and memory. Natalie discovers Leonard's tattoos and explains her recent loss of Jimmy. They go to bed and Leonard muses about his loss.
Q	7/6	28:28	FIRST SCENE OF DAY THREE: Leonard wakes up at Natalie's. She offers to find out about John G's

Story (scenes listed in the order in which they occur in the fictional world)

Scene	DVD Chapter (Regular/ LE)	Time	Story
			license plate. They arrange to meet later in the day. When Leonard leaves, Teddy is waiting for him.
R	6/5	22:54	As Leonard leaves Natalie's place, Teddy is waiting for him. Leonard and Teddy discuss the unreliability of memory over lunch. Leonard returns to the Discount Inn and discovers he's been checked in to two rooms. He discovers his note from Natalie and goes to meet her at a restaurant.
S	5/4	16:57	Leonard meets Natalie at a restaurant. She gives him a copy of Teddy's driver's license and registration. They discuss the point of Leonard's quest for a revenge he won't remember. Natalie gives Leonard directions to a derelict building as a place for Leonard to take John G. Leonard goes to the bathroom and sees his "remember Sammy Jankis" tattoo.
T	4/4	11:05	In the bathroom, Leonard sees his "remember Sammy Jankis" tattoo. He returns to the Discount Inn and, examining his evidence, infers that Teddy is John G. He calls Teddy, who says he'll come over. He writes "HE IS THE ONE/KILL HIM" on Teddy's Polaroid.
U	3/3	7:00	Leonard writes "KILL HIM" on Teddy's Polaroid. He goes down to the lobby, discusses his condition with Burt, and pays for his room. Teddy arrives.
V	2/2	2:57	Teddy arrives at the Discount Inn. He and Leonard drive to the derelict building. Leonard shoots Teddy.
			(Approximate total time of color scenes: 1:23:06)
Ω	1/1	0:43	Leonard shoots Teddy and takes a Polaroid of Teddy's body.

Chapter 1

Michael McKenna

MORAL MONSTER OR RESPONSIBLE PERSON? *MEMENTO*'S LEONARD AS A CASE STUDY IN DEFECTIVE AGENCY

C HRISTOPHER NOLAN'S psychological thriller Memento is an
impressive cinematic achievement. Although many films can be used
to illustrate philosophical ideas, few are intentionally philosophical.
Memento is. In it, we are struck by several philosophical questions that the
film is clearly designed to raise.[1] Before proceeding to a discussion of
these questions, I shall begin with a brief comment on the film itself.

As is often observed, Memento is nearly impenetrable on first viewing.
Even a straightforward, unambiguous interpretation of the film, sup-
posing one could find one, involves an extremely complex plot. Add to
that the duplicitous innuendos and other built-in ambiguities, and we
are provided with resources to doubt an unambiguous rendering. Finally,
present the entire storyline using the intricate temporal structure Nolan
developed, and the net effect of Memento is simply baffling, at least the
first time through it.

If Nolan's efforts were merely self-indulgent showmanship, it would
be easy to dismiss this film. Intriguing as it is, it would be a fair criticism
to complain that the film demands too much of its viewers, and that a
finely crafted story in the fashion of Hitchcock or Bertolucci easily
trumps all Nolan's smoke and mirrors. But in my estimation, this com-
plaint is misguided. Those pressing it fail to see the genius in what Nolan
has accomplished. In terms of its complexity, I would argue that Nolan's

Memento is similar to Faulkner's masterpiece *The Sound and the Fury*. In both cases, the formal structure of the artwork—which no doubt completely overpowers its audience upon an initial encounter—provides a commentary on, or illustration of, the thematic subtext of the story. Only after revisiting the work can we come to see this, and in our revisiting we assign richer significance to the various pieces constituting the whole.

In *Memento*, Nolan has, in essence, demanded that his audience make use of mementos in order to follow his film. We, like Leonard, have to leave notes to ourselves to decipher the proper temporal order, think through the credibility of Leonard's telling of the story of Sammy Jankis, scrutinize the veracity of Teddy's revelations, understand the motives of characters such as Natalie, and so on. As we begin to question the stability of a single right interpretation of the film, we are led to reflect upon core philosophical themes in *Memento*, which turn on the nature of knowledge, mind, personal identity, and practical as well as distinctively moral agency.

Philosophical issues in Memento

Eventually I shall turn to an extended treatment of first practical and then moral agency. Here I wish to comment briefly on several other closely related issues.

Global skepticism

As the intelligent critic of *Memento* recognizes, Nolan has not given us enough textual evidence to settle what is to be taken for reality and what is not. Did Leonard kill his wife with an overdose of insulin, as Teddy alleges, or was it the assailant Leonard is seeking? How much of what we see is just a hallucination or, more innocuously, maybe a daydream, unfolding inside the confines of Leonard's mind? Furthermore, how are we to sort through all of this, given the elaborate temporal ordering Nolan creates? Because of our uncertainty, we are placed in a position similar to Leonard's. Thus, our relation to the film, like Leonard's relation to the world he confronts, leaves us as Descartes found himself at the beginning of his second meditation, before he was able to convince himself that there was an external world. In this moment, he was uncertain as to how to interpret the status of his beliefs. He wrote:

So serious are the doubts into which I have been thrown as a result
of yesterday's meditation that I can neither put them out of my mind
nor see any way of resolving them. It feels as if I have fallen
unexpectedly into a deep whirlpool which tumbles me around so
that I can neither stand on the bottom nor swim up to the top.

(1641: 16)

If we take all of the ambiguous interpretive data seriously, the effect Nolan
creates with Memento is analogous to that created by unresolved Cartesian
global skepticism. Given the available evidence, there simply is no settled,
proper interpretation of reality. As between competing and inconsistent
interpretations, we are completely ill-equipped to settle on which, if any,
is veridical.

Descartes attempted to argue his way out of his skeptical predicament,
and as we cast about for anchors in the film to rule out some evidence
and retain other pieces, we are attempting to do likewise. We start with
certainties, the ones closest to home and least subject to doubt. (Descartes
claimed to find his first certainty in the mere fact of his own thought.)
With this in mind, recall the scene in which Leonard has a meltdown in
front of Natalie, whereupon, in a moment of tenderness, she takes him
to bed (P). In that scene, Leonard insists that there are certainties, such
as knowing what it will feel like when he picks up an ashtray. The
practical predicament for him, as cast in that scene, is whether there are
enough crumbs of certainty scattered about to build a bridge to his past,
and to his future. For Descartes, his solipsistic predicament was whether
he had enough to build a bridge to knowledge outside of his own mind.

But is Leonard really involved in this struggle while sitting in Natalie's
living room? Or is he just insane, imagining the entire thing from an
asylum? Just as Descartes in his early stage of skeptical doubt could
interpret all of his experiences as consistent with veridical judgments
about the world, or instead as fabrications fed to him by a demon, so
we in watching the film can interpret what Nolan presents for us as
consistent with Leonard actually out hunting down a killer, or instead
as delusional daydreams fed to him by his own insanity. The uncertainty
that Nolan engenders does a far better job of illustrating the Cartesian
skeptical predicament than a film such as the Wachowski brothers' The
Matrix, in which the audience is easily clued into which interpretation is
reality and which is an artifice.[2]

Self-knowledge, and knowledge of other minds

A striking fact about the human condition, at least in the normal case, is that there is a crucial asymmetry between knowledge of our own minds and knowledge of others' minds. Admittedly, there is room for self-deception. Sometimes, maybe even often, people do not understand themselves nearly as well as they think they do. But the default assumption is that persons have a privileged relationship to their own beliefs about themselves. No doubt, the degree of credence that we ought to assign to their convictions varies depending on the beliefs in question. We regard people as completely authoritative about sincere pain reports, slightly less so about their visual impressions, less than that about what they claim to see, and so on. Once we get to things such as sexual preferences and how people really feel about their mothers, well, all bets are off. But along this spectrum, awareness of one's own basic biography, at least in simple details, such as what one had for breakfast earlier in the day, or whether one cut the grass yesterday, are certainly regarded as beliefs about which one has a greater authoritative claim in comparison with third parties. My knowledge about what I had for breakfast this morning is more reliable than my knowledge of what *you* had for breakfast this morning. In the case of knowledge of my own history, I can consult my own "memory-record" of my experiences. But I do not have access to your experiences, to your memory-record. I have to infer knowledge of what you did without direct access to your mind.

The classical philosophical problem of knowledge of other minds is posed as a restricted kind of skepticism. Set aside the skeptical challenge that we do not know that there is an external world. Suppose that problem is solved; we do know there is an external world. A distinct problem is how we know there are other minds, and even if we do, how do we know the content of those other minds? Since we cannot have another's thoughts or feelings, cannot experience her pains, and so on, all we can do is infer from her external behavior that she is having thoughts and experiences. But maybe she is not. Maybe she is a hollow zombie who just acts like we do when we have experiences. Or maybe she has them but, unlike in our case, there is no correlation between her conduct and her thought, so that no matter how she behaves, we are forever ignorant about what she is really feeling and thinking.

Although Leonard does not entertain full throttle skeptical doubts about knowledge of other minds, his relation to his own recent self is just like his relation to another person. He has to infer what he had previously thought without access to any memories that would give him a privileged basis for any beliefs he might form. In this way, Leonard stands diachronically to his own recent self as he does synchronically to another person. The primary Socratic edict is to know thyself. Now recall Teddy's skeptical challenge to Leonard, "You don't even know who you are" (H, 1:07:52). For Leonard, knowing himself will always involve gigantic obstacles, ones that will make it nearly impossible for him ever to figure out what to do, since this requires some appreciation of what he has done (a point I will explore in more detail later).

The extended mind

What constitutes a mind? Put differently, what constitutes a subject of mental states or processes? Many philosophers, myself included, are physicalists. We believe that minds are physically *realized*. There is a good bit of technical philosophical machinery required to get clear on what physicalism does and does not commit one to. Setting all of that out is far beyond the scope of this essay, but a central idea is something like this: This mind of mine, Michael McKenna's mind, whatever it comes to, is dependent upon physical states and processes, and is, in some loose sense of "is," a physical state or process. So, roughly, my mind is located where my brain is located, inside my cranium. As peculiar as it might seem, saying this much, committing to physicalism, does not amount to the stronger thesis that my mind is *just* a physical state or process, where the "just" suggests the idea that mental states and processes can be *reduced* *to* physical states and processes. To explain: Though I contend that my mind is a physical state or process, and that, for instance, my beliefs, desires, intentions, values, and so forth, are all physical, it does not follow that they are *simply* physical, or that they are "no more than" physical. It might be that, though they are physical, what makes them mental states is that they function in certain ways. So if my mind were, say, built out of some different material, or if a small part of my brain quit working and could be replaced by a silicon chip that would perform the functional tasks now performed by the operative grey matter in my brain, it would still be *my* mind. Hence, while my brain does duty for how *in fact* my mind is "realized," it is possible (even if not now technologically realistic) that it *could* be realized by some other physical material.

Nevertheless, on this view, when we point to my brain we point, for all practical purposes, to my mind. Stick my brain in a blender, reducing it to a frosty shake, and you do the same to my mind.

Given the assumption of physicalism, here is a striking puzzle brought out by *Memento*: If a mind is, in some sense, a physical system, then why assume that it is located only in the cranium, or under the skin? (Clark and Chalmers 1998) Why can't it be extended outside of the skin to, for example, my computer, which retains articles I have written but have long since "forgotten?" Why is it not also extended to my weekly planner? What about snapshots of my father, long dead now? If this photo on my desk of him and me as a kid walking in the park sustains a memory of my time with him, why is it not part of my mind rather than something that can affect my mind? If you were to destroy it, my computer, or my daily planner, would I be entitled to say that you destroyed a part of my mind?

If the mind extends beyond the skin, then Leonard's mementos *are* part of his mind. In fact, to the extent that he relies upon others to aid him in his planning (as Teddy has aided him), his mind is, in part, constituted by those others, just as if my daily planner is part of my mind, so too is my wife, who helps me to remember when to have the car scheduled for an oil change, or to decide what investments are most prudent, and so on. Alluding to his memory condition, at one point Teddy says to Leonard that he (Leonard) does not know anything. But assuming a theory of the extended mind, Leonard *does* know various things. It is just that he cannot use memories to get to them. Nevertheless he has access via other routes, and, as Leonard points out in arguing against Teddy, memories are overrated anyway. They are not records of the facts, he protests, but interpretations that can be deceiving.

Personal Identity

What makes a person the very same person that she is at a particular time and over time? By "the very same" I mean numerical identity. When we say things like "She is not the same person she used to be" we (almost) never mean that there was this one person, Cindy, but Cindy no longer exists, that is, that very entity—that person—is gone, and in her place is a completely numerically distinct person, Cindy*. What we mean is something like, one single person, Cindy, has changed so much that she, that same person Cindy, has acquired very different qualities from the ones she used to have. She used to be unkind and selfish, but she—that same person—is now generous and sensitive. This kind of change is known as qualitative change, and is philosophically unproblematic (or at least less problematic). But numerical change, or rather numerical sameness—that is, lack of numerical change over time—is much more challenging. How do we track a being's alterations across time such that, though that being does undergo qualitative changes, it remains numerically the same one? We can ask this question about any object, such as a car or a bicycle, as well as a person. If I buy replacement parts for each piece of my bicycle and have them all in boxes right by my bike, replacing just one part, like my handlebars, do I now have a numerically distinct bike? Of course not! It is my same bike with new handlebars. But what if I replace every part, one right after the other, in two hours? The bike before me after two hours shares no part with the earlier bike. Do I now have a numerically distinct bike? Of course! What could possibly explain these different answers? This illustrates the problem of explaining numerical identity over time.

When applying the problem of numerical identity over time to persons, philosophers have proffered various theories to account for how the same person can change radically over time and be the same person. One theory is the *bodily continuity theory*. If some person, say Leonard, is a particular human body, then he remains the same person across time so long as that body exists (albeit always changing). In *Memento*, on the bodily continuity theory, there is no problem about Leonard's identity over time. The same animal body does all of these different things, so Leonard does them. But like many other philosophers, I find the simple bodily continuity theory highly implausible. Suppose that a demon were to completely erase all of my memories and psychological states overnight and replace them in this body with the memories and other states of the actress Betty Davis. I would regard this as an identity-destroying change. Michael McKenna would no longer exist, and some very confused man would be in his place. Or consider a real-life case, one that bears on memory-retention. Many family members of Alzheimer's patients claim that, in the last stages of the disease, when a person's memories are wiped clean and there is no memory of the person who was, "Grandpa has already gone; he's not there anymore." I think these claims should be taken literally. The person suffered an identity destroying change at some point, and this person, or this human shell, is no longer that person, is no longer Grandpa.[3]

Reflections like these have led many philosophers to endorse some version of a *psychological continuity theory* of personal identity. A person remains the same person over time if and only if there is some sort of "identity grounding" relation between her psychological states across time. The philosopher John Locke first proposed memory as the crucial requirement (1689: bk. 2, ch. 27). And if we develop Locke's suggestion so that (most of) the memories have to be genuine (and not false), then we can link a person's identity across time like we link shorter strands of twine together to form a longer rope. I might have no memory now of my experiences when I was five years old, but I do have memories of my twenty-year-old self, and this self had memories of my ten-year-old self, and so on.

On a psychological continuity theory, Leonard's situation *appears* to raise deep metaphysical problems for him, aside from his gigantic practical problems. If Leonard in his current state has no recent memories of his recent past, then is he no longer the person who was assaulted, the one who was an insurance agent, and who was married? In one scene, Nolan raises this question when he has Teddy say to Leonard that he does not even know who he is, that he used to be Leonard, but is not any longer (H, 1:08:00). Here, it seems to me that Teddy is confused (maybe Nolan is too). Leonard has memories of his former self (before his accident), and so even on a psychological continuity theory, he is that same person. That he does not have memories of what he did an hour ago is of no matter, since he does have genuine memories that link him to his earlier self. No version of a psychological continuity theory could be true if it set the bar for identity over time so high that at each moment in time, a person at later times had to be linked to a genuine memory of that earlier time. Every dreamless sleep would result in a death, as would a serious alcohol bender, or a dance with the magic mushroom fairy.[4]

So, if *Memento* is to pose a puzzle about personal identity, it cannot quite be the one that Teddy (or Nolan?) thinks it is. The problem must be a more subtle one, and I think that there is one to be seen in the film. The key is to realize that a good theory of personal identity will not just account for how a person at one time is the same person she was in the past. It must explain what will be required for her to be the same person in the future. In the normal case, this will allow a person some stable practical basis for caring about her future self. The problem for Leonard is not the fear that he will not be in the future. He knows that, unless he dies, he will be, and he knows that the ground for his being the same person in the future is that his future self will have access through his memories to the same history as he has now in his present state (access to his memories before his accident). Leonard's problem is that, as he is now, he knows that his future self will not be able to know the present part of his biography. He knows that he will (probably) have a future, but he also knows that his future self will forever be a stranger to its recent biography, that is, to him as he is now. Thus, he cannot act now in the normal ways one might to help shape one's future self, so that one might be able to grow or mature as a person. And this makes it especially hard for him to care about what he does now in terms of how it will bear on who he will be or how he will think of himself later. This is brilliantly illustrated in his fleeting, clear-eyed decision to set himself on Teddy.

Practical agency

I now turn to the issue of practical agency. As will become clear, the previous philosophical considerations will have some bearing on how we understand this topic, as well as the more narrowly focused topic of moral agency (to be discussed in the following section).

What is an action? What distinguishes it from a mere event in the world? Like many philosophers of action, I endorse a liberal view of what makes an event an action. Anytime a being's behavior can be understood as purposeful by attributing to it even the most rudimentary beliefs and desires, we have action. This allows for actions by agents that are very far down on the zoological pecking order. If a bird is searching on the ground and moves off the pavement into the dirt, we can see his behavior as purposive to the extent that we can see it as minimally rational. The bird believes that the worms are in the dirt and not the pavement, and he desires some food. This explains his act of pecking.

But the actions characteristic of human agency are certainly more complex, and it is a difficult question just what is distinctive about the practical agency of comparatively sophisticated creatures like us. An especially challenging problem is to explain what makes an action intentional. On a simple view—one that I think is indefensible—for each act, there is an intending that goes with it, a particular kind of mental state or event. Earlier today I drove to the gym. According to the simple view, if this was an act, then I intended to do it. So far, so good. But on the way to the gym I had to use my turn signals five times. On the simple view, if each use was an act, then I intended to do each. That seems a stretch, but not too outrageous. However, note that each time I directed the car in any new direction, I had to move the steering wheel ever so slightly. Each of these were surely actions of mine, but did I intend to do each? Was there a corresponding intention—a discrete mental state or event—for each of these acts of steering wheel manipulation? The view begins to sound implausible, and it is.

Intentional action and planning agents

Here is a rough sketch of a better view, due to the philosopher Michael Bratman (1987). Not every intentional action is one that a person intends. What makes an action intentional is that it fits within a broader plan, and what practical agents like us intend is to execute certain plans. So, in my action of driving to the gym, I intended to drive to the gym. When I used my turn signals and turned the steering wheel several times, each of those acts I did intentionally, but I did not intend them. All I intended in executing them was to drive to the gym. They were done intentionally by virtue of their figuring in how it was that I planned to get to the gym. Thus, our intentions are plans, and they can themselves be embedded in larger, and ever more complex plans. (Going to the gym is embedded in the larger plan of remaining fit, or training for a bicycling race.) What we do intentionally is to perform various acts in an effort to execute our sometimes immensely elaborate plans. Some of what we do intentionally is what we intend to do (e.g., go to the gym), but the majority of what we do intentionally (e.g., turn the steering wheel) is not what we directly intend. We only do these latter things (intentionally) in an effort to achieve what we do intend.

Well-functioning practical agents like us have elaborate legislative and executive resources for forming and carrying out our plans. We must, since our plans require on-the-spot modifications and adjustments, reassessment of the reasonableness of goals, and so on. New information can get us to revise how we execute a plan, or get us to reconsider whether we should sustain a commitment to a plan in the first place. If on the way to the gym I learn that one route is closed due to road construction, I must be able to alter the details of my plan in order to sustain my commitment to the larger goal. If it is announced on the radio as I am driving that the gym is closed today, then I need to be able to abort the mission and revise my goals, and so on. Furthermore, this plan might need to be coordinated with others that could be assigned a higher or lower priority. Perhaps I also have a plan to get to the doctor's office, and if on the way to the gym I learn that I can only do both by rearranging the time I will be at the gym, then I will likely revise accordingly. On a planning theory of intentions, our practical agency is seen to be distinctive of creatures like us due to our ability to apply sophisticated patterns of practical reasoning to develop, sustain, coordinate, and carry out elaborate plans. All the while, our procedures need to be sufficiently plastic that we are able to remold them on a dime, based on the possibility of constantly changing bits of information, newly emerging preferences, reconsidered values that speak to the desirability of our goals, and so on.

Because, on this theory, intentions figure in a wider diachronic picture of an agent's goals, intentional action is best understood as intelligible only insofar as it is spread out over time. If so, it is easy to see that this makes problems for Leonard. The mementos Leonard uses are meant to facilitate his planning as best as he is able. And the different types of mementos that he leaves for himself are categorized into varying levels of importance—the most important of which he has tattooed on himself. Leonard's entire elaborate process, including his reliance on habituation, is all part of his seriously handicapped effort to sustain and coordinate his intentions, and embed them in plans that outstrip the limits of his memory's impoverished temporal horizon.

To call into relief just how impaired Leonard's practical agency is, Nolan has the hotel clerk, Burt, remark that Leonard's problem is the reverse of most people's (U, 0:09:15). Most people know what they have done, but don't know what they want to do. (In Bratman's terms, they have yet to settle on their plans.) Leonard seems to know what he wants to do next, but doesn't know what he just did. Recall also that at one point Natalie comments on Leonard's sorry system for coordinating his plans. She says that it must be hard to live your life "according to a couple of scraps of paper. You mix your laundry list with your grocery list and you'll end up eating your underwear for breakfast" (S, 0:18:04).

Because of Leonard's condition, the prospects for exercising his agency are starkly limited. In a normal human life, the possibilities for meaningful action are varied, and they offer the prospect of many different rewarding paths into the future. Not so for Leonard. Think about his agency in terms of his relation to the future. The only way, it seems, that he can coordinate his agency so as to embed his immediate intentional conduct in a more expansive diachronic plan is by relying upon some single, simple thing to give his activity a purpose, an organizing goal around which the details of his immediate actions could make sense. This is what Teddy has done for him, sweet guy that he is. Now think about Leonard's agency in relation to the past. Our present plans for how to act are shaped by our understanding of our recent history. It is on the basis of the recent events in our lives that we figure out what to do next. Our diachronic agency not only stretches forward in time, but reaches toward the future in light of an understanding of what the immediate past has made salient. If, indeed, the last thing he remembers is his wife dying, then intelligible options for Leonard will forever be from that moment forward. There are, therefore, very few options for him, other than to consider some act to aid in grieving (like hiring a hooker to help him say goodbye), or some way of seeking revenge. One can only wonder what will be left for Leonard once he offs Teddy. Maybe Leonard will be able to sustain a more expansive diachronic plan with no more than his mementos to guide him. But it seems very likely that, without Teddy's competent mind aiding him, he'll quickly crash and burn.

Truth, desire, and self-deception

So Leonard's abilities as a planning agent are severely impaired, and this is due in large part to the fact that he is ignorant of so much. But that does not alter the fact that he still has a strong desire to regard himself as appropriately anchored in the world. This calls attention to a further feature of competent planning agents like ourselves. We set goals for ourselves—make plans—in light of our beliefs about how attempts to achieve those goals will fit with the facts of an independent world. This is partially for the instrumental reason that otherwise we'll fail to achieve what we set out to do. But it is also because the goals we set for ourselves are often based upon reasons that presuppose values and a reality independent of our preferences. Leonard, for instance, rejects the relevance of Natalie's suggestion that his quest for vengeance is futile since he'll never be able to remember achieving it (scene S). It won't matter to him, she tells him. But he'll have none of this. It doesn't matter if he won't know, if he will be unable to reap the enduring satisfaction of being able to recall his righteous vengeance. He says that it still matters that the guilty man, John G (whoever he is), pay for killing his wife. She deserves to be avenged. Leonard's desire that his actions be anchored in the truth is also revealed when he reacts with panic to the fear that he might have just killed an innocent man (Jimmy Grantz). In this moment, Teddy tries to reason with Leonard just as Natalie did: "So you lie to yourself to be happy—there's nothing wrong with that!" (A, 1:42:28).

Thus, we see in Memento an illustration of the value of truth for a planning agent, even one whose relation to it is so very fragile. This aspect of planning agency is, however, often pitted against another, against desire.[5] We form plans in order to achieve goals so as to make the world conform to what we wish. As it is often explained, one distinguishing feature between belief, whose goal is truth, and desire, whose goal is satisfaction, is the proper relation of fit between each and the world. In the case of belief, it aims to fit the world. In the case of desire, it aims to make the world fit it. Thus, these two ingredients, both necessary constituents of intentional agency, are uncomfortable bedfellows, often at odds with each other.

Nolan illustrates this tension with Leonard's struggle. His desire for revenge has outstripped what is true, and at one point Teddy accuses Leonard of not wanting genuine truth, but of fabricating it so that he can live a dream of carrying out his campaign to avenge his wife. So furious is Leonard upon hearing this, and learning of Teddy's manipulation of him, that he intentionally deceives himself, setting himself up to find and kill Teddy. In this moment, Leonard forsakes his allegiance to the truth, as he cynically says to himself, "Do I lie to myself to be happy? In your case Teddy, yes I will" (A, 1:48:15).

What Nolan offers us in the case of Leonard is either a tragic or a comic magnification of our predicament as planning agents, as practical agents trying to live in a world that is not our making. Our desires are sometimes at odds with our allegiance to the truth. Still, needing the latter to achieve the former, we are forced to constrain desire accordingly.

Nevertheless, sometimes the incentive for self-deception is extremely strong, so strong that we judge it worth the cost of forsaking truth, as Leonard does in that fleeting moment of clarity when he decides to give Teddy a taste of his own medicine.

It may well be that some degree of self-deception in human agency is a good thing. We are probably all a lot better off believing that we are a little better looking, smarter, more interesting, kinder, and more thoughtful than we really are. Were we to live in the constant light of the unvarnished truth about ourselves, we'd likely be so burdened that it would be hard to get up in the morning. All the same, as the case of Leonard illustrates, it is also clear that the limits of healthy or harmless self-deception are fairly constrained.

Meaningful lives and narrative structure

The fact that, as planning agents, our practical agency is spread out across time also helps to make sense of how we evaluate the meaningfulness of a life. By and large, we presume that a meaningful life is one that involves the pursuit and achievement of goals that sustain one over the relatively large span of a life. The relative worth of a life is a matter of its unfolding history, whether it is lived in pursuit of a reputable body of published work, an artistic oeuvre, or a career in a profession, trade, or even sport. So, too, for raising a family, investing one's life in the love of a spouse, or cultivating lasting friendships that color and enrich life. How such things unfold over time will speak to the value or meaning they offer to a life lived. A career that starts gloriously and then crashes on the rocks due to embezzlement and professional infidelity will be regarded as wasted not just for the later bad acts, but because the promise shown in its infancy was squandered. A career starting out from meager beginnings, with little hope for success, that then takes off and is sustained through many difficulties will be regarded, by contrast, as well-lived not just for the later successes, but because the earlier failures made the later successes all the sweeter. Those successes will be understood as part of a larger struggle to overcome adversity. Hence, the value of our lives, their meaning, for good or ill, is partially characterized by their narrative structure.

As is obvious, the prospects are very limited for Leonard's life having any meaning that would involve sustained narrative development. For this reason, so many of the things that make a human life meaningful are beyond Leonard's reach. Consider grieving. Grieving involves a process of coming to accept and heal from the pain of loss. It can also be the source of future growth and possibility. The loss of a husband or a wife in an accident or due to an illness, while a source of pain, is also the source of the enriching possibilities that a future human life can offer, in the possibility of a new love, or a life lived in homage to the one who has passed. Because Leonard cannot forget, he cannot grieve, and so this distinctive pattern of healing and self-discovery is unavailable to him. As noted above, the same applies to the desire for vengeance, which for Leonard can never be quenched. Even if we find it an ugly, barbaric, primitive desire, part of its role in the unfolding of the life of the avenger is to facilitate a process of resolving the outrage of having been deeply aggrieved.

Even the one meaningful task Leonard seeks to achieve, one that would have narrative structure—the hunting down and killing of his wife's murderer—is undermined as something that could be meaningful for Leonard *once achieved*. Suppose he does leave evidence to himself that he succeeded, with a tattoo reading "I've done it" (Figure 1). He is nevertheless easily able to wonder if he had been deceived, and so did not really do it. Thus, concerns about the truthfulness of his mementos are likely to rob him of the little bit of meaningful narrative development his life could have.

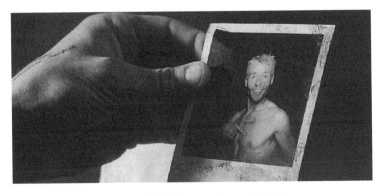

Figure 1 Space for Leonard's final tattoo (12, 1:22:17)

Moral agency: moral monster or responsible person?

Is Leonard a moral agent? When he murders the drug dealer Jimmy Grantz, or later Teddy, or the various other John G's that he has presumably killed, is Leonard morally responsible for what he does? Or is he a moral monster, a being capable of moral evil, but not really a candidate for competent responsible agency, perhaps like Doctor Frankenstein's creation?

The foregoing treatment of the philosophical issues leading up to this topic offers a considerable part of the answer, or so it seems. It is reasonable to assume that morally responsible agency presupposes competent practical agency. And as I have been at pains to bring out, Leonard's capacities for competent agency are severely restricted. March down through each topic: Leonard is living a life like the one Descartes described in the midst of global skeptical doubt. His knowledge of his own recent self is no better than his knowledge of the minds of others. Even assuming his mementos serve as part of his mind, on an extended-mind view, then so do Teddy's machinations. And while his personal identity *per se* is not threatened by his memory condition, his ability to care about his current relation to his future self is hamstrung. Further-more, as a planning agent he is highly limited, and to the extent that his actions can be coordinated around a long-term plan, he's at the mercy of people like Teddy and Natalie. His commitment to the truth about the world—whether his wife is really avenged or not—is one he cannot reliably confirm, and he has a strong incentive to deceive himself, which eventually he does. Finally, the prospects for his life ever unfolding meaningfully in a way that could have the sort of narrative structure that others naturally value is beyond his reach. How could a person so off the radar, so impaired in his practical agency, be considered a competent moral agent, one who is responsible in any way for his actions?

Even if all of the above hurdles could be overcome so that we could still take seriously the claim that, in his very acts of murder and violence, Leonard is morally responsible for them, there is the further hurdle that we could never see Leonard as a candidate for our blame or punishment, nor could he even see himself as a candidate for guilt. The philosopher David Hume presented a famous puzzle about the gap between an act and an agent (1740: bk. 2, pt. 3, §2). When we blame and punish, we are led to do so because of the act. But if the act is over, then why punish the agent? Hume's answer is that the act flowed from the bad character traits of the agent, and so we punish the agent as a way of responding to these traits. But not surprisingly, an agent who simply could not remember his acts could not see the blame or the punishment as responding to the character traits in him as they were revealed in his actions.

Still, it might be insisted, though we cannot ever meaningfully blame or punish Leonard, it does not follow that, in those very moments of his violent murders, he is not blameworthy, that he is not morally responsible for what he does then and there. True, we cannot blame him since he cannot remember, but we also cannot blame a man who murders and then drops dead immediately thereafter. Though dead, it does not follow that in murdering, the man was not worthy of blame. If he were to have lived, then it would have been perfectly fitting to punish him. So too, one might say, Leonard, in acting as he does, impaired as he is in various ways, is blameworthy, and were he able to remember, it would be perfectly fitting to blame him. The mere fact that we are impeded from blaming him does not detract from the credibility of the judgment that in acting he was worthy of blame.

Can we take this possibility seriously? Surprisingly, some philosophers endorse an ahistorical theory of morally responsible agency that would make good sense of how we could think of Leonard as morally responsible for his actions at the very times that he acts. They allow for the possibility that a person could come to be in a particular condition in a very bizarre way, one that subverted her agency and autonomy (that is, her self-government) altogether, but if, in the moment of acting, her agency works properly with respect to the here-and-now decision and action undertaken, then she can be morally responsible for what she does. Consider this famous quote from the philosopher Harry Frankfurt:

> [T]o the extent that a person identifies with the springs of his actions, he takes responsibility for those actions and acquires moral responsibility for them; moreover, the questions of how the actions and his identifications with their springs are caused are irrelevant to the questions of whether he performs the actions freely or is morally responsible for performing them.
>
> (1988: 54)

Leonard fully identified with the springs of his actions, and though he came to acquire them in deviant ways, according to the ahistorical theory defended by Frankfurt, that is of no importance as to the question of whether Leonard is morally responsible for what he did. When he acted, his mental life was, in the here-and-now sense, largely cohesive, organized as it was around a commitment to a campaign of revenge. And while his reasons for killing, in the case of Jimmy Grantz, for instance, were the products of others' acts of deception, nevertheless he still acted on them. Furthermore, he was well aware, as he notes several times, and as others note to him, that his evidence was fairly shaky for who did what and which clues he could rely upon. Nevertheless, on the basis of this very thin evidence, he was all too prepared to kill. These sorts of in-the-moment decisions reveal deeply morally objectionable ways in which Leonard exercised his agency. And so, why not, as Frankfurt's thesis would have it, respond to these aspects of Leonard's agency as grounds for judging that, indeed, he was morally responsible for what he did at those different moments of action?[6]

Numerous other philosophers writing on morally responsible agency defend an historical account of moral responsibility, arguing that an agent's history matters as to whether she is morally responsible for what she does at that time. Indeed, they would argue that if you were to imagine some other character, Leonard*, who had no memory problem, who was not hoodwinked by others into believing all of these things about Jimmy, but who had come to a decision to murder Jimmy out of revenge under his own rationally competent steam, then Leonard* would be morally responsible. Leonard, however, would not, even though Leonard and Leonard* would be just alike in all of their ahistorical (or "current time-slice") properties at the moment of action. At best, they would argue, Leonard is a moral monster, but surely not a morally responsible agent, and so not morally responsible for his actions.

I confess that between the historicists and the ahistoricists, I have remained ambivalent about who is right. I see the force of Frankfurt's thesis that we evaluate people as they are, regardless of how they came to be that way. The poor kid from nowhere and the wealthy kid from privilege, once they have hit a certain threshold of competent agency, should be evaluated just based on who they are and what they do now, not how they came to be that way. On the other hand, it stretches imagination to think that, in the moment of action, we could really regard

Leonard to be just as blameworthy as Leonard*. In an earlier publication (McKenna 2004), I floated a way to try to make more plausible the idea that someone like Leonard is just as responsible for what he does as someone like Leonard* would be. I argued that a character like Leonard*, unlike Leonard, is morally responsible for more than the mere fact of his action. He is also morally responsible for the character that he freely formed on his own, the one that led to his coming to be the guy who, just like Leonard, performed such and such act of murder. Thus, we can make sense of our thought that Leonard* deserves more blame than Leonard deserves. On the current proposal, it is not because Leonard deserves nothing and Leonard* deserves to be blamed for the bad act of murder. Rather, both deserved to be blamed for the bad act of murder, but only one, Leonard*, deserves to be blamed for being the person he is and for coming to be the person who performed this bad act.

Thinking carefully about the case of Leonard has actually led me to be less comfortable about my previous proposal. If Leonard is morally responsible and blameworthy for his acts of murder, and so is not a moral monster but, in those moments, a morally responsible agent, his moral responsibility is so vanishingly minimal that it seems not to amount to much. If Leonard could be morally responsible for his acts of murder despite the numerous and colossal impairments to his states of knowledge, self-understanding, and practical agency that I have enumerated in the preceding discussion, then one wonders how much responsibility he could bear, how much it would be reasonable to say that he shared with a Leonard* who by contrast is a largely normally functioning human person. Very little, I think. Very little indeed.

A fine film, like a fine novel, if it is of the right sort, can provide especially vivid thought experiments designed to test philosophical intuitions. I close by reporting that because of Memento, I have been led to revise my earlier commitment to a defense of the ahistorical thesis. Even if there is any life in it, the moral responsibility that could be attributed to an agent like Leonard strongly suggests that it's not worth the ink spilt to discuss it.[7]

Notes

1   In what follows, I will assume familiarity with the film, and I will operate under the assumption that the film does create interpretive challenges that

make any unambiguous rendering of it contentious. I should also note that I have profited from Andy Klein's impressive essay "Everything You Wanted to Know about *Memento*," (2001) although I am not in complete agreement with it.

2   In this way, *Memento* is like Brian De Palma's *Body Double* (1984). Chris Grau has also recommended David Cronenberg's *eXistenZ* (1999) and Joseph Rusnak's *The Thirteenth Floor* (1999).

3   For an opposing view, see Williams (1970).

4   For another film that explores interesting questions of personal identity, see Paul Verhoeven's *Total Recall* (1990).

5   On this topic, I have profited from Hibbs (2003). I am indebted to Chris Grau for calling my attention to this essay.

6   The points considered in the preceding paragraph are owed to Matthew Talbert's judicious comments.

7   I am grateful to Christopher Grau for his thoughtful and extensive comments on an earlier draft of this paper. Matthew Talbert, acting as a reader for Routledge, also offered excellent suggestions, and so I thank him here. Finally, I would like to thank Andrew Kania for inviting me to contribute to this volume, and for his wise and patient editorial advice.

References

Bratman, M. (1987) *Intentions, Plans, and Practical Reason*, Cambridge, MA: Harvard University Press.

Clark, A. and Chalmers, D. (1998) "The Extended Mind," *Analysis* 58: 7–19.

Descartes, R. (1641) *Meditations on First Philosophy*, trans. J. Corringham, R. Soothoff and D. Murdoch (1984) *The Philosophical Writings of Descartes*, vol. II, New York: Cambridge University Press.

Frankfurt, H. (1988) *The Importance of What We Care About*, Cambridge: Cambridge University Press.

Hibbs, T. (2003) "A Neo-noir Filmmaker Echoes a Philosopher's Quest for Truth," *The Chronicle of Higher Education* 50 (12), November 14: B14.

Hume, D. (1740) *A Treatise of Human Nature*, L.A. Selby-Bigge (ed.) (1960) Oxford: Oxford University Press.

Klein, A. (2001) "Everything You Wanted to Know about *Memento*," online. Available at: http://archive.salon.com/ent/movies/feature/2001/06/28/memento_analysis/index.html (accessed 15 October 2008).

Locke, J. (1689) *An Essay on Human Understanding*, A.D. Woozley (ed.) (1974) New York: Meridian.

McKenna, M. (2004) "Responsibility and Globally Manipulated Agents," *Philosophical Topics* 32: 169–92.

Williams, B. (1970) "The Self and the Future," *Philosophical Review* 59: 161–80.

Further reading

Dennett, D. (1987) The Intentional Stance, Cambridge, MA: MIT Press. (A liberal view of action of the sort I endorse.)

Fischer, J.M. (2006) "Responsibility and Self-expression," in My Way, New York, NY: Oxford University Press. (An application of the idea of the narrative structure of a meaningful life to considerations of moral agency.)

Fischer, J.M. and Ravizza, M. (1998) Responsibility and Control: An Essay on Moral Responsibility, Cambridge: Cambridge University Press. (An historical theory of moral responsibility.)

Grau, C. (2005) "Bad Dreams, Evil Demons, and the Experience Machine: Philosophy in The Matrix," in C. Grau (ed.) Philosophers Explore the Matrix, New York, NY: Oxford University Press. (An illuminating discussion of the topic in relation to The Matrix.)

Mele, A. (1995) Autonomous Agents, New York, NY: Oxford University Press. (An historical theory of moral responsibility.)

—— (2001) Self-deception Unmasked, Princeton, NJ: Princeton University Press. (A thorough treatment of the topic of self-deception.)

Perry, J. (1978) A Dialogue on Personal Identity and Immortality, New York, NY: Hackett. (By far the best way to learn about the topic of personal identity.)

Russell, B. (1948) "The Argument from Analogy for Other Minds," in Human Knowledge: Its Scope and Limits, New York, NY: Simon and Schuster. (An excellent article on knowledge of other minds.)

Sher, G. (2006) In Praise of Blame, New York, NY: Oxford University Press. (A contemporary treatment of the problem of the act/agent gap, along with a critical discussion of Hume's resolution.)

Velleman, D. (1991) "Well-being and Time," Pacific Philosophical Quarterly 72: 48–77. (An intriguing treatment of the relation between a meaningful life and its narrative structure.)

Williams, B. (2002) Truth and Truthfulness, Princeton, NJ: Princeton University Press. (A treatment of the relation between truth and desire.)

Wilson, G. (2007) "Action," in E.N. Zalta (ed.) The Stanford Encyclopedia of Philosophy, Fall 2008 edn, online. Available at: http://plato.stanford.edu/archives/fall2008/entries/action/ (accessed 4 August 2008). (A helpful overview of the challenging topic of action theory.)

Chapter 2

Joseph Levine

LEONARD'S SYSTEM: WHY DOESN'T IT WORK?

NEAR THE BEGINNING OF MEMENTO, Leonard argues forcefully that his disability, his inability to lay down new memories, isn't really all that disabling after all (scene R). He claims that memory is overrated, and that his system of writing everything down and constantly checking his notes provides him with sufficient information to get by successfully. He contrasts most peoples' reliance on memory with his reliance on "the facts," that is, what he's written down. Given the research that shows memory to be much more a process of construction than of pure retrieval,[1] and given the relative permanence of what is written down, it might seem offhand that he has a point. Most of us don't bother to write down most of what we want to remember, since, after all, we can remember it. But maybe Leonard is right. Perhaps if we were to rely more on what we could write down, and less on memory, our epistemic situation—the level of justification that our current beliefs achieve at any given time, as well as the range of facts with which we would be acquainted—would improve. Or, at least, it wouldn't be much, if at all, worse.

As anyone who has seen the movie knows, the plot is presented backwards, with each new scene depicting events that occurred before those of the preceding scene. While this technique has been used before, it is especially interesting in this case since it puts us, in a way, in the same epistemic situation as Leonard. During any scene we have as little to go on as he has. All we know is what is right there in the moment, including the notes about past events that are available. Leonard can't remember, and we're in the same boat since we haven't seen the past yet.

When Leonard makes his little speech about how he doesn't need memory to get by, that he does just fine with his notes and his "facts," the movie encourages us to take what he says seriously. At that point we've seen him kill someone who seemed to be a threat to him—according to his notes, anyway—and in general he appears to be functioning fairly well. So maybe we're not really going to buy this "memory is overrated" argument—it is just a movie, after all—but the picture presented has a definite air of plausibility about it.

Of course, by the end of the movie it becomes all too clear that, far from functioning fairly well with his notes and his "facts," Leonard is totally clueless. As we learn the course of events that led up to the initial scenes in which he seemed to be doing okay, we realize that his epistemic situation in those early (that is, fictionally later) scenes is so weak as to render him powerless to control his life in any meaningful way. The notes that were supposed to provide his link to the past serve to consistently mislead him. None of his inferences about his present situation or how it came about are reliable. The world is worse than a buzz of confusion to him, since he thinks he knows what's going on while suffering massive delusion. For Leonard, "everything he knows is wrong."

So now the question presents itself: What was wrong with his method? Why is memory so crucial to maintaining an epistemic position that allows one to function, even minimally, in the world? Why don't his notes and strategies for getting by succeed? What epistemological lessons can we learn from Memento concerning the crucial role that memory plays in providing a cognitive subject with a belief system that adequately mirrors the world around her?

In this essay I want to explore three approaches to answering these questions: I call them the "qualitative-difference" approach, the "mere-quantitative-difference" approach, and the "architectural" approach. I will begin by discussing the first two approaches, showing why I think they do not adequately explain Leonard's problem. I will then describe the third approach, which incorporates some features of the first two, but in a way that properly explains Leonard's epistemic disability. In the course of defending the architectural approach I will discuss the bearing of Leonard's case on an extremely provocative view in the philosophy of mind, championed by Andy Clark and David Chalmers (1998), called the "extended mind" hypothesis. On this view it is wrong to think of the skull, or the nervous system, as a principled boundary between the mind and the outer world. On the contrary, information that we write down, store in our computers, or just possess in our library, is a part of our minds in the same way as what is stored "inside." This view of the mind should find nothing in principle wrong with Leonard's system, so an advocate of the extended mind hypothesis is likely to adopt the mere-quantitative-difference approach to explaining Leonard's epistemic deficit. My argument against that approach will also constitute an argument against the extended-mind hypothesis itself.

The qualitative-difference and mere-quantitative-difference approaches

On the qualitative-difference approach, the problem Leonard faces is, as the name suggests, a qualitative one; that is, in principle, nothing that is written down as a mere historical record can play the epistemic role that memory plays. By a "mere historical record" I mean to distinguish cases like Leonard's from more mundane cases where people write things down—like shopping lists—in order to aid or jog their memories. When I consult a shopping list and see that it says "milk," I don't just then learn that I need milk, but rather remember that I do. What's written down functions to prompt a memory experience. With Leonard, however, the notes he writes for himself are not prompts or aids of this sort. They don't remind him of anything. Rather, he is in the position of an historian discovering a document from the past and attempting to figure out what it reveals about events at the time. On the qualitative-difference approach, then, though historical records are of course a valuable source of data about past events, they cannot substitute for memory. Memory provides a different kind of support for our beliefs about the world, without which genuine knowledge (except of the most trivial kind concerning current experience) is not possible.

On the mere-quantitative-difference approach, on the other hand, there is nothing principled about Leonard's weak epistemic position. Historical records don't differ in kind from memories. The problem Leonard faces is purely quantitative in nature. Simply put, he just can't write enough down. If somehow he could write faster, or speak fast enough into a tape recorder (or tattoo himself faster—ouch!), he could in principle use his system to overcome the disabling effects of his memory loss on his epistemic relation to the world. However, as a matter of fact, it isn't possible to write or talk fast enough, and too much data gets lost. The difference between his epistemic position and our own is like the difference between an historian who studies a recent period of Western history, with tons of archival material available to her, and one who studies an ancient period from which only fragments survive. They are both engaged in the same kind of enterprise, one just has much more to go on than the other.

Let's begin now to consider the qualitative-difference approach. What difference in kind might there be between memory and other forms of information storage that might bear on their epistemic status? Tyler Burge's (1995) idea of "content preservation," which he applies both to memory and testimony, might provide the basis for making just such a principled, qualitative distinction. So let's take a digression from Leonard's predicament just to get clear on Burge's view. Afterward, we'll see if it helps to explain why Leonard is so epistemically disabled by his memory loss.

Burge's discussion starts from consideration of a puzzle. But first a few preliminaries. Traditionally, philosophers distinguish *a priori* knowledge from *a posteriori* knowledge. The former includes mathematics, logic, and purely definitional propositions, such as that all bachelors are unmarried. The latter includes most of what we know, from where our keys are to highly theoretical claims in science. While there are many different definitions of the terms "*a priori*" and "*a posteriori*" around, let's follow Burge in using the terms in the following manner. One possesses an "*a priori* warrant" for one's belief if no perception of a specific situation plays a role in providing the justification for the belief. One possesses an "*a posteriori* warrant" just in case an experience of a specific situation does provide part of the justification. So, for instance, if my basis for believing that there's a computer screen in front of me right now as I type is that I see it, then my belief that there is a computer screen in front of me right now possesses an *a posteriori* warrant. However, if my basis for believing that the Pythagorean theorem holds is my seeing a proof, this particular written expression of the proof is not really part of what justifies my belief, even though of course I accessed the proof through seeing it.

Rather, once I understand it, it's my cognitively appreciating the relation between the premises and the conclusion that does the work. Hence, though vision plays a causally necessary role in this case, my warrant for believing the theorem is still *a priori*.

Now comes the puzzle. Suppose one comes to believe a mathematical theorem on the basis of a fairly long proof. Perhaps the proof itself is, say, fifty lines long, and the conclusion is derived by a valid inference rule from lines 49 and 25. Granted, if the rule used to derive line 50 from the other two is logically valid, then one's warrant for believing the proposition expressed by line 50 is *a priori*—so long as one's warrant for believing the immediate premises, the propositions expressed on lines 49 and 25, is also *a priori*.

But now consider one's warrant for believing line 25. True, at the time one derived it, one could see how it followed validly from earlier premises (which, we'll assume, were warranted *a priori*). But that information is now gone. One remembers deriving it validly, and now remembers the result, line 25, and so one uses it to derive the conclusion, line 50. The puzzle is, does this reliance on memory to furnish the premise for the last step render one's warrant for the conclusion *a posteriori*? If so, very little of what we normally consider *a priori* knowledge will survive.

Why might the reliance on memory undercut the *a priori* status of one's warrant for belief in the conclusion of the proof, the theorem? The idea is that memory, like perception, is an experience. Just as an answer to the question, "How do you know there's a computer screen in front of you?" is "I see it"—that is, I'm having a particular experience of the computer screen—so too an answer to "How do you know that the proposition expressed by line 25 is true?" might be "I remember proving it"—that is, I'm having a particular experience of a previous mental state. In both cases, one might argue, I am currently relying on an experience of some particular situation or event—what's outside me in one case and what happened earlier in my mind in the other—to support my current belief. If the one case counts as *a posteriori*, goes the argument, so too should the other.

Burge argues, however, that the role of memory in the proof case is quite different from the role of vision in the computer screen case. In the latter case, vision is supplying new information, adding to whatever justificatory force might or might not have previously attached to the proposition that there is a computer screen in front of me. In this sense it is correct to say that my belief that there is a computer screen in front of me is epistemically based on the visual experience; it relies on the visual experience for its justification, or warrant. However, in the proof case, where memory, as it were, "delivers" the proposition from line 25 to my current state of mind, to be used in the derivation of line 50, memory isn't adding a new content, or providing justificatory force; rather, the role of memory in this case is purely "preservative" (hence the name of his article, "Content Preservation"). The idea is that memory functions to preserve information that might be needed for later reasoning within my "belief store," and the preservative process of memory functions not only to maintain the propositional content itself, but also its level and kind of warrant. Memory isn't adding to, or subtracting from, the warrant that attaches to the proposition. It is preserving it from its earlier presence in one's conscious awareness, transferring it, and presenting it to one's current conscious awareness. Of course one relies on the mechanism of memory when using the earlier line in a current bit of reasoning, but, for Burge, that is no different from the way we use what's written down on the page to follow the proof. In neither case is the experience itself, of seeing the proof or remembering the line, explicitly part of the justification for the conclusion. We might put it this way: What is remembered plays a role, but not the remembering itself.

Let's get back to Leonard and his predicament. Suppose Burge is right and memory "preserves content" in the way he suggests. How might this make a difference to Leonard? Well, what we are imagining is the situation in which a piece of information that would have been available to Leonard via memory, had he not suffered the trauma to his brain, is now available in written form. Since he has to perceive the note—whether on a piece of paper or on his body—Burge's notion of content preservation doesn't apply. The information isn't immediately available to him, but rather must be perceived and interpreted. Perhaps this then is the crucial difference between a normal person's ability to rely on memory to make her way in the world and Leonard's need to rely on a written record. For the normal person who remembers what she's seen and heard, the information so acquired is "preserved" by memory, whereas for Leonard, relying on his written records, it must be accessed again through perception and interpretation.

Of course, Burge's account of the way memory "preserves content" is quite controversial, but even if we accept it, I don't see how it helps to explain Leonard's problem. What Burge's account can explain is why Leonard's beliefs about the past, and what's going on in the present to the extent this is conditioned by the past, perhaps have a different epistemic status than those of a person with intact memory. Perhaps Leonard couldn't know a theorem that took many steps to prove in the way a normal person could. Perhaps every belief about the past is burdened with an extra layer of required justification, since each bit of information must be perceived and interpreted. But all of this may be true even though the information recorded in his notes is every bit as reliable as that which others get by memory, or what he himself would have obtained by memory had he not suffered from his condition.

One issue is the kind of justification or warrant a belief has: Is it *a priori* or *a posteriori*? Is it "preserved" by memory or based on current perception? This might matter for certain issues, such as the status of mathematical knowledge, as Burge's discussion suggests. But so long as the information is relatively reliable, what kind of justification it has shouldn't matter for the prospects for success in acting on it. For action, what matters is reliability. True, Leonard's information, given its written form, must first be perceived and interpreted before he can make use of it, and these added steps do also add some degree of risk of getting things wrong. But if this were the only problem Leonard's condition wouldn't seem to be so debilitating as it clearly is. After all, the perceptual and interpretive mechanisms he employs—his visual and language systems—are tremendously reliable. The added epistemic risk that attends the need to perceive and interpret what would otherwise have been remembered seems marginal. And let's not forget, as Leonard reminds us, that memory mechanisms themselves are not always tremendously reliable. After all, that is why we make shopping lists for ourselves. I conclude that Leonard's problem cannot be explained by the different epistemic status possessed by what's remembered and what's perceived (even if, as Burge argues, there were such a difference).

What's the alternative explanation? Well, the mere-quantitative-difference approach pins Leonard's deficit totally on the quantity of information he misses by losing his short-term memory. As I put it above, we can think of Leonard as an historian of the ancient world, with only fragments to go on. There is, after all, just so much he can write down, and that amount is so much less than what a normal person can remember, it's no wonder he finds himself at such an epistemic disadvantage. Perhaps that's all there is to it.

While I think it's right to say that the small quantity of information he has available is crucial to explaining Leonard's epistemic deficit, we need to put a little more emphasis on the term "available" here to get a full explanation of what's going on. True, he can only write down so much. But even if he could write down everything a normal person would remember, he would still have a problem. The problem is that it doesn't do him any good sitting on paper. It has to get inside his mind, where his memories would have been, to be of any use to him. So while the qualitative-difference idea concerning the special "preservative" status of memory proved irrelevant to explaining his deficit, the fact that what's written down has to be perceived and interpreted before it can be of use is quite relevant. In this sense I want to claim that both the qualitative-difference and the mere-quantitative-difference approaches possess a grain of truth. As the qualitative-difference approach emphasizes, the fact that Leonard must perceive and interpret what's written down—steps not necessary for what's remembered—is crucial to explaining his epistemic deficit. On the other hand, as the mere-quantitative-difference approach insists, the issue in the end does come down to a matter of how much information is available to Leonard. The way to incorporate both of these insights is through the architectural approach, to which I now turn.

The architectural approach

The architectural approach is based on the idea that the mind is a kind of information processing device with a computational architecture, as is the case with your computer. Computers contain central processors, working memory, hard drives, input devices (keyboards, microphones, cameras), and output devices (monitors, printers, speakers). According to the currently popular "computational model," minds also possess an architecture, which it makes sense to investigate empirically. While there are a number of issues here that fall under the heading of cognitive or computational "architecture," the one that I want to exploit for the purpose of explaining Leonard's disability is the architectural distinction between cognitive "modules" and "central processes." Let me explain this distinction, and then show how it helps in understanding Leonard's predicament.

Jerry Fodor (1983) divides mental operations into two basic kinds: those that take place within input systems, which he calls "modules," and those that take place within what he calls "central systems," which are not modular. To simplify, assume that we have six input systems—one each for the five senses, and one for interpreting and producing language. According to Fodor, each of these systems is modular, in the sense that it works largely in isolation from the other input systems, as well as from the central systems. The idea is that an input module (say, vision) takes stimulations of nerve endings as input and delivers a description of the relevant part of the environment as output. One of the crucial features of a modular processor is that it doesn't have access to information that is available to the mind as a whole, but only to a restricted range of information that is stored within it.

One way to see what Fodor means here is to consider a visual illusion. You look at a stick partially submerged in water and it looks bent. After lifting it out of the water you see that it's really straight; it's just that the refraction of the light as it travels through the water makes it look bent. But now, when you stick it back in the water, it still looks bent, even though you know perfectly well that it's straight. What's going on? Well, according to Fodor, the persistence of the illusion that the stick is bent reflects the fact that your visual system is modular. In computing the shape of the stick from the light hitting the retina, the visual system doesn't know about the refraction of light in water. What's more, your visual system also doesn't have access to the information that you, as a matter of what's stored in your central system, have available; namely, that it's a straight stick. The point is that seeing isn't believing after all. What you see is determined by what your visual system figures out, but what you end up believing on the basis of what you see takes account of everything else you know as well. In this case, you will believe the stick is straight even though it looks bent. You know, as it were, much more than your visual system does about this.

This distinction between how things look to you in the stick-in-the-water case and what you actually believe about the shape of the stick highlights the particular way in which modular processing differs from central processing, the non-modular system in the mind within which all-things-considered belief is determined. We can put it this way: Modular processing is "local" in character, whereas central (non-modular—I'll let this be understood from now on) processing is "global." Taking the visual system as our example again, the information processing taking place within it applies to two sources of data for delivering verdicts about the spatial layout of objects in the subject's environment: the light hitting the retina, and whatever information is stored within the visual module. In deciding how to visually represent the shape of the stick— that is, present how the stick looks—the visual system only consults these two local sources of data. What you know about its shape from having examined it before isn't part of its database.

On the other hand, central processing, the kind that determines what you actually believe, seems to be global in character. When trying to figure out what to believe about a particular situation, almost anything you believe about any other topic—whether it be general knowledge, memories of particular events, or current experiences—is potentially relevant. What's more, when deliberating between two mutually exclusive possibilities for what to believe, a large part of what decides between the two hypotheses are certain global features of the overall belief system one would have were one to adopt one or the other to believe.

Perfectly mundane matters as well as highly theoretical ones exemplify both points. For example, suppose you are driving on the highway and you see a sea of brake lights in front of you all of a sudden. What you see is just that—a lot of red lights coming on in your visual field. But what you come to believe depends on all sorts of other things you might happen to believe at the time. If you believe you are on your way into Washington, D.C., and you also believe that an al Qaeda video has just been released, you might come to believe that there is a police roadblock ahead, checking for weapons. A belief about something that happened half way across the world was brought to bear on how to interpret the import of red lights flashing in your visual field.[2]

As for how global features of entire belief systems affect which particular belief we adopt in a particular situation, consider how most of us react to reports of supernatural events, even if we ourselves perceived the allegedly supernatural event. We refuse to believe it. Why? Well one way of explaining our reluctance to believe that a genuinely supernatural event has occurred is that doing so would conflict with deeply held common sense and scientific beliefs. But of course we could remove the conflict by making an ad hoc adjustment in our overall belief system, perhaps by believing that normal laws of nature were suspended in this instance. While this may remove the formal contradiction between our general common sense and scientific beliefs on the one hand and the belief that a supernatural event has just occurred on the other, the resulting belief system as a whole becomes clearly less simple and elegant than the alternatives, namely, that the report was false, or that we ourselves suffered from an illusion. Features such as generality, simplicity, and elegance, which clearly play a large (though not very well understood) role in how we decide what to believe, are global features of whole belief systems, not merely features of individual beliefs or the relation between small sets of data and conclusions drawn from them.[3]

It's important to note that there are two sides to the global character of central processing, both of which bear on Leonard's situation. First, independently of how we in fact reason, canons of good reasoning demand that we take account of both the potential relevance of almost any belief to any other and the global features of entire belief systems. By saying that this is a rational demand, what I mean, in the first instance, is that reasoning in accordance with this demand yields beliefs that are much more likely to be true than reasoning in violation of it. Processes that determine beliefs according to these global principles are highly reliable.

Secondly, not only is following such a globally sensitive procedure a rational demand, but we seem in fact, to a very remarkable extent, to follow such procedures. That is, the kind of information processing that goes on in our central system, the kind that determines what we believe all-things-considered, does seem sensitive to these global features of our belief system. Our thinking seems responsive both to the relevance (and irrelevance) of information from widely disparate areas and to the relative simplicity of vast bodies of beliefs. How we are able to do this is still not well understood at all.[4] Nevertheless, we do do it, and given the way the world is put together, our ability to do it seems to be crucial to our tremendous success in arriving at largely true beliefs about the world.

There is one more element that needs to be added before the architectural approach to explaining Leonard's epistemic problem can be presented—the notion of the "domain of an operation," or, equivalently, the "set of representations over which an operation is defined." An operation in an information processing system applies to a representation (or a set of representations), taking it (or them) as input to the operation, and yielding a representation (or set of representations) as output. If one reasons, say, from the belief that the stick looks to be bent to the belief that the stick is bent, we can think of this as an operation that took the first belief—a representation of the way the stick looks—as input, and delivered the second belief—a representation of how the stick is—as output. The domain of an operation, then, is just the set of representations that the operation is capable of accepting as inputs.

With this idea in mind, one way to characterize the function of an input system is this: Input systems serve to transform information from a form that is not in the domain of the central operations or processes into a form that is.[5] So again, consider a simple case of looking at a stick in water. The world contains this information, that the stick is submerged in the water (and that it is straight). Suppose I want to know what's going on with the stick in question. This information is out there in the world—the straight stick is right there in the water—but the central processes responsible for determining what to believe about the stick and its shape can't access this information; their operations don't work on information in that form, at that location. (Rather, they work on representations in the relevant portion of the brain.) But when I look at it, my visual system takes that information[6] and puts it into a form and location that make it accessible to the central processes whose job it is to figure out what's going on with the stick.

These features we've been discussing—the modularity of input systems, the global nature of central operations, and the constraints on which representations are included in the domain of the relevant operations—all fit under the rubric of cognitive or computational architecture. So the architectural approach to explaining Leonard's disability is the approach that explains it in terms of these features. Let's see how this works.

Applying the architectural approach

I said above that two elements from the first two approaches would be employed in this approach: the fact that Leonard has to perceive and interpret the information that he's written down (along with the snapshots he's taken, of course) and the fact that he has access to much less information than he would have had had his memory been intact. To see how the architectural approach works, incorporating both of these elements, let's start by imagining a somewhat different scenario. Suppose that Leonard—contrary to what is in fact feasible—is able to write down every bit of information he might have stored in memory had he not suffered from his disability. To draw out the contrast I want to focus on, imagine as well that Leonard has a duplicate, Leonard*, who is just like Leonard in every respect except that his memory systems are all intact. So for every item that Leonard* learns (by perception, testimony, reading, or whatever) and remembers, Leonard learns the same item, but instead of remembering it he writes it down. Thus, if we include all the information that Leonard has written down in his "database," we can say that he doesn't suffer from a quantitative deficit of information when compared to Leonard*.

Now let's consider a situation in which Leonard or Leonard* has to decide what to believe. Suppose he has to decide whether or not to trust what someone is saying to him. For instance, consider scene G, in which Natalie, after leaving her house, returns and tells Leonard that Dodd beat her. For Leonard*, who can remember Natalie and his history with her, it would be obvious right away that he can't trust what she says. For him, the task of deciding whether or not to trust what he's being told is the usual one we all face. Most of us can come up with a pretty reasonable idea of whether to trust what we're being told most of the time.

Now let's look at Leonard's situation. Remember, everything in Leonard*'s memory that provides him with evidence concerning Natalie's trustworthiness is available in written form to Leonard. So in one sense he has all the evidence he needs. Leonard* employs that evidence by applying whatever central operations are relevant to such a decision directly upon the evidence. His memory store contains representations that (or enough of which) are included in the domain of those operations. But how is Leonard to use his information? What's written down on paper, no matter how closely he places it to his head, is not within the domain of the operations that figure out what to believe. Hence that information is useless unless it is first transformed into a form, and into a location where the relevant operations can make use of it (i.e., in his brain). To do that he needs to see it and interpret it. This is precisely the problem.

Quantity of information *per se*, given our fiction that he can write down everything relevant, is not the problem. Instead, the problem is the inaccessibility of that information, or, to put it another way, the format in which the information is stored. Since Leonard has to perceive and interpret each individual piece of information—all of which is already in the right form and location for Leonard*—he has two severe limitations on his ability to use it: (1) There is a channel limitation on how much information can be processed through his perceptual input systems at a time, and (2) when something gets in there it doesn't stay very long—after all, the mechanism that stores information in long-term memory is broken. So Leonard never is in the position of being able to utilize all the information, or evidence, that bears on the question at hand at one time. Thus what his central operations are so good at, detecting these global features of extremely large sets of data, never get the chance to be employed. During the course of any central reasoning operation Leonard is always limited to the information that has most recently been perceived.[7]

Let me sum up the main points of the architectural approach. Figuring out what to believe involves central processes that somehow operate on large stores of information at once, information that is stored in a designated location and represented in the appropriate form. Memory is precisely that store of information. Since Leonard must perceive and interpret—that is, process through an input system (actually two, vision and language comprehension)—each piece of information he's stored on paper or on his person, his central processes never get the opportunity to operate on all of it at once. Thus even if he can write fast enough, he suffers from insufficient quantity of information, because of the necessity of perceiving and interpreting what he's written. In this way, as I claimed earlier, the architectural approach does incorporate elements from the first two approaches.

The extended-mind hypothesis

I want now to turn to the bearing of Leonard's case on the "extended mind" hypothesis. As I said earlier, I think that for an advocate of that hypothesis, only the mere-quantitative-difference approach really makes sense, and the limitations of that approach for explaining Leonard's problem show what's wrong with the extended-mind hypothesis itself.

I will first briefly present the view in a little more detail, and then explain how it conflicts with the architectural approach to Leonard's problem defended in this paper.

In an influential paper, Clark and Chalmers (1998) defend the claim that the mind isn't confined to what's enclosed within the skull, or even the central nervous system. Rather, instead of there being a principled division between the mind and the world, better to think of the mind as spreading itself out into the world, including within it information that is written down, stored on computer disks and hard drives, and, perhaps, even what's contained on the internet. While clearly we tend to distinguish what's "inside" from what's "outside" for practical purposes, their idea is that this isn't a theoretically principled division. The information that I can read on a piece of paper is just as much a part of my mind as what's stored in my memory.

To make their case they describe an example involving two people, Inga and Otto, both of whom form the intention to go to a certain location to see a museum exhibit. However Inga remembers where the museum is, so once she forms the intention to see the exhibit she relatively immediately forms the intention to go to the relevant location. Otto, on the other hand, is suffering from Alzheimer's, so he has to write everything down in a notebook that he keeps on his person and consults constantly. So when he forms the intention to see the exhibit, he first looks up the address in the notebook, and then forms the intention to go to that location. Their claim is that, given his mode of interaction with the information in his notebook, Otto should count as believing that the museum is at the address in question even before looking at the notebook, just by virtue of his having the information stored there. In terms of what they believe, Clark and Chalmers maintain, there isn't a principled difference between Inga and Otto. Except for details that don't matter for the question at issue, their case of Inga and Otto is strikingly similar to our case of Leonard and Leonard* (see Figure 2).

The extended-mind hypothesis might seem to be a natural extension of "semantic externalism," a doctrine that has many adherents in both philosophy of mind and philosophy of language. Semantic externalism is the view that the contents of many of our cognitive states—our beliefs, desires, thoughts, etc.—are partly determined by the world around us. To get the idea, consider Hilary Putnam's famous thought experiment involving "Twin Earth" (1975). Putnam asks us to consider

Figure 2 Just part of Leonard's system, or part of his mind? (22, 1:34:21)

a world just like ours, at least superficially, that he calls "Twin Earth." On Twin Earth there is a substance that looks, tastes, and behaves just like water does on Earth, except it's made of a totally different chemical compound, "XYZ" for short. Here's the question: When I think, here on Earth, that water is liquid at room temperature, is my thought about our water only, H_2O, or also about Twin-water, XYZ? Putnam argues, convincingly, that my thought is only about H_2O. That is, what my thought is about, what determines its content, is partly a matter of what stuff I interact with. In this sense, the external world plays a role in determining the content of my thoughts.

Suppose one accepts this view (not everyone does, of course,[8] but, as I mentioned above, it's widespread among philosophers of mind and language). If what's outside my mind plays a role in determining what my thoughts mean, then is it such a stretch to say that my thoughts *themselves* literally extend out into the world beyond my skull? If the nature of water, that it's H_2O, partly constitutes what I'm thinking about when I think about water, then why couldn't what's written on a piece of paper, or tattooed on my arm, not count as part of my mind?

In fact, I think there is a world of difference between the doctrine of semantic externalism and the extended-mind hypothesis.[9] While the former is quite plausible (though still controversial), it lends no support that I can see to the latter. Furthermore, I think our reflections on Leonard's disability show what's wrong with the extended-mind hypothesis. Let me take these points in order.

First, externalism about the contents or meanings of thoughts embodies the following idea. Many of an object's properties or features are determined not only by what it's like in itself, intrinsically, but also by how it is related to other objects. So, to borrow an example from Antony (1995), while Michael Jordan is over six and a half feet tall in his own right, he is (or was) a basketball player by virtue not only of his intrinsic features, but also by virtue of there being an institutional setting, involving thousands of others, within which he can play basketball. In this sense one is an externalist about the feature of being a basketball player.

However, despite the fact that Michael Jordan wouldn't be a basketball player without thousands of others related to him in a complex way— the way that constitutes the institution of basketball—it is still clear where the boundaries of being a basketball player are: the boundaries of Michael Jordan himself of course. Basketball players are individual, discrete entities, with limits that coincide with the limits of individual human bodies. There is no "extended basketball player" hypothesis that follows from being an externalist about the feature of being a basketball player. So too, just because which thought a mind has is determined partly by facts outside the skull, doesn't mean that the mind itself extends beyond the skull.

The foregoing was meant to show that adopting externalism about the contents of mental states does not in fact lead naturally to the extended-mind hypothesis. But from our discussion above concerning Leonard, we see specific reasons for rejecting that hypothesis. First of all, to the extent that the distinction between an input system and a central system is principled, that enforces a distinction between the "inside" and "outside" that the extended-mind hypothesis rejects. After all, what is an input system, if not a mechanism for getting what is outside the mind inside the mind? Calling something an "input" entails there is a boundary to cross.

What then determines the boundary of the "inside," the mind's central system? The natural answer is this: The central system includes the mechanisms that embody its principal operations together with the objects upon which those processes operate. Central-system operations are those globally sensitive computational operations that determine what we believe, and the only objects on which they operate are those that have been properly processed through one of the input systems. Thus memories of what's been seen, heard, and the like count as within the mind, but what's written on pieces of paper, no matter how constantly close to hand, do not. Leonard's problem is precisely that the information is not inside the mind, where it needs to be to do him any good. The same consideration would seem to apply to Otto as well.[10]

Interestingly, Clark and Chalmers do consider the objection that what makes it the case that Otto's notes do not count as part of what he believes—as information in his mind—is the fact that he has to perceive it before he can reason with it. They do not think that this fact grounds a principled distinction between what's inside and outside the mind, because, they argue, one can just consider perception as a kind of internal channel of information flow within the mind. However, if we take seriously the differences discussed above between the global central processes that determine what we believe and the modular input processes that transform information out in the world into a form usable by central processes, I think the basis for a principled distinction between what's inside and outside the mind exists. Leonard can't function precisely because, no matter how fast he can write, what he writes isn't in a form, or at a location, that his central reasoning can use in the particular way necessary for developing a reasonable common sense picture of the world around him. And that's why Leonard's system doesn't work.

Notes

1 For a good overview of the research on memory, see Reisberg (2006: 139–247).
2 For a really nice example of this idea of potential relevance from anywhere as it applies in science, see Antony (2003).
3 For a classic discussion of this issue, see Quine and Ullian (1978).
4 Fodor (1983, 2000) argues, in fact, that we haven't a clue how this is done, and that the problem threatens the viability of a computational model of such processes. Others argue the problem is not nearly so intractable. See Ford and Pylyshyn (1996) for several papers that take opposing views on this question.
5 This leaves out an important aspect of what input systems do, which is to figure out what information is in fact out there. That they don't do this perfectly is why there are illusions. But for present purposes this can be ignored.
6 Again, this isn't quite right. What the visual system does is take the information concerning the light hitting the retina, which, in the normal situation, preserves the information concerning the shape and location of the stick.

7 Of course he also has available, within the domain of the central operations, all of the information stored in memory from before his trauma. Indeed, without that, he would be altogether unable to make it through the day. But the point is that so much of the information upon which his most recent decisions need to be based postdate the trauma, and so is usually unavailable to the relevant operation.

8 For a particularly well-developed critique of externalism, see Segal (2000).

9 Clark and Chalmers themselves note the difference, so they don't argue that the extended-mind hypothesis just follows from semantic externalism. They do see it as an extension of that doctrine, though, albeit a radical one.

10 Of course there is a significant difference between Leonard and Otto. Otto's memory deficit is very small in comparison with Leonard's, so his reliance on his notebook does not put him in the impossible epistemic position that Leonard occupies. But with respect to the question of whether to consider what's in the notebook as "in" his mind, the two cases are identical.

References

Antony, L.M. (1995) "Sisters, Please, I'd Rather Do It Myself: A Defense of Individualism in Epistemology," in S. Haslanger (ed.) "Feminist Perspectives on Language, Knowledge, and Reality," special issue of *Philosophical Topics* 23: 59–94.

—— (2003) "Rabbit-pots and Supernovas: The Relevance of Psychological Evidence to Linguistic Theory," in A. Barber (ed.) *The Epistemology of Language*, Oxford: Oxford University Press.

Burge, T. (1995) "Content Preservation," *Philosophical Issues* 6: 271–300.

Clark, A. and Chalmers, D. (1998) "The Extended Mind," *Analysis* 58: 10–23.

Fodor, J.A. (1983) *The Modularity of Mind*, Cambridge, MA: MIT Press.

—— (2000) *The Mind Doesn't Work That Way*, Cambridge, MA: MIT Press.

Ford, K. and Pylyshyn, Z. (eds) (1996) *The Robot's Dilemma Revisited: The Frame Problem in Artificial Intelligence*, Norwood, NJ: Ablex Publishing.

Putnam, H. (1975) "The Meaning of 'Meaning'," in K. Gunderson (ed.) *Language, Mind, and Knowledge*, Minneapolis, MN: University of Minnesota Press.

Quine, W.V. and Ullian, J.S. (1978) *The Web of Belief*, 2nd edn, New York, NY: McGraw-Hill.

Reisberg, D. (2006) *Cognition: Exploring the Science of the Mind*, New York, NY: W.W. Norton.

Segal, G. (2000) *A Slim Book About Narrow Content*, Cambridge, MA: MIT Press.

Further reading

Adams, F.A. and Aizawa, K. (2001) "The Bounds of Cognition," *Philosophical Psychology* 14: 43–64. (Adams and Aizawa consider the extended-mind hypothesis, or what they call "transcranial cognition," arguing that though there is nothing conceptually incoherent about the idea, nor does it violate natural law, still there is no good reason to believe that this sort of cognition actually exists.)

Clark, A. (2001) "Reasons, Robots, and the Extended Mind," *Mind and Language* 16: 121–45. (Clark, the principal defender of the extended-mind hypothesis, explores the implications of new paradigms in cognitive science, such as "situated" and "embodied" cognition, for our view of rationality and the evolution of advanced human cognition.)

Garfield, J.L. (ed.) (1987) *Modularity in Knowledge Representation and Natural Language Processing*, Cambridge, MA: MIT Press. (This is a fairly technical compilation of articles both in favor of and against the view that language processing and perception is modular.)

Goldman, A. (1986) *Epistemology and Cognition*, Cambridge, MA: Harvard University Press. (Alvin Goldman, a leading epistemologist, systematically reviews the bearing of research in cognitive psychology on epistemological concerns. He defends a naturalistic account of knowledge and justification. Chapter 10 concerns memory.)

Martin, C.B. and Deutscher, M. (1966) "Remembering," *The Philosophical Review* 75: 161–96. (This classic article attempts to provide an analysis of what it is to remember. The authors propose a causal theory that they claim addresses various epistemological concerns about memory.)

Pinker, S. (1997) *How the Mind Works*, New York, NY: W.W. Norton. (This is a popular work by an eminent psychologist and psycholinguist, in which he presents a view of the mind as a system of innate modules shaped by evolution. Unlike Fodor, he argues that central cognition is largely modular as well.)

Chapter 3

John Sutton

THE FEEL OF THE WORLD: EXOGRAMS, HABITS, AND THE CONFUSION OF TYPES OF MEMORY

"I don't want to live backwards,
I don't even want to look backwards . . . "
—Kristin Hersh, lyrics from "Your Dirty Answer,"
featured on the album *Sunny Border Blue* (2001)

Introduction: the feel of the world

MY PAST REMAINS ALIVE FOR ME in my explicit memories of single events, of particular shared experiences, moments of embarrassment or joy. But my past also still marks me in all the things I know about the world yet don't need to think about right now—in the way other people interact with me, in the way I drive and the music I sing along with as I do, in the state of my teeth, in my clothes and my smile, in the scar on my elbow and the condition of my internal organs. History animates complex dynamical systems like people, bodies, brains, and groups at many different timescales and levels. Christopher Nolan's film *Memento* dramatizes the extraordinary variety of ways in which the past is absorbed and drives us even when it isn't consciously accessible. In this chapter, I argue that *Memento* relies on a sophisticated taxonomy of types of memory that it simultaneously and successfully challenges. The film explicitly teaches us about differences between *personal memory*, for specific episodes in one's past, *factual memory*, or general knowledge about the past, and *habit* (or *procedural* or *embodied*) memory, through which we remember how to do things. Yet at the same time, brilliantly, Nolan complicates these neat distinctions by constantly playing with the many forms of interaction, coordination, or (more often in *Memento*) confusion of different types of memory, of the different ways the past drives us.

As we work out the story told backwards in *Memento*, we decode layers of history built in to artifacts and bodies, often in wayward forms or through deviant causal pathways. Struggling to make sense of the events revealed in the reverse sequence of color scenes, we partly share Leonard's inability explicitly to grasp or tap into that history. This primary narrative device rests on and coexists with a whole range of clues and residues of "actual" fictional-world time, little revelations of the asymmetric causal structure of reality: scars open up, clothes and cars get cleaner.

One example will serve to introduce my central theme: the richly layered, not always comfortable interweaving or co-presence of different forms of memory. When we first see Leonard tending to Natalie's swollen, bruised face, gingerly wrapping ice for her (scene G), both he and we are unaware that it was Leonard himself who hit her, just minutes earlier, not Dodd as she now claims.[1] But—as, I'll argue, throughout the film—Leonard is also still affected in various ways by what he can't recall. In a brilliant short sequence suggested by Guy Pearce, Leonard here experiences sensations in his hand and knuckles, as if he's hurt himself in some way he doesn't understand: looking down, puzzled, he clenches his fist and unfurls it in an insert shot from Leonard's point of view. When we then cut back to Leonard's face, his bewilderment has a slightly different quality (see Figure 3.1).

Figure 3.1 Leonard puzzled by his sore hand (G, 1:12:31)

Bodies, and the traces they conceal, carry the past, whether it is explicitly and fully detected or not. In other cases in the film, I'll suggest, there's even more highlighting of the possible seepage or bleeding of information across personal, factual, procedural, visceral, affective, material, and social aspects of memory and history.

I have two complementary aims, hoping that philosophy and film can here be mutually illuminating. On the one hand, we can better understand the pervasive roles in our lives of those aspects of memory that Leonard has lost, by focusing on the precise nature, range, and difficulty of what he has to do to manage or bypass the narrative gulfs in his life. Here, we treat *Memento* as a brilliant thought experiment that vividly reveals memory-related features of ordinary mental and social life that usually escape notice in their unquestioned ubiquity. On the other hand, we can read back in to the film a more subtle, fascinated interrogation of the distinction between explicit personal memory and habit memory. In this more ambitious mode of analysis, we use independently motivated theoretical concerns to help us see real features of the film that might otherwise remain invisible.

Not all aspects of past experience are eliminated or irrelevant even with the selective and dramatic loss of conscious access to it. Leonard still knows how wood will sound when knocked, how glass will feel when he picks it up. As he tells Natalie, "it's the kind of memory you take for granted" (P, 0:34:12). In a range of circumstances, Leonard knows what to do, how to use things, and what's likely to happen when you do. As a philosopher might say, he has an enduring mastery of sensorimotor contingencies, maintained by reliable ongoing interaction with everyday objects (Noë 2004). Like many people who can no longer convert or consolidate new experiences into long-term personal or factual memories, Leonard nonetheless retains the know-how needed to dress and to drive, to walk and talk.

Christopher Nolan found himself always knocking on the table when describing the project to actors.[2] This concrete action on a brute physical object helped to communicate the film's texture, inside Leonard's world of things and present sensations, operating often from his own point of view or close by, in the claustrophobic space and time he must inhabit. In the pivotal scene in which Leonard describes these remaining sensory certainties, he tells Natalie that despite his condition he still knows "the feel of the world" (P, 0:34:19). By the time of this rare brief moment of peace between scenes of more frenzied action, the film has already familiarized us with the idea that there are distinct types of memory. We've heard Leonard repeatedly explain the nature of his condition and his system, and we've heard enough from him of the parallel story of Sammy Jankis to know the difference between true memory, affected by possible damage to the hippocampus, and forms of "instinct" or "conditioning." Sammy should still have been able to learn through repetition, as we learn to ride a bike: "you just get better through practice" (7, 0:31:54). Sammy's failure to demonstrate the right dissociation between memory and instinct got Leonard's smug past self a big promotion, and Leonard's present confidence that conditioning works for him as it didn't for Sammy, that habit and routine do make his life possible, is itself pat or routinized. As Nolan says, Leonard has reduced his condition to a series of soundbites.

The theory that thus seems, on first impressions, to drive the film assumes a sharp distinction between different types of memory. It suited Leonard then to accept this theory from Sammy's doctors and from his own research, and he needs it now as he seeks to cope with his own temporally broken situation, to find strategies to tie together his fragmented experience in service of his driving urge for revenge. The idea that memory comes in fundamentally independent forms is heavily reinforced in Memento's early scenes, in part to train the audience in the plot's ground rules. Before we ever have doubts about the relationship between Sammy's and Leonard's stories, we know that the abilities to learn new information or to retain new personal experiences for more than a short period can be lost, even while procedural skills and know-how remain.

This chapter considers the complex roles played, at the heart of Memento, by this taxonomy of memory. Although the taxonomy is of considerable independent interest for both theoretical and practical reasons (Sutton 2007, 2008), here I stick closely to the film. I first examine habit and knowhow, the range of embodied memory capacities that Leonard labels "conditioning" or "instinct" but that actually include some sophisticated skills. I argue that in Memento, as in some complex real-world contexts, information and experience do not remain neatly bounded within independent memory systems, as personal memory and embodied memory interact in subtle ways. Next, I discuss the links between personal or autobiographical memory, on the one hand, and the capacity for genuine action and choice, on the other, examining the nature, emotional valence, and use of those fragmentary personal memories that Leonard retains. Finally, I address the use in Leonard's "system" of objects and mementos, which I'll call "exograms" or external memories, adopting Merlin Donald's term for the worldly counterparts to "engrams," our inner neuro-biological memory traces (Donald 1991; Sutton forthcoming). Leonard's attempts to extend his own mind, which involve a diverse array of aids, are vulnerable but partly successful. I focus on Leonard's habitual modes of engagement with different parts of this distributed system, arguing that his particular relation to his tattoos—those most embodied of exograms—strikingly reveals Nolan's depiction of the interaction or confusion of distinctive forms of memory and history. In sum, my case in this chapter is that *Memento*'s attention to the interaction or confusion of forms of memory brings the "mind–body" problem to practical life by revealing the multiplicity of forces normally hidden behind each term.

Habit, skill, and history

Leonard's spared capacities—the skills that he retains after the incident—extend much further than acquaintance with the basic properties of things and the common requirements of daily life. He also knows and inhabits "the feel of the world" in more unique ways. He believes that he has unusual skills in interacting with both objects and people. In his previous life as an investigator, we hear, Leonard learned how to read eyes and body language effectively, so that he still has the vital ability now to see through people's bullshit (scene 5). Although Leonard officially attributes his remaining capacities to "conditioning" or "instinct," they are in no way rigid or stereotyped. He uses "a practiced hand" to slip the lock on Dodd's room at the Mountcrest Inn (scene M, Nolan 2001: 159). He has the expertise to assess certain kinds of traces even under conditions of high arousal and emotional intensity: arriving with Teddy at the derelict building, he inspects the tracks of the pick-up that he himself had earlier abandoned there with "a methodical, practiced eye" (scene V, Nolan 2001: 106). Despite Teddy's nonchalant claim that the vehicle has been there for years, Leonard is confident that the tracks aren't more than a few days old.

Although large tracts of Leonard's personal history are otherwise as inaccessible to him as to us, we can thus see that it included various forms of "useful experience," in which these more idiosyncratic skills were honed. Further, the ongoing employment of Leonard's "system" requires a host of context-sensitive procedures and "well-practiced, efficient movements," like those with which he sets up his wall chart in room 304 (scene I, Nolan 2001: 169). His ability to use this range of embodied and external memory aids relies on the broader realm of spared skills provided by procedural or habit memory.

The acquisition of both skills and habits tends to be gradual rather than one-off. Such training does not require memory for each specific learning episode: if I've ended up with a competent tennis backhand, half-decent ability at jazz piano, or the dazzling sleight-of-hand of a stage magician, I don't have to think about particular lessons or past exercises of my skill as I act. In fact my smoothly-grooved performance is often disrupted if I do consciously access specific past occasions whilst in the thick of things.

Leonard tells us in a practiced narrative that, in a "graceful solution to the memory problem," he has successfully mobilized habit and routine to substitute for the free-ranging conscious access to the personal past that he's lost (scene 4). This fits a standard view, in both Western philosophy and common sense: the smooth exercise of established skills and habits operates along autonomous and automated embodied lines, independent of attention, awareness, control, deliberation, and explicit memory. On Hubert Dreyfus's influential phenomenology of everyday expertise, for example, absorbed action is the smooth direct engagement of body and world, so that conscious access to the causes or mechanisms, the processes or principles involved, can only interfere with the grooved routines: "mindedness is the enemy of embodied coping" (Dreyfus 2007: 353). According to practitioners' lore in music, dance, and sport, top-down care or attempted control disrupts flow and rhythm: as one elite performer wrote, "when you're playing well, you don't think about *anything*" (quoted in Sutton 2007: 767). Sandy Gordon, long-time psychologist with the successful Australian cricket team, describes "a critical skill in cricket" as the capacity "to absorb yourself in the moment and have a present focus" (2001: 20). On this view, history and practice must have their effects directly on and in the present flowing embodied activity, without cognitive mediation.

Yet, as I've noted, the idiosyncratic skills that Leonard can still exercise, despite his lack of explicit personal or factual memory, are not mindless. Nolan repeatedly underlines the richness and flexibility of these remaining embodied and habitual resources, something that these standard views (including Leonard's) perhaps mask. Leonard is no mere engine of reflex, even though he doesn't need to set his skillful actions in motion deliberately, to reflect on the basis or mechanisms of his ability, or to consider explicitly the source of his skill. The slow processes of incorporation through which embodied skills develop are, in the main, "traceless practices" (Connerton 1989: 102). For most of us, such procedural skills are complemented by and integrated with quite different forms of memory, in which history animates present dynamics more directly. My personal memories are *about* the past events or experiences that also caused them, whereas my current memories of how to use a credit card to slip a lock, how to dance the tango, or how to prepare a homemade tattoo, derive from past experiences that are not themselves part of their content: nothing in the occurrent practice *refers* in any straightforward way to its history.

But, in principle at least, I can coordinate my remembered auto-biographical episodes with my practiced know-how. Leonard's mental and affective life since the incident, in contrast, exhibits an agonizing gulf between a disrupted personal memory and a preserved habit memory. When Leonard is supposed to recognize someone, to access a personal memory, he knows that his failure to show the appropriate signs of recognition may cause offence, and so—like Sammy, perhaps—he's developed the tendency habitually, automatically, to fake it, to bluff.

Humor is just one of a number of ways in which Nolan repeatedly signals the uneasiness and experiential complexity of this reliance on habit without autobiography, scripts without specificity. Leonard's sudden realization (scene Q) that he's in bed with someone else, someone he doesn't recognize, is the most striking of the many scenes of waking in *Memento*. As we imaginatively relate to Leonard's mixture of politeness and confusion, we remember that *he* can't slowly piece together from memory what might have happened with this woman—Natalie, he discovers from his Polaroid—as we might have done if ever in a similar situation. In more comic mode, Leonard's revealingly practiced skills in breaking and entering are undercut when—misreading Natalie's note—he erroneously first opens the door of room 9 at the Mountcrest instead of Dodd's actual room 6. Leonard himself is able to mock his reliable, conditioned awareness of what he'll find in a motel room—"the Gideon Bible, which I of course, read, religiously" (2, 0:06:32). Just doing what you always do can be marked as funny, or embarrassing, from inside the space of reasons, because such behavior is not considered, not the product of deliberation, and thus in a sense beyond the range of normative evaluation. Teddy's attempt at humor when Leonard reads the age of the pick-up's tracks seeks to locate Leonard as some kind of outsider for relying on skills over memory—"Tracks? What are you, Pocahontas? . . . C'mon!" (V, 0:04:40).

Embodied habits and autobiographical experience are often thus entangled, in the many activities involved in real-world remembering. The Japanese discourse psychologist Kyoko Murakami (2003), for example, reports on similarly awkward attempts at lightness as distinctive forms of memory are layered together in particular occurrences and actions. In the course of her work on reconciliation, Murakami interviewed British veterans who'd been held as prisoners of war in WWII on the Thai-Burma railway and in a copper mine in Japan. Murakami notes that troubled interactions arose at moments of shifting from the exchange of pleasantries into interview mode. The British veterans, in search of some jocularity as they position the Japanese researcher as the giver of orders, often used isolated Japanese phrases such as "kyotsuke," "ichi-ni-san-shi," or "sagyoo sagyoo" ("stand to attention!," "one-two-three-four," and "work, work!"). These terms, verbal residues of that very different time, bring the wartime past directly to the present. They have an incorporated, affective force beyond their surface meaning as an entire embodied and moral order arrives with a "visceral shock" (Middleton and Brown 2005: 134–5).

The veterans are unlike Leonard in that they do retain highly charged autobiographical memories of their wartime experiences: but those recollections are not, it seems, directly animating current behavior (Murakami 2003). There is no deliberate reference to particular past events in enacting this word "kyotsuke" ("stand to attention!") so that in one sense the habitual and embodied residues of the veterans' history are independent of explicit personal memory. But, as in Leonard's case, we can still identify the thorough and pervasive layering of levels, as bodily practices, autobiography, and big history are interwoven. As in Memento, the past may be fully, viscerally alive and aching even when it isn't cleanly captured in declarative thought or focused awareness.

In other real-world contexts, when explicit thought can't easily get a grip, other ways of absorbing and using information sometimes step in. Consider H.M., the celebrated patient whose speculative neurosurgical treatment for epilepsy lies at the source of the modern sciences of memory. H.M. became tragically unable to encode new factual or personal memories after the summer morning in 1953 when "central portions of his brain were sucked out by a silver straw" (Hilts 1995: 21) in the removal of his hippocampus, the organ subsequently identified as playing a key role in these forms of memory (Milner, Corkin, and Teuber 1968). Yet H.M. not only has residual memories of his life *before* the surgery, as we'll see below: he also famously retains the capacity to learn new skills despite his loss of explicit memory. Moreover, in the kind of seepage of information across memory systems that we're exploring here, in an apparent anomaly H.M. successfully came to remember the detailed layout of a house he lived in only after his operation. This is surprising because spatial memory usually requires *explicit* memory capacities, in order to form an objective representation of a particular place. In H.M.'s case, though, this information was perhaps learned slowly over an extended period of time, in the course of many repeated movements between rooms in an emotionally significant place (Corkin 2002: 156). Another example comes from Clive Wearing, an Englishman who had been a celebrated early music expert and conductor before sadly suffering a more extreme and all-encompassing amnesia than H.M.'s or Leonard's. Wearing can't remember what's happened moments before the present, and continuously feels as if he's just come to consciousness. Nevertheless, after 18 months in a new home where he was taken for a daily walk to feed the ducks, he started to ask, "when prompted to put his coat on, "Aha, do the ducks want their tea?"" (Wilson and Wearing 1995: 27).

These examples demonstrate that information can seep through from other systems, variously driven by peculiar cocktails of affect, familiarity, and habit, to influence awareness or action. Just as autobiographical and embodied memories are ordinarily intertwined, so "amnesia is not an all-or-nothing condition" (Corkin 2002: 157). Nolan, I am suggesting, seeks to depict this extra complexity across a number of parallel strands of *Memento*. I'll discuss later the way in which Leonard repeatedly (re)discovers his tattoos: here we can consider the end of the story of Sammy Jankis, so vital a narrative prop for Leonard. We see Mrs. Jankis's

final, extreme test of Sammy's condition (scene 21) just after we've seen
Natalie assessing Leonard's own memory with a quick and cruel test
involving a polluted beer (scenes D and C). Sammy continues to inject
Mrs. Jankis with insulin, administering more and more: but at the
moment when he finally sees its effect, Sammy does not register total
surprise or shock. As Nolan puts it in his commentary on this scene,

> There's some underlying awareness of what's going on, whether it's
> just on an emotional level, or whether there's some greater
> awareness, because it was very important to me, the idea of the
> confusion of different types of memory. I wanted to not make it
> as simple as Leonard describes the condition. . . . You can't reduce
> the human mind to this incredibly simple separation of different
> functions, different brain parts, and a lot of the film deals with
> Leonard's conscious journey through the story being informed by
> emotion that he doesn't quite understand, that underlies that, and
> that's, you know, a different part of his mind doing that, and it's
> the interaction between them, the conscious mind and the emotional
> memory . . . that is so difficult for him, so confusing for him.

Perhaps what's at stake here is not best described as simply a two-pronged
interaction between consciousness and emotion—perhaps each of these
aspects of the embodied mind is itself multiple. The film dramatizes the
complexity of these coordination problems that are ordinarily solved, for
most of us, by the smooth interaction of the components of our minds,
bodies, and brains, well enough to get by, most of the time.

Autobiography, time, action, and emotion

The leaking of Leonard's blood and mind onto the bathroom floor
(scene E) has left him unable to form new personal or factual memories.
As in the case of H.M., this is anterograde, not retrograde amnesia:
it's new or ongoing information, not Leonard's entire past, that is lost
to him. But as time passes and more new post-incident events occur,
they become past. It's this missing back-story, in which experience
has failed to stick, the time between the incident and the present—a
period unspecified in the film—that fascinates and frightens. What might
Leonard have done?

Much of the intense scrutiny of plot and coherence that Memento encourages has dealt with Leonard's residual knowledge: not just his spared skills and practical capacities (discussed in the previous section), but also his ongoing knowledge of how to operate his "system" (discussed in the next section), and the fact that he even remembers that he has a condition. Within my overarching focus on the variety of ways in which history and information can be absorbed and retained, in this section I discuss the extent to which Leonard (like real-world anterograde-amnesic patients) retains a grasp of the concept of time on the basis of what remains of his autobiographical memories. Drawing on work by Christoph Hoerl, I suggest that it's appropriate to describe Leonard as temporally disoriented only against the background of a residual understanding of the significance of time: this line of thought helps to explain not just Leonard's insight into his impairment, but also the peculiar and tragic nature of his approach to his own actions and choices. This discussion then helps us consider the peculiar nature of those personal memories of Leonard's that we see in flashback, deriving from his life before the incident, and to see how Nolan depicts Leonard actively using these remaining fragments to motivate his own present actions.

In a rich and original paper "Memory, Amnesia and the Past," Hoerl (1999) develops an analysis of the grounds for and consequences of having a concept of the past. Hoerl notes that in most cases, anterograde amnesia leaves patients with some awareness of their situation, although this leads to many different emotional responses. Even if their amnesia deprives them of information about their condition, they can still (to some degree) understand it, because the ideas of the past and of a connected, directed life still make sense. On Hoerl's account, this is because they can still remember some specific events from before the period covered by the amnesia: they have at least some genuine episodic memories for particular past actions and experiences. So if H.M. "has good insight into his memory disorder" (Corkin 2002: 158), this must be anchored in his long-retained personal memories of particular events and sequences from his early years. In Philip Hilts' moving portrait, H.M. smilingly describes a pair of "shoe skates with fiber wheels" he owned as a child, and shyly tells of dropping his girlfriend Mildred Carpenter for Beverly McDonald (Hilts 1995: 86).[3] In episodic memory, as Hoerl argues, we are not just influenced by the past, but are having thoughts about the past:

the ability to have such thoughts, also revealed in our command of the past tense, is required for a grasp of the concept of the past.

In contrast, the few reported extreme amnesias in which patients do seem to "lack the conceptual resources for capturing what is wrong with them" are characterized by an absence of genuine episodic memories. S.S., for example, tended to recall only "the general idea of a past event," so that his knowledge of his whole biography (not just the time after the onset of amnesia) appeared to be exclusively factual rather than truly personal (Cermak and O'Connor 1983: 230). Such patients, suggests Hoerl, "do not have an adequate concept of time" (1999: 240–1). This is a psychological rather than evaluative judgment: responses of distress or confusion or acceptance at their temporal disorientation only appear in patients who still know why and how the passage of time matters.

> We would not describe a subject as temporally disoriented for whom it did not have any significance what time it is. Being aware of one's own temporal disorientation thus requires that one can still make sense of oneself as occupying a particular location in an objective time series, even though one may not be able to make out this location on the basis of one's own resources.
>
> (Hoerl 1999: 231)

Leonard is acutely aware of his temporal disorientation, on this view, just because he can still recall particular past events and experiences from his own past, however imperfectly. He still knows how time works, in other words, but can't reliably place himself and his actions or experiences within it. This is why we occasionally see him still trying to remember, aware that he's lost something. Our narrative dislocation within the film thus gives us not just insight into his loss but an experience that echoes it: we feel at a loss, as if all the pieces are there but we can't grasp them, all the memories and exograms in place, if only we could inhabit them.

With Hoerl's help, we can push a little harder on this point that Leonard still knows how time works: this isn't a merely theoretical awareness, but an agonizingly practical influence on his sense of himself as an agent. Hoerl notes that many amnesic patients with insight into their condition realize that they cannot aim easily toward long-term goals, goals that would rely on each action building cumulatively on earlier actions and their effects. N.A. is typical in, as a result, striving "for a rigorously stable environment as an aid to his memory," and avoiding even the attempt at life-changing progress toward such goals (Kaushall et al. 1981: 387). Hoerl's comment on N.A. affords a striking comparison with Leonard's response:

> [N.A.] realizes that any kind of progress he might make can mean a potential danger to him, since, as a consequence of such progress, he might find himself in an environment which he can no longer recognize.
>
> (1999: 242)

In Leonard's world, these dangers have become actual. He knows perfectly well that what he does makes a difference, and that things may not be the same after any particular action, even though he won't remember how they were before or understand what's changed. Under normal circumstances, he is thus reluctant to transform momentary feelings into action, and fears the effects of his own anger. But, unlike N.A., Leonard cannot protect himself from the world of time, because his single driving passion makes one particular action obligatory. This drives the intensity of his information-gathering and his urge to trust "facts, not memories" (R, 0:24:04). This high-level stability of planning doesn't justify attributing to Leonard full temporally extended agency in Michael Bratman's sense (2000): Leonard's attempts to develop and coordinate his policies and activities through reflective temporal cross-referencing are severely compromised by the executive disruptions brought on by his inability to attend for any substantial span, or across pressures and distractions like the slamming of a car door.[4] But Hoerl's analysis offers an alternative notion of agency that perhaps gives us more of a grip on Leonard's plight and choices: Leonard is a full-blooded agent at least in the sense that, because he shares our concept of time, he too is "sensitive to the irrevocability of certain acts" (Hoerl 1999: 243). He understands the uniqueness and unrepeatability of events, and has insight into the causal structure of the world, the significance of the fact that actions cannot be undone (Hoerl 1999: 245).

It's true that Leonard can't reliably track his own position within these causal sequences. But the point, which we have drawn from Hoerl's analysis, that Leonard nonetheless grasps the singularity of time also helps us better appreciate the climactic end of Memento. In scene A, by writing a new message on Teddy's Polaroid, burning the photos of himself and Jimmy, and writing a note for a tattoo of Teddy's license number, Leonard is manipulating his future self, tampering with the records and exograms on which he knows he will later rely. His decision here to alter the course of future events is momentous—it's a genuine and perhaps horrifying choice, rather than a random or reflex response—precisely because it depends on and demonstrates Leonard's residual understanding of the irrevocability of action. We come to realize that we have already seen, at the beginning of the film, the fatal effect of these decisions: while Leonard himself couldn't later assess the outcome of these actions, we now hold the burden of both tracing and understanding the lines of causal and moral responsibility for Teddy's death.

At least two other key sequences in Memento also show Leonard exploiting his remaining capacity for personal memories. Consider again those surviving memories from Leonard's earlier past to which we gain access. Leonard repeatedly insists on his psychological continuity with his previous self, and on his access to autobiographical information from before the incident—"I know who I am, I know all about myself," as he tells Burt (U, 0:08:25). But the only signs of the more recollective, sensory-perceptual phenomenology of true episodic memory are in his flashbacks. We become familiar with the first-person point of view characteristic of his memories of his wife, which he typically recalls in "field" perspective, as from the original vantage-point, rather than in "observer" mode, seeing himself in the remembered scene (Nigro and Neisser 1983), as in his memories of the Jankis case. They are vivid but isolated memories—Leonard looks down toward his wife reading in bed or turning in her chair to look at him, or up across her side of the bed to the clock and the bedside table.

These personal memories are fragmentary: the contents of Leonard's churning engrams, his remaining inner memories of his wife, are no more woven in to any fuller, clean life-narrative than are the assortment of external, artifactual relics with which he seeks to mourn her. The emotional valence of these fragments is not always unambiguously positive. Whatever their accuracy, this mode of presentation from a "field" point of view underlines their affective intensity. Memento offers intriguing opportunities to work through such questions about vantage-point in memory and imagination, topics on which discussions in philosophy, psychology, and film studies so far remain disconnected (Berntsen and Rubin 2006; Debus 2007; Smith 1997; Wollheim 1984). Here I merely note one aspect of the use and motivational function of these first-person fragments. In hiring an escort to recreate momentary belief in his wife's presence (scenes I and J), Leonard exploits his amnesia by re-occupying his first-personal vantage point: when he wakes as the woman goes to the bathroom, he again looks across the warm bed at her worn paperback and hairbrush, for a brief moment "utterly content" (scene J, Nolan 2001: 166). He seeks to coordinate his biological memory fragments with his bag of mementos (bra, hairbrush, book, toy, clock) in a desperate quest for brief comfort. The strategy fails, as it must have failed before, for even with more immersive sensory memory (smelling her book) and ceremonial ritual (burning his memorial props in a desolate lot), Leonard can neither obliterate her death nor "remember to forget" her (scene K). The sequence both demonstrates Leonard's capacity for self-manipulation, on a more minor scale here than the grand decision to lie to himself at the end of the film, and further underlines his lament to Natalie, "How can I heal . . . if I can't feel time?" (P, 0:37:33).

One effective message of Memento is that a wider range of emotions and interpersonal practices than we usually notice depends on a constantly, more-or-less reliably updated personal memory. The class of temporally extended emotions, which Leonard can only at best approximate, includes not only grief but love and probably hate, regret, anticipation, and (according to Natalie) fear (scene F). Leonard's condition also rules him out of the ordinary social practices of working successfully with contracts and trust and promises, as Teddy and Natalie both realize. It's not just that relevant information often fails to make it across episodes of Leonard's waking awareness, but that—at temporal scales below the grand search for John G—such connections, for him, don't automatically matter in their own right. Anger, however, remains available under pressure, and if Leonard can still be scared it's at the things he might have done under its influence and then forgotten. It's interesting that H.M. too went through more periods of high emotional intensity and anger than might be apparent from the public scientific record (Hilts 1995: 152–7).

But there's a suggestion in another vital scene of Memento that—in the absence of the kind of abuse Natalie doles out in scene F—Leonard has to incite or provoke his own rage, using his disconnected engrams to manipulate himself into action. In watching Jimmy arrive at the derelict building (scene 22), as Leonard works up to killing him—just before the timelines meet as the photo of the dead Jimmy morphs into color—Leonard mobilizes a series of flashbacks of his wife, allowing the version of her he carries with him to sanction or request or drive his violence. The first-person or field perspective in these fragmentary, apparently mundane episodic memories, before a final flash of her head thrashing during the incident, is complex. As well as having his wife turn in her seat to urge him on with her direct look, somehow drawing these images from his available stock, Leonard almost becomes her momentarily as he and she both move to the window when Jimmy's vehicle draws up outside (22, 1:37:18). The blurring between Leonard and his wife is rendered even more striking because these are color flashbacks intruding into a black and white scene.

Embodied exograms

One pleasure of increasing familiarity with Memento is gradually to trace the idiosyncratic provenance and trajectories of the array of objects and artifacts on and around Leonard over time. Leonard is desperate to give certain sanctioned things their own cognitive life, while still controlling their history and contacts. His "system" has a glorious baroque precision, with different levels of information allotted to different storage media, particular pockets assigned to particular items, and different handwriting employed for information that needs later scrutiny.

But we see Leonard's wishful confidence in his system of notes and photos, chart and file and so on, under pressure from the start. Cognitive artifacts are twisted, or adapted for other purposes; or they roam free of their designer's plans, living out unauthorized biographies or off on a frolic of their own. One tattoo reads "notes can be lost" (T, 0:14:11); Leonard's retort to Teddy that memory too can be unreliable doesn't refute Teddy's point that notes are (scene R); and our realization that one of Leonard's vital photo annotations has been scribbled out (scene S) immediately suggests the potential for his system to unravel or be undermined. We are trying throughout to decode the (reverse) history of bodies and bruises, keys and coasters and cards, guns and clocks and bullets and bags, a jacket and a Jaguar, as well as the various components of Leonard's explicit symbolic system of words and images and inscriptions. The cognitive environment for Leonard is everywhere: anything can become a trace, following Leonard across contexts or media whether he is currently aware of its significance or not. His field of possible inference includes not just others and objects, skin and system, but also his own inner states: he has to assess his sobriety when he comes to holding a whisky bottle, or (as we've seen) treat his own residual neurally encoded memories as useful prosthetic tools to help provoke action.

Many of Leonard's exogrammatic traces are unreliable in these ways, or (in some cases) detachable and thus imperfectly accessible. In these respects the information in the external parts of Leonard's system differs from the usual ways that beliefs are held and accessed by those without such a condition, though of course various non-standard conditions such as forgetfulness, drunkenness, or enduring repression can render engrams too hard to reach. But we can close this discussion of coordination between forms of memory by pointing to two more successful aspects of his use of exograms: the transparency of Leonard's "system" when in use, and the way he repeatedly discovers his tattoos.

Many parts of Leonard's network of traces, carrying him across repeated gaps in consciousness, do function with remarkable success much of the time. Just as his practiced eyes and hands retain and develop certain practical skills, so he has achieved an impressive level of procedural efficiency in more or less unobtrusively hooking up to his photos and notes. Under many circumstances, he can quickly work out who someone is, or which car to get into, or where to go: always flipping through his photos, he has routinized the means to encode relevant basic information about people extra-neurally, to store this information in accessible spots about his person, and to retrieve it when needed. When this all goes well—when his externalized cognitive equipment is genuinely transparent in use, requiring no reflective mediation—he is (arguably) simply remembering. An observer might think that Leonard must first activate an inner belief that the information needed is on the notes or photos before looking at them. But this would be a mistaken or at best awkward interpretation of his behavior: it is more economical to see Leonard as simply accessing the relevant information in one step, given his extensive practice, when the system of exograms is in fact operating roughly as desired. This case no more requires an explicit prior belief about what's in his pockets than does our ordinary use of on-board biological, engrammatic memory (Clark forthcoming).

But there are, as we've noted, significant limits to the transportability, security, flexibility, and resistance to pressure of Leonard's system. Where he hasn't yet incorporated particular artifacts into that system, his lack of flexible executive control and attention can halt him: Leonard could easily have left the restaurant, after lunch with Natalie, without his room key and the brown envelope containing Teddy's registration details, which he'd forgotten to take with him to the restroom, if the waiter hadn't stepped in as a transient memory support (scene T). Habit and routine, Leonard's "graceful solution to the memory problem," don't do all the work he might wish. But he has successfully internalized at least a basic range of proceduralizations. He doesn't have to think first before taking or checking his Polaroids, or even before destroying them by burning, the only way possible: in each case, he just does it.

Leonard's relative ease in working with his photographs and notes, however, contrasts with his more complex interactions with his tattoos: this provides our last example of the film's rich depiction of the subtle interfaces between memory, habit, bodies, objects, and emotions. Leonard's tattoos are less ready to hand or eye than his photos and notes. We are primed by Leonard's own genuine surprise at finding the message "remember Sammy Jankis" on the back of his hand to be indelible— this happens twice, in what is for us quick succession, though in fact at opposite ends of the fictional-world chronology (scenes 2 and T). Thus schooled from the start into thinking, as Natalie does, that Leonard doesn't seem the tattooing type, we find the extraordinary revelation of Leonard's panoply of tattoos later in scene T engrossing, as we try to piece together fragmentary clues to help our narrative orientation. While we are still trying to assimilate Leonard's writing "KILL HIM" on Teddy's picture at the end of scene T, Nolan works us further—in "a bit of a reinforcement," as he puts it in the commentary—by immediately showing us Leonard discovering his tattoos *again* as for the first time at the start of scene 4.

The tattoos we see revealed on Leonard's body in these scenes are all different, in style, script, and provenance as well as content. Some have to be viewed in the mirror, some are read rightly by looking down, and so on. Just as, within the time span of the film, one of his new tattoos is self-administered and the other tattooed in a parlor, so the great variety of other tattoos suggests the longer back-story, the history to which we and Leonard equally lack direct access. Where the (re)discovery of the Sammy Jankis tattoo on his hand does puzzle Leonard each time, his response to finding the rest across his body is not so easy to read. Nolan plausibly describes Guy Pearce's performance here as capturing Leonard as both knowing and not knowing something at the same time.

Though lacking explicit memories of the appearance, history, or content of his tattoos, Leonard is nevertheless neither entirely surprised nor nonplussed. In these sequences, a number of layers of memory or experience or history are present simultaneously, in uneasy cooperation or confusion or competition. Familiarity, repetition, habit, and his affective engagement with his quest as mapped out on his chest, over the period in which he has had these tattoos, have had their indirect effects on Leonard despite his overt ignorance. What's written on the body does make sense to him, and this is a body he can inhabit or reinhabit fully rather than simply occupy. While we as first-time viewers are scrambling for each item of incorporated information, Leonard is simply caressing his skin, allowing the words again to acquire their affective significance for him (see Figure 3.2).

One could suggest that here Leonard's hands remember more than he does. But even this formulation, still hankering after the two terms of the mind–body problem, would reinscribe the dualism that *Memento* dismantles. Neither body nor self is singular and unified. While personal memories and embodied memories do make their distinctive

Figure 3.2 Don't trust your weakness (T, 0:14:10)

contributions to action, habit, and identity, they constantly shadow and inflect each other, not as isolated and neatly dissociable as we, or Leonard, might think.[5]

> "I don't want to live backwards,
> I don't even want to look backwards.
> It's not my fault,
> It's not my fault you don't love me.
> It's not my fault you don't love me when I'm drunk."
> —Kristin Hersh, "Your Dirty Answer,"
> from *Sunny Border Blue* (2001)

Notes

1   Scenes are referenced using the standard scene tables as explained in Andrew Kania's introduction to this volume. Quotations are from the film and from the screenplay (Nolan 2001) as appropriate.

2   Christopher Nolan, Limited Edition DVD commentary. I rely heavily on this informative commentary. It diverges into three distinct versions over the final scenes, but my references derive from the scenes before the switch point.

3   Like every case of amnesia, of course, H.M.'s is unique. Many of the personal events H.M. seems to have retained for a long time have a slightly generic, unspecific feel. They are not clearly single, particular, temporally unique events and may be somewhat "semanticized," more factual than truly personal (Corkin 2002: 157). And in recent years, as H.M. has got older, his remote autobiographical memory has deteriorated rapidly, even though he "could still demonstrate impressive recall of old and even new semantic knowledge" (Salat *et al.* 2006: 944).

4   However, in a fascinating recent discussion of *Memento*, Marya Schechtman argues that Leonard exhibits at least a basic, practical unity of agency while being entirely fragmented as an experiencing subject (2008: 412ff). For Schechtman, Leonard's virtuoso manipulations of his future self are both evidence of and mechanisms for his ongoing constitution as a continuing agent (417).

5   Many thanks to Andrew Kania for his help throughout. He, Will Sutton, and an anonymous referee offered extremely helpful comments that I've tried to incorporate. Doris McIlwain has strongly influenced my views on the relations between skill and memory, movement and thought. Thanks also to Amanda Barnier, John Buckmaster, Wayne Christensen, and Ed Cooke.

References

Berntsen, D. and Rubin, D.C. (2006) "Emotion and Vantage Point in Autobiographical Memory," *Cognition and Emotion* 20: 1193–215.

Bratman, M.E. (2000) "Reflection, Planning, and Temporally Extended Agency," *Philosophical Review* 109: 35–61.

Cermak, L.S. and O'Connor, M. (1983) "The Anterograde and Retrograde Retrieval Ability of a Patient with Amnesia Due to Encephalitis," *Neuropsychologia* 21: 213–34.

Clark, A. (forthcoming) "Memento's Revenge: The Extended Mind, Extended," in R. Menary (ed.) *The Extended Mind*, Cambridge, MA: MIT Press.

Connerton, P. (1989) *How Societies Remember*, Cambridge: Cambridge University Press.

Corkin, S. (2002) "What's New With the Amnesic Patient H.M.?," *Nature Reviews Neuroscience* 3: 153–60.

Debus, D. (2007) "Perspectives On the Past: A Study of the Spatial Perspectival Characteristics of Recollective Memories," *Mind & Language* 22: 173–206.

Donald, M. (1991) *Origins of the Modern Mind*, Cambridge, MA: Harvard University Press.

Dreyfus, H.L. (2007) "The Return of the Myth of the Mental," *Inquiry* 50: 352–65.

Gordon, S. (2001) "Reflections on Providing Sports Psychology Services in Professional Cricket," in G. Tenenbaum (ed.) *The Practice of Sport Psychology*, Morgantown, WV: Fitness Information Technology.

Hilts, P.J. (1995) *Memory's Ghost: The Nature of Memory and the Strange Tale of Mr. M.*, New York, NY: Simon & Schuster.

Hoerl, C. (1999) "Memory, Amnesia and the Past," *Mind & Language* 14: 227–51.

Kaushall, P.I., Zetin, M., and Squire L.R. (1981) "A Psychosocial Study of Chronic, Circumscribed Amnesia," *Journal of Nervous and Mental Disease* 169: 383–9.

Middleton, D. and Brown, S. (2005) *The Social Psychology of Experience: Studies in Remembering and Forgetting*, London: Sage.

Milner, B., Corkin, S., and Teuber, H.-L. (1968) "Further Analysis of the Hippocampal Amnesic Syndrome: A 14-year Follow-up Study of H.M.," *Neuropsychologia* 6: 215–34.

Murakami, K. (2003) "Orientation to the Setting: Discursively Accomplished Intersubjectivity," *Culture & Psychology* 9: 233–48.

Nigro, G. and Neisser, U. (1983) "Point of View in Personal Memories," *Cognitive Psychology* 15: 467–82.

Noë, A. (2004) *Action in Perception*, Cambridge, MA: MIT Press.

Nolan, C. (2001) *Memento*, in Memento and Following, London: Faber and Faber.

Salat, D.H., van der Kouwe, A.J.W., Tuch, D.S., Quinn, B.T., Fischl, B., Dale, A.M. and Corkin, S. (2006) "Neuroimaging H.M.: A 10-year Follow-up Examination," in *Hippocampus* 16: 936–45.

Schechtman, M. (2008) "Diversity in Unity: Practical Unity and Personal Boundaries," *Synthese* 162: 405–23.

Smith, M. (1997) "Imagining from the Inside," in R. Allen and M. Smith (eds), *Film Theory and Philosophy*, Oxford: Oxford University Press.

Sutton, J. (2007) "Batting, Habit, and Memory: The Embodied Mind and the Nature of Skill," *Sport in Society* 10: 763–86.

—— (2008) "Between Individual and Collective Memory: Interaction, Coordination, Distribution," *Social Research* 75: 23–48.

—— (forthcoming) "Exograms and Interdisciplinarity: History, the Extended Mind, and the Civilizing Process," in R. Menary (ed.), *The Extended Mind*, Cambridge, MA: MIT Press.

Wilson, B.A. and Wearing, D. (1995) "Prisoner of Consciousness: A State of Just Awakening Following Herpes Simplex Encephalitis," in R. Campbell and M.A. Conway (eds) *Broken Memories: Case Studies in Memory Impairment*, Oxford: Blackwell, pp. 14–30.

Wollheim, R. (1984) *The Thread of Life*, Oxford: Clarendon Press.

Further reading

Clark, A. and Chalmers, D. (1998) "The Extended Mind," *Analysis* 58: 7–19. (The classic statement of the extended-mind thesis in philosophy—the idea that cognition is sometimes literally distributed across objects and world as well as brain and body.)

Dreyfus, H.L. (2002) "Intelligence Without Representation: Merleau-Ponty's Critique of Mental Representation," *Phenomenology and the Cognitive Sciences* 1: 367–83. (A further attack on the idea that high-level thought is involved in embodied practice.)

Hoerl, C. (2008) "On Being Stuck in Time," *Phenomenology and the Cognitive Sciences* 7. (More discussion of the ideas of agency and personal memory.)

Sacks, O. (2007) "The Abyss," *The New Yorker*, September 24. (A powerful meditation on amnesia.)

Sutton, J. (2002) "Porous Memory and the Cognitive Life of Things," in D. Tofts, A. Jonson and A. Cavallaro (eds) *Prefiguring Cyberculture: Informatics from Plato to Haraway*, Cambridge, MA: MIT Press, pp. 130–41. (Further discussion of extended-mind issues.)

—— (2003) "Memory," in E.N. Zalta (ed.) *The Stanford Encyclopedia of Philosophy*, Fall 2008 edn, online. Available at: http://plato.stanford.edu/archives/fall2008/entries/memory/ (accessed 3 October 2008). (A more detailed introduction to the standard taxonomy of memory in philosophy and psychology, and discussion of the terminology.)

Toth, J. and Hunt, R.R. (1999) "Not One Versus Many, But Zero Versus Any: Structure and Function in the Context of the Multiple Memory Systems Debate," in J.K. Foster and M. Jelicic (eds) *Memory: Systems, Process, or Function?*, Oxford: Oxford University Press, pp. 232–72. (A trenchant critique of the idea of memory systems in psychology.)

Wheeler, M. (2005) *Reconstructing the Cognitive World: The Next Step*, Cambridge, MA: MIT Press. (A brilliant integration of phenomenological ideas with up-to-date scientific theorizing about embodied cognition.)

Chapter 4

Raymond Martin

THE VALUE OF MEMORY: REFLECTIONS ON *MEMENTO*

What a great faculty memory is, how awesome a mystery! It is the mind,
and this is nothing other than my very self.
—Augustine (1997: 213)

You have to begin to lose your memory, if only in bits and pieces, to
realize that memory is what makes our lives. Life without memory is
no life at all. . . . Our memory is our coherence, our reason, our feeling,
even our action. Without it, we are nothing.
—Luis Buñuel (1983: 4–5)

WITHOUT QUESTION, MEMORY MAKES an extraordinary
contribution to the value of our lives—one so important that it
would be difficult to overstate its value. Difficult, but not impossible.
Augustine and the Spanish film-maker Luis Buñuel seem to have
accomplished the feat!

Roughly speaking, memory makes two contributions to our lives: an
instrumental contribution, in helping us to function more effectively in
pursuit of our goals, and an *intrinsic* contribution, in enriching the quality
both of our subjective experience and what I shall call the moral texture
of our lives (such things as our ability to love, to appreciate art and nature,
and to be morally good).

As important as these contributions are, memory is not everything. Whether the other things besides memory that make us up and contribute to our lives might be enough to enable us to function effectively and to have worthwhile lives are interesting questions. In the present paper I shall argue that the answer to suitably qualified versions of both of these questions is, yes.

Leonard on the instrumental contribution

In *Memento*, there are two interpretations of Leonard's condition that matter: his own, and Teddy's. According to Leonard's own, due to his head injury he has normal memory access to events prior to his head injury, but only fleeting memory access to later events. So far as specific event memories are concerned, Leonard thinks that he remembers that his wife died in the assault that led to his head injury. According to Teddy's interpretation, Leonard has blocked his event memories of some of what happened after the assault, and this not for physiological, but for psychological reasons. In particular, Leonard has blocked his remembrances that his wife did not die in the assault, but only later, due not to injuries sustained in the assault but to Leonard's own actions. Independently of Teddy's testimony, there is even a suggestion toward the end of the movie that Leonard has fleeting memory access to interactions between himself and his wife after the assault, including some memory access to his giving his wife the insulin shots that may have killed her. For the sake of simplicity, in what follows I shall ignore this latter suggestion.

Whatever the truth about the two main interpretations, throughout the period covered by the movie, all of which, except for flashbacks, occur after the death of Leonard's wife, Leonard is a man on a mission. It would be true, but an understatement, to say that this mission is the main thing in his life. It would be closer to the truth, even if a slight overstatement, to say that it is the only thing. Most people rely on memories to weave their lives into a coherent whole. To some extent Leonard does this too. It's just that after he sustained his head injury he seems to have lost the ability to retain new event memories for longer than five minutes.

Nevertheless, post-trauma Leonard is not overly impressed with the instrumental contribution that memory makes to our lives. According to him memory is both unreliable and interpretive. What's needed in order to function effectively, he says, is not more memories, but access to facts (that is, true information).

Whether it's true that what's needed in order to function effectively is not more memories, but access to the facts, depends on the answers to two questions:

1   If one has enough access to facts, can one function as well in pursuit of practical objectives without event memories as with them?
2   Assuming that one can function as well without event memories, can one have enough access to facts?

Leonard thinks that the answer to the first of these questions is, yes. I agree. He does not address the second question. The answer to it, I think, is that currently people with a normally diverse range of objectives, but without normal memory abilities, cannot have enough access to facts to function as effectively as they could have with normal memory abilities. As Leonard's example makes clear, external memory aids can help, but they cannot provide a sufficiently high level of access to facts.

But what about in the future, when in all likelihood memory-aid technology will have improved dramatically? Might external aids then provide enough access to facts? If they might, then the instrumental contribution that memory makes to our lives is a mere byproduct of the current state of our technology. To assess the value of memory, one must determine whether it is a mere byproduct. I shall argue that it is.

Event vs. procedural memory

Under post-traumatic circumstances similar to those in which Leonard finds himself, many real-life people, like Leonard, continue to remember how to do some things they previously knew how to do, such as understanding, speaking, thinking, playing a musical instrument, and driving a car, and some are able to enhance abilities like these and even learn new ones. This is one of the lessons to be drawn from the famous case of H.M., an epileptic who, after brain surgery in the 1950s, was no longer able to form event memories. H.M. would forget everything minutes after experiencing its occurrence. He lost his sense of time passing. Yet he was still able to learn games, and to improve his performance at perceptual-motor skills, even though he had no idea each time he did such things that he'd ever done them before.

It seems, then, that event memories of what a person experiences and so-called procedural memories are monitored by different systems in the brain. Yet, as John Sutton explains, these systems interact in complicated ways that are not currently well understood:

> [N]either philosophers nor psychologists have a clear grip on the various ways that personal [event] memory and other high-level cognitive processes interact with remembered embodied skills. Competition and coordination between the different memory systems can both occur. On the one hand, skilled performers in dance or sport know that their motor habits often run best in a groove, when not consciously or verbally controlled: yet the skills involved are robust and flexible, unlike more primitive forms of procedural memory, and can sometimes be directly shaped by mood, context, verbal instruction, and conscious decision.
>
> (Sutton 2006: 123)

H.M. lost his hippocampus in the brain surgery. We do not know whether Leonard's hippocampus was intact. Otherwise it seems that Leonard's problem was pretty much that of H.M. Might he nevertheless have functioned effectively in pursuit of his goals?

Post-trauma Leonard has just one goal: to avenge his wife's death. Worries about his subjective experience and the moral texture of his life

Figure 4 Some of Leonard's memory aids (T, 0:15:39)

aside, the problems posed for him by his having a greatly diminished capacity for forming event memories are entirely practical, the main one (dramatically depicted in the movie) being that in pursuit of his one goal he cannot rely on his memory to keep things straight, but instead has to rely on external aids (tattoos, notes to himself, inscribed photographs). These aids can take him only so far. But far enough, he thinks, to achieve his goal. He is wrong. The external memory aids that are available to him are not up to the task of giving him enough access to facts for him to effectively pursue his goal. As a consequence his life is a pitiful exercise in futility. But what if he had had better external memory aids?

Technology to the rescue

It is virtually certain that in the future, with technological advances, external memory aids will provide better access to facts than they do now. Whether they could ever provide enough access to facts for people to function as well without event memories as they now function with them depends in part on what sorts of goals people pursue. In general, peoples' goals are many and varied. Since Leonard's situation—with just one overriding goal—is so much simpler, let's consider it first. Our question, then, is whether in a technologically more advanced future, external memory aids might have done as well as event memories in the service of Leonard's one goal.

It would seem that in *certain respects* at least, if not also overall, external aids could not only have done as well as event memories in providing Leonard with access to facts, they could have done even better. And for this result, we don't even need the qualifier, "in a technologically more advanced future." This should not be news. Like most people, I have more confidence in the spellchecker on my computer than I do in my own ability to remember how to spell most words. And if when writing something I forget a fact, like who wrote "The Five Modes of Agrippa," often Google will quickly provide the answer—in this case, Sextus Empiricus.

Even so, it will seem to most of us that technological memory aids are not all that impressive compared to event memory itself. I agree. In any case, the examples just given deal more with what is called *semantic* memory than with the sort of *episodic* memory deficit that plagues Leonard. Yet, we need to remember that memory-aid technology is in its infancy.

Soon—indeed, very soon—much more will be possible. Eventually, perhaps, unimaginably more will be possible.

Currently, for instance, in response to the growing epidemic of Alzheimer's and other forms of dementia, technologists are busy trying to design eyeglasses that have pattern recognition devices built into them. The way these eyeglasses may someday work is that as you approach someone whose look and name have been encoded into the computer in your glasses, his or her name appears, visible only to you, on the inside of your glasses. In one projected elaboration of this memory aid, in addition to the name you are provided with information about your most recent conversations with the person you are approaching. "Hi Joe, how are you? Say, whatever became of that trouble you were having with the IRS?" Ignorant of your hi-tech memory aid, Joe smiles back, pleased by your interest. Leonard could have put glasses like these to good use. We can imagine a more elaborate version of such a memory aid in which the identification of Joe and information about your recent conversations with him is conveyed not by being printed on eyeglasses, but by being transmitted directly to the "memory centers" of your brain. With the aid of the device you could remember such things not only just as well as you would have had you had excellent event memory, but in the same way, at least so far as phenomenology is concerned.

Extended consideration of such possibilities would blur the issue under consideration, which is whether external aids might *supplement* a faulty memory from the *outside*, so to speak, not whether they might *repair* it from the *inside*. For now, it's enough to note that Leonard is at least partly right. What's needed for many of life's purposes that are ordinarily served by event memories is not necessarily event memories, but access to the facts (e.g., his name is "Joe," he's been having trouble with the IRS, and so on). In this respect, event memory is like any other natural capacity—for instance, those afforded by one's circulatory and visual systems—the exercise of which affects one's ability to function. When, due to some defect, a capacity fails to perform, an external way might be found to accomplish the same end.

"Memory that" vs. pattern recognition

We have been focusing on two of the most common ways in which event memories provide factual information: what's called "memory that," for instance, the remembrance that Joe said he has been having trouble with the IRS, and pattern recognition, for instance, one's recognition that the person approaching is Joe. Memory-that is just a propositional version of the sort of information that Leonard writes on his body and on photographs—information such as, "This person [the one depicted in the photograph] is a liar."

For most people, most of the time, memories, including pattern-recognition memories, provide easy access to a rich array of facts. Leonard is atypical. Because he has a seriously deficient memory he is short on facts. But, as we have seen in the eyeglasses example, advances in technology could easily have provided Leonard with access to a much richer array of facts, delivering information to him externally on appropriate occasions. So the answer to one of the central questions that the portrayal of Leonard provokes—how much of the access to facts that event memories contribute to our lives might be provided by external aids—would seem to be: quite a bit.

Background information

Leonard not only lacks normal access to propositional memories and pattern recognition, he also lacks normal access to background information that would allow him to ensconce newly acquired information in a meaningful interpretive context. In people with normal memory abilities such background information is constantly being updated, and it plays a crucial role. For instance, in order for factual information about a prior acquaintance to have much significance in everyday transactions, normally it would not be enough to recognize the name of the person approaching and what you had talked about the last time you met. You would also need accurate, continually updated background information, for instance, about the person, about people in general, about the topic of your conversation, say, the IRS, and so on.

Could external memory aids provide such a context? To do so, they would have to be much more sophisticated than those we have so far imagined. But if technology continues to develop throughout the twenty-first century and beyond, such aids may someday be available. Even now, with much of the information we receive, we have low-tech versions of the sort of thing that would be required. For instance, in a newspaper or a novel we read about something unusual and unknown and our source suggests not only what it is, or what happened, but how to contextualize it. That is, the source suggests why and how the unusual event should or should not be regarded as meaningful.

Of course, we mentally ensconce this sort of background information in an even broader web of background information that, as a function of memory, we carry around in our heads. One couldn't do this if one's mind were a complete blank. But if one's mind were a complete blank, one wouldn't be able to assimilate either the new information or the context in terms of which one could make sense of it. One could not even understand language. So, the case in which one's mind is a complete blank is not the interesting comparison. The point is that even without a great deal of the sort of access to facts that event memories normally provide, external aids could take up much of the slack.

Recollecting experiences

Ordinary event memory, however, is much more than just a mechanism for access to propositional memories, pattern recognition, and contextual information. It also includes memories of *having had* experiences, say of having watched a sunrise from Uhuru Peak on Mount Kilimanjaro, the so-called "roof of Africa." Such memories include a powerful and meaningful phenomenological component—the subjective feel of what it was like to have had a remembered experience. This feature of event memories goes a long way toward making them truly personal.

Anyone with internet access can call up an image of the view from Uhuru Peak, but currently no such image can realistically capture the feel of what an actual experience of that view is like. A photograph that one took at the time from the same perspective from which one actually experienced the view might do better at capturing this more personal form of information, but more by stimulating event memory than by replacing it. An Imax movie can sometimes come close to capturing a realistic sensory feel of dramatic views (at least it can scare and amaze us), so we can expect technology to continue to narrow the gap. Perhaps one day it will be able to close it.

John Sutton has aptly characterized personal or event memories as "the most striking manifestation of the peculiar way human beings are embedded in time" (2006: 122). As such, they go a long way toward giving us a sense of our identities. They provide not only a sense of our continuing presence but also an internal impetus to identify with the person we remember ourselves to have been and imagine ourselves becoming. And, as Richard Wollheim has stressed, memory communicates affective tone from the past to the present and the imagined future, thus giving things a significance to us that they would not otherwise have (Wollheim 1984). All of this is included in what I earlier referred to as "subjective experience and moral texture." Together, such features and functions of event memory give shape to our lives and provide a phenomenological context for virtually everything we do. Perhaps, regardless of technological advances, external aids could never provide such shape and context, but it's hard to be sure.

Closing the gap

In any case, the question of whether external aids to memory could take up enough of the slack created by the loss of normal event memory abilities to allow us to function effectively is not so much about how close we might come to a life with normal memory abilities, but about how functional we might become in pursuit of our goals, regardless of the effect that the mechanism enabling us to function has on our subjective experience and the moral texture of our lives. As Memento effectively dramatizes, there are all sorts of ways to function and all sorts of goals people might pursue. If it is just a question of functioning, the deficit in facts left by a diminished memory can sometimes be compensated for in ways that circumvent the facts.

Consider, for instance, the contribution sometimes made by imagination to functioning effectively in pursuit of one's goals. It is well known that people with memory deficits tend to confabulate, to make things up. Often they even seem to believe the stories they make up. It may seem that confabulation—the invention of imaginary facts, or imaginary contexts in which to ensconce real facts—could not help someone to function in the real world. But whether it helps or not depends on one's purposes. One of the purposes that people with memory loss often have is to retain their dignity in social situations. And that's where confabulation can be handy. If one can't play a good game, at least one may be able to fool others into thinking that one can. And for the purpose of fooling others well enough to maintain one's dignity in what otherwise might be an embarrassing social situation, confabulation may be enough.

For people with memory loss, every social interaction is a test. If others think that one is OK, then, for *some* of one's purposes at least, one may be OK. This is one of those rare situations in which mere thinking—not ours, but theirs—can make it so.

There are, of course, many other things besides event memories and imagination that we need in order to function at what in normal circumstances would count as our full potential. We need to be able to see well, have a good sense of touch, a healthy brain, and so on. In addition, there are things, such as mind-reading, that ordinarily most of us cannot do, no matter how healthy and fit we are, but that it would sometimes be useful to be able to do. If, as may one day be the case, there were a pill we could take that enabled us to mind-read, taking it might enhance our ability to achieve some of our goals—it would certainly at least be entertaining. So, when it comes to the question of what we need to obtain our goals, in one way at least there is nothing special about memory. How well our memories function profoundly affects our ability to reach our goals. But the same is true of lots of other aspects of our bodies and minds.

Enhancement

Leonard's observation about the priority of facts over event memory encourages one to think of ways of compensating for an impaired memory. But if we're focusing on the contribution that external memory aids could make to effective functioning, it's not just a question of compensating for impairment, but one of enhancement. As we saw, external aids can often outperform event memory, even now. And, as was suggested, the transition from an *external* memory aid to an *internal* enhancement of memory may someday be a natural, welcome progression.

Imagine a person whose event memory is good by any ordinary standard. Yet, there is a pill that he can take to make it better. After taking the pill, simple tasks, such as working crossword puzzles and performing on academic examinations, become much easier. Imagine that such a pill were available, that it were free of cost, and that taking it had no bad side effects. As seems likely from the frequency with which athletes take steroids and college students take Ritalin and Adderall, probably ordinary people would be clamoring to take such a pill.

A little more exotically, consider genetically engineered memory enhancement. Currently its promise, and problems, are on the minds of scientists who study memory. In March 2006, for instance, researchers at the University of California announced their discovery of the first known case of *hyperthymesia*, the ability to perfectly and instantly recall details of one's past. AJ, the subject of their more than five-year-long study is a forty-year-old woman who can reputedly recall her event past "with astonishing accuracy" (*Science Daily* 2006). What seems to make AJ different from others with superior event memory who have been studied is that AJ does not use mnemonic devices, such as rhymes or visual imagery, to help her remember. According to the researchers, AJ's "recall is instant and deeply personal, related to her own life or to other events that were of interest to her" (*Science Daily* 2006). The researchers believe that when it comes to event memory AJ has a genetic advantage over the rest of us. They are trying to figure out the exact source of this advantage.

Interestingly, for present purposes, the researchers studying AJ concede that there are serious limits to her memory. Apparently she has difficulty with rote memorization and with organizing and categorizing information. And AJ sometimes complains that her ongoing remembering is "a movie in her mind that never stops." As a consequence, the researchers say, AJ "is both a warden and a prisoner of her memories, which can at times be a burden because they cannot be controlled." Nevertheless, AJ said that if she had a choice, she would not want to give up her extraordinary ability to recall (*Science Daily* 2006).[1] However, in a more recent interview, she also said "that whenever she hears a date, memories from that date in previous years flood her mind like a running movie" (CNN 2008). The phenomenon, she lamented, "is nonstop, uncontrollable and totally exhausting." She said that while most people "have called it a gift," she herself calls it "a burden." How much of a burden? AJ writes, "I run my entire life through my head every day and it drives me crazy!!!" (CNN 2008). One is reminded of Borges' story, "Funes, the Memorious," in which an accident causes a man to have perfect memory, so that he forgets nothing that he's seen or heard, no matter how minor. His blessing turns out to be a curse.[2]

Leonard, of course, has a different problem. He is not so much a prisoner of the past as he is of the present.

A life that's worth living

We've been talking about the contribution that memory makes to human functioning. What about the contribution that it makes to the value of our lives? Without event memories, or the ability to form new ones, would our lives still be worth living? Apparently Leonard thinks that his is still worth living (he isn't suicidal, just driven). So, perhaps his heartfelt purpose by itself, even with his lack of event memories, is enough to make his life worth living.

Some philosophers would dispute that if one *thinks* one's life is worth living, then it *is* worth living. They think that there are objective values, and for one's life to be worth living it must possess these values. Although philosophers who think this way disagree among themselves about which values are objective, many think that things such as autonomy, the ability to give and receive love, creativity, knowledge, beauty, and moral goodness are on the list. As objective values, they say, these are things that a person *ought* to desire.

Post-trauma Leonard, of course, does not have much access to these goods. He is not able—at least not in a normal fashion—to love, to help others in need, to make discoveries about the nature of reality, to rear children, to create most sorts of art, to be autonomous, or even to appreciate as a continuous expression any form of music that lasts more than five minutes! Some may think that if one cannot do any of these things, then one's life is not worth living. In my view, that judgment is harsh.

Even if one grants that all of the things said to be objectively good really are, it doesn't follow that they are the only good things. Surely there are other good things as well, some of which don't require a capacity for event memory that extends longer than five minutes. One of these things is a heartfelt purpose in living. Leonard has that in spades. He also remembers having had many of the things on the objective-goods list, which is itself arguably an objective good. In this respect, he is like someone who once was healthy but is now disabled. But what else beside a heartfelt purpose and fond memories might contribute to making one's life worth living?

Animal enjoyment

How about the mere experience of living? Compared to humans, animals seem to have many fewer event memories and a greatly diminished capacity for forming new ones, yet their lives often seem worth living. Probably we have all heard someone joke to a pet-loving friend that in their next life they want to come back as that person's pet. Is it obvious that if being reborn as a human were an option, such a wish, if it were serious, would necessarily be irrational?

On the face of it, the lives of some humans seem not to be worth living and the lives of some non-human animals seem to be worth living. So, it is hard to see why being transformed into a non-human animal whose life was worth living would *necessarily* be worse than being transformed into a human whose life was not worth living. If you had the choice, which would you choose? Perhaps both seem so awful that you would rather just cease to exist. But what if someone did not feel that way? (I once knew someone who said she would have preferred to be a wolf.) Would choosing to be a non-human animal necessarily be irrational? It's hard to see why it would.

If a non-human animal's life might be worth living, then why not also the life of a human with a capacity for forming event memories no greater than that of a non-human animal? In this regard, it's important to remember that while event memories can be a great blessing, they can also be a burden. We've seen this in the case of AJ, but it's also true of normal people. Henry Hawks, a sixteenth-century traveler, wrote of the Philippines, "If there is paradise upon earth, it is in that country. Sitting under a tree, you shall have such sweet smells, with such great content and pleasure, that you shall remember nothing" (quoted in Hakluyt: 292).[3] And Anaïs Nin once wrote, "The loss of memory was like the loss of a chain. Without memory I was immensely light, vaporous, fluid. The memory was the density which I could not transcend" (1948: 217). Probably most of us can appreciate such sentiments. It would seem, then, that occurrent memories, however beneficial they may be most of the time, are sometimes, for some people, a burden. By contrast, "living wholly in the present," whatever exactly that means (and it seems to mean at least that one is not *at that time* having occurrent event memories), is widely regarded, particularly in some meditative traditions such as Buddhism, as a great boon.

No doubt what proponents of the view that memory abilities exceeding those of an animal are essential to a life worth living really mean to suggest is not that *continually* experiencing event memories is necessary for a life worth living, but that *being able* to experience them, and/or to form new ones, is necessary for a life worth living. Unquestionably, having event memories and the ability to form new ones is a great blessing. The question is whether and, if so, in what ways it is necessary.

Pleasure

Suppose, for instance, that one's life were constantly suffused with pleasure, but that one didn't have the ability to remember the pleasure for more than five minutes. Wouldn't being constantly suffused with pleasure still be a great good? It would seem so, yet some doubt whether pleasure all by itself, without the ability to remember it, would be a great good. Those who doubt this should consider analogous cases of how we judge the badness of pain.

In the 1940s, curare, purified as d-tubocurarine, was used as a general anesthetic. Later it was discovered that the drug did not block, or even diminish, a patient's experience of pain, but merely blocked his or her ability to express pain. Many who had major surgery under these circumstances claimed later that they could remember experiencing the pain of surgery and that it was horrible. But since the people who said this tended to be children they were not believed. When doctors finally discovered that d-tubocurarine did not inhibit pain, they were shocked. Its use as an anesthetic was immediately discontinued.

Daniel Dennett asks us to imagine that

> one were to add to curare a smidgin of *amnestic*, a drug that (we will hypothesize) has no effect on experience or memory during n hours after ingestion but thereafter wipes out all memory of those n hours.
>
> (1978: 209–10)

Patients administered curare-cum-amnestic, Dennett imagines,

> will not later embarrass their physicians with recountings of agony, and will in fact be unable to tell in retrospect from their own experience that they were not administered a general anesthetic. Of course, *during* the operation they would know, but would be unable to tell us.
>
> (1978: 210)

Surely this is a horror story.

Imagine that you were to discover that curare-cum-amnestic was used as the anesthetic in your child's recent major surgery. Any normal parent would be understandably outraged—what we are imagining would be horrible. But if extreme pain that one cannot remember would be horrible, why wouldn't extreme pleasure that one cannot remember be wonderful? Admittedly, memory matters, but how much? And, however much it matters, why should it matter so much more when it comes to pain than pleasure?

It's not necessary for the larger point I'm trying to make that pleasure all by itself be sufficient to make one's life worth living, just that it could importantly contribute to that end. As we've seen, there are other things in addition to pleasure that, even in the absence of the ability to form long-lasting event memories, might contribute to making one's life worth living. The question is whether *all of these together* might be enough to make one's life worth living.

Unity

Some, including, it would seem, Buñuel, seem to think that the disunity in a life without the ability to form new event memories would be a deal-breaker. In their views, Leonard's post-trauma life, whatever other benefits it might include, *could not* be worth living, because it lacks a kind of unity that memory provides. But what kind of unity is that?

Leonard's post-trauma life has many sources of unity. He has access to event memories of his life prior to the assault. And he has the ability to form new short-lived event memories. He has the ability to draw upon old procedural memories and perhaps even the ability to enhance them, and to form new long-lasting procedural memories. Moreover, he has a forward-looking project to which he is fiercely committed.[4] Each of these contributes importantly to unifying his post-trauma life. Admittedly, compared to normal people, his life after the assault is still pretty chaotic. An important part of what's missing is the continuous reality check that normal memory abilities provide. Leonard has his current experience as a reality check. He also has maybe five minutes' worth of the sort of check that normal memory provides for most people. But that's not much compared to what people with normal memory abilities have.

A source of unity that many philosophers and psychologists have claimed is crucial to human flourishing is the ability that every adult with normal memory has to generate a reasonably robust autobiographical narrative that weaves together events in his life from the remote past to the present. Leonard cannot do that, at least not without external aids. The unity in question that normal people have, and that he lacks, is what is sometimes called "narrative unity"—the memory-nourished sense that one's life forms a story-like whole. But how important is narrative unity as a determinant of whether one's life is worth living?

Galen Strawson has suggested recently that in the lives of some people such narratives may not be all that important. In contrast to the prevailing opinion among academics that the unity provided by autobiographical narratives is vital to one's well-being, Strawson claims that an "episodic," non-narrative lifestyle is a perfectly good route to human flourishing. Using himself as an example, he says:

> I have a past, like any human being, and I know perfectly well that I have a past. I have a respectable amount of factual knowledge about it, and I also remember some of my past experiences "from the inside," as philosophers say, and yet I have absolutely no sense of my life as a narrative with form. Absolutely none. Nor do I have any great or special interest in my past. Nor do I have a great deal of concern for my future . . . [I]t seems clear to me, when I am experiencing or apprehending myself as a self, that the remoter past or future in question is not my past or future, although it is certainly the past or future of GS the human being.
>
> (Strawson 2005: 64)

It seems that aside from the practical value of remembering what happened to GS (that is, to Galen-Strawson-the-human-being) Strawson does not regard either the remembering of his past life, or the sort of unity that this remembering might contribute to his current life, as a thing of much value.

Of course, unlike Leonard, Strawson has an undiminished ability to form event memories and he could, if needed, produce at will an autobiographical narrative that—without the sort of gaps that would plague Leonard's similar attempt—would link his remote past to the present. So, in spite of Strawson's apparent lack of interest in his autobiography, when it comes to retaining memory *abilities*, there may be a line that one cannot cross and still have a life worth living, and Leonard, but not Strawson, may have crossed that line. But, if we take Strawson at his word, it would seem that it is possible to live closer to that line than most people seem to think and still have not only a life worth living, but one in which one flourishes. In any case, *Memento* does not depict Leonard as suffering much from a lack of narrative unity. If we suppose that temperamentally Leonard is like Strawson then that lack may not be much of a problem for him.

Where all of this leaves us

At the least, the discussion to this point should leave all of us with a heightened appreciation of the case to be made for three contentions:

1   that, practical problems aside, it may be possible to live one's life in a way that is extremely valuable both to oneself and to others, even though one has a seriously diminished capacity to form event memories;

2   that it's likely that, in the future, memory aids will become available that provide factual information "from the outside" that greatly diminishes these practical problems; and

3   that the life of someone who had to rely on these memory aids in lieu of event memories, though radically different and in many ways less "personal" and perhaps less "meaningful" than a normal human life, might nevertheless still be a life worth living.

With luck, our discussion may also leave a few of us convinced that even without the ability to form new event memories, but with sophisticated external memory aids, one might function reasonably effectively in pursuit of one's goals and even have a rich and satisfying subjective life. There are things one would have to do without, but nothing, it seems, that would necessarily preclude one from having a life worth living.

Looking to the longer picture, technology promises to change not only how easily and in what form one has access to information about the past, but even what it means to be human. Indeed, already on the horizon, darkly looming, is the prospect that due to continuing technological advances humans will eventually become obsolete. If this happens, of course, not only event memories as we know them, but human life itself may go by the board. Yet, some sort of humanlike "lives" may go on, perhaps ones that are not only worth living, but exemplary. In *The Tempest* (Act V, scene 1) Shakespeare has Miranda say, "O brave new world, that hath such people in't!" How prophetic. If we humans don't destroy ourselves first, and thereby end the prospects for continuing technological advancement on Earth, a brave new world does indeed seem to be on its way—one that may be populated by a new sort of humanlike being, but which is perhaps not less valuable than the one it replaces.[5]

Notes

1 Recently it has come to light that AJ is not alone. According to the Associated Press, radio news anchor Brad Williams, of LaCrosse, Wisconsin, is believed to have autobiographical memory abilities comparable to those of AJ. It is also reported that since Williams began to talk on the air more about his memory abilities fifty people who have heard his broadcasts have called in to claim that they have similar memory abilities (CNN 2008). I am grateful to Lynn Gray for bringing this article to my attention.

2 I am indebted to Felmon Davis for reminding me of the Borges story.

3 The remarks quoted are from a manuscript written in 1512.

4 For an interesting discussion of the importance of forward-looking projects, including some discussion of the late Russian neuropsychologist A. R. Luria's view of their importance, see Sorabji (2006: 175–77, 303).

5 Thanks to Emily Brunelle and Bruce Connolly for assistance with references, and to John Barresi, Felmon Davis, Harry Marten, and Marya Schechtman for helpful comments on an earlier draft.

References

Augustine (1997) *The Confessions*, trans. M. Boulding, New York, NY: Vintage Books.

Borges, J.L. (1942) "Funes, the Memorious," reprinted in J. Sturrock (ed.) (1962) *Ficciones*, trans. A. Kerrigan New York, NY: Grove Press.

Buñuel, L. (1983) *My Last Sigh*, trans. A. Israel, New York, NY: Knopf.

CNN (2008) "Amazing Memory Man Never Forgets," online. Available at: www.cnn.com/2008/HEALTH/02/22/memory.man.ap/index.html (accessed 27 February 2008).

Dennett, D. (1978) *Brainstorms: Philosophical Essays on Mind and Psychology*, Cambridge, MA: Bradford Books.

Hakluyt, R. (undated) *The Principal Navigations, Voyages, Traffiques, and Discoveries of the English Nation*, London: J.M. Dent & Co.

Nin, A. (1948) *Under a Glass Bell, and Other Stories*, New York, NY: E.P. Dutton.

Science Daily (2006) "Researchers Identify New Form of Superior Memory Syndrome," online. Available at: www.sciencedaily.com/releases/2006/03/060314085102.htm (accessed 19 December 2007).

Sorabji, R. (2006) *Self: Ancient and Modern Insights about Individuality, Life, and Death*, Chicago, IL: The University of Chicago Press.

Strawson, G. (2005) "Against Narrativity," in G. Strawson (ed.) *The Self?*, Oxford: Blackwell, pp. 63–86.

Sutton, J. (2006) "Memory," in D.M. Borchert (ed.) *Encyclopedia of Philosophy*, 2nd edn, Farmington, MI: Thomson Gale, pp. 122–8.

Wollheim, R. (1984) *The Thread of Life*, Cambridge: Cambridge University Press.

Further reading

Baier, K. (1988) "Threats of Futility: Is Life Worth Living?," *Free Inquiry* 8: 47–52. (An argument that one's life can be worth living even if it is not meaningful.)

—— (1997) *Problems of Life and Death: A Humanist Perspective*, Buffalo, NY: Prometheus Books. (A prominent philosopher contends that rational humanism is the best alternative to theism.)

Benatar, D. (2006) *Better Never to Have Been: The Harm of Coming into Existence*, Oxford: Oxford University Press. (Argues that coming into existence is always a serious harm.)

Papanicolaou, A.C. (2005) *The Amnesias: A Clinical Textbook of Memory Disorders*, Oxford: Oxford University Press. (Includes a psychological overview of different types of memory.)

Sacks, O. (1985) *The Man Who Mistook His Wife for a Hat and Other Clinical Tales*, London: Picador. (Includes fascinating accounts of memory and other psychological disorders.)

Sutton, J. (2003) "Memory," in E.N. Zalta (ed.) *The Stanford Encyclopedia of Philosophy*, Fall 2008 edn, online. Available at: http://plato.stanford.edu/archives/fall2008/entries/memory/ (accessed August 22, 2008). (An excellent overview of the philosophy and psychology of memory.)

Trisel, B.A. (2002) "Futility and the Meaning of Life Debate," *Sorites* 14: 70–84. (A consideration of (i) what it means to claim that life is futile, and (ii) whether life still might be worth living, even if human striving is always futile.)

—— (2007) "Judging Life and Its Value," *Sorites* 18: 60–75. (What does it mean when someone claims that life is worth living, and is it true?)

Chapter 5

Richard Hanley

MEMENTO AND PERSONAL IDENTITY: DO WE HAVE IT BACKWARDS?

Introduction

I MEAN MY TITLE BOTH LITERALLY and metaphorically. Metaphorical first: Philosophers commonly deny what seems commonsensical, arguing that the ordinary folk in fact have it backwards. This happens a lot in the metaphysics of personal identity, as we shall see! Second, as a philosopher who works on the metaphysics of time travel, I ponder whether or not one could live a life literally backwards. Thinking about Memento will inform both of these "backwards" hypotheses, starting with the metaphorical one.

As with any other piece of popular culture, we shouldn't get too carried away thinking that a movie like Memento has anything special or new to say. What Memento does do is get you thinking. That is a great gift, and if you want to keep thinking, philosophy is waiting.

Survival and identity

In Memento, Leonard Shelby has survived something very traumatic: a severe head injury compounded by a terrible psychological blow. Leonard lost his wife when he lost the ability to lay down new memories. Or at least, that's what he thinks. It's also possible that he didn't quite lose either in that incident in the bathroom—the incident.

It's not my purpose here to decide exactly what's true in the story, and I am going to employ both main versions of events in what follows. I shall use them to investigate one of my main metaphysical interests: what is personal survival, whether in an extraordinary case like that of Leonard, or in the presumably more typical cases like yours and mine? When we say *Leonard survived*, what does that mean?

You might say it just means that he didn't die. But that's imprecise at best. *Most* of us when pressed think or hope that we'll survive death. It's *that* sense of "survive" that I'm interested in. Your next answer might be that you survive if and only if you do not cease to exist. What matters to your survival, then, is that *you persist* into the future, and you persist just in case there is a future person that is numerically identical with— one and the same person as—you.

This isn't beyond argument. Derek Parfit has famously claimed, most prominently in *Reasons and Persons* (1984), that commonsense is making a mistake: Although we *think* identity is what matters to survival, we have it backwards, and what *really*, objectively, matters is something else, which he calls Relation R.[1] We'll see just what R consists in, but it will do for now to note that it is a *psychological* relation, which can in principle hold between numerically distinct persons.

We'll consider four different answers to the question of what personal survival really is:

1　The Body View: that your body, or enough of it, persists.
2　The Mind View: that your psychology persists.
3　The Soul View: that something other than your body or mind persists.
4　The Parfitian View: that Relation R holds, whether or not you persist.

According to Views 1–3, commonsense is correct, and personal identity is what matters to survival. But they disagree about what personal identity consists in. For instance, in the case of Leonard Shelby, if the Body View is correct, then Leonard unproblematically *survived* his trauma. Same body, same person.[2]

The modern philosophical debate is between the Body View and Views 2 and 4, which both focus upon psychological relations. That is, the debate is between those who reject the Soul View. Let's see what motivated the Soul View in the first place, and why it seems inadequate.

View 3: Persistence, change, and souls

In scene B, Leonard gets Fact 6 tattooed on his thigh. In scene A he has no such tattoo, and in chronologically later scene C, he does. It seems two things are true: first, Leonard's body persists from scene A to scene C, and second, Leonard's body has changed from scene A to scene C. But how can one and the same thing both persist *and* change?

It may surprise you to learn that until relatively recently the dominant view in philosophy was that it *can't*—that is, it's *impossible* for a thing to both persist and change. Once again, we have philosophers arguing that commonsense has it backwards. In this case, I think commonsense is right after all, but those philosophers definitely have a point that needs to be countered. Consider how we ordinarily distinguish one thing from another. I ask you if this is your pen that I have in my hand, and you say No it isn't, because *your* pen has your name on it. Here you are employing this principle:

> If object *A* has intrinsic property *F*, and object *B* lacks *F*, then *A* is not one and the same object as *B*.[3]

Note that the principle connects our two ordinary concepts of "identity," qualitative identity (a matter of shared properties) and numerical identity. The principle tells us that from qualitative difference we rightly infer numerical difference.

Now consider Leonard again. Leonard's body in scene A is qualitatively different from Leonard's body in scene C, so according to the tradition, it *couldn't be* one and the same body. As Thomas Reid writes in 1785:

> [I]dentity . . . has no fixed nature when applied to bodies; and questions about the identity of a body are very often questions about words. But identity, when applied to persons, has no ambiguity, and admits not of degrees, of more and less . . .
>
> (Reid 1969: 344)

Reid's view, then, seems to be that whatever bodies do, they don't actually persist, whereas *persons* do.

Can Reid instead adopt the Mind View, holding that personal identity consists in psychological identity? No, because exactly the same problem arises all over again. Any individual psychology—even an abnormal one like Leonard's—undergoes intrinsic change over time. Consider memory. Leonard can remember things in the short term, such as what just transpired with Natalie in scene F, the scene where he hits her. But by the time Natalie comes back in the front door in scene G, Leonard no longer remembers having hit her. By the principle above, it seems that Leonard's psychology in scene F is numerically distinct from Leonard's psychology in scene G. So Reid ought to say that psychologies, like bodies, don't actually persist. *Persons* must be something else again, which brings us to the Soul View.

You can see why the Soul View is tempting. If only, you might think, there were something intrinsically unchanging, then we could hang our persistence hat on it. But the Soul View will not do. Consider what it implies, given its Reidian motivation: Underneath (or above?) all the flux in body and mind, there lies some unchanging thing that is the real *you*.[4]

The problem is that were the Soul View true, then bodies and minds, and whatever bodies and minds do, would be strictly *irrelevant* to judgments of personal identity over time. If what is relevant is the presence of the (relevant) soul, how is one to judge (a) whether any soul is present in, or associated with, a particular body or mind (including one's own!), or (b) whether a soul present in, or associated with, a particular body or mind at another time is one and the same soul as before?

Since we don't have a soul detector, the only criteria we *actually* employ in making personal identity judgments are bodily and psychological ones. That this practice has no justification whatsoever on the Soul View is sufficient reason to reject that view.

View 1: Connectedness and continuity of body

We seek, then, a criterion of personal identity that vindicates common-sense and common practice, one that renders persistence compatible with change. Let's revisit the Body View, and begin with a definition: Two bodies are *connected* if and only if they *overlap*; that is, if and only if they have parts in common. For instance, as Leonard ages, skin cells are routinely lost, and when he shaves his thigh, he loses extra skin and hair cells, which are more or less replaced by new ones. ("More or less" because growth involves more replacement, and shrinking involves less.)

But from moment to moment, minute to minute, hour to hour, day to day, the ratio of cells lost to the number of total cells is fairly small. So on a particular day Leonard's body is very strongly connected to Leonard's body the day before, and to Leonard's body the day after.

Is bodily identity the same thing as bodily connectedness? No. Suppose the old saw about total cellular replacement turned out to be true, and in, say, every seven-year period, a human body completes the recycling of all of its cells. Then Leonard's body in scene A would be unconnected with Leonard's body ten years earlier. Nevertheless, we surely would judge it to be one and the same body.

And we can't just shrug and say: Oh well, I guess his body didn't persist after all. Because bodily identity just *couldn't be* bodily connectedness. The problem is that (like any numerical identity), bodily identity is *transitive* (if body X = body Y and body Y = body Z, then body X = body Z) and bodily connectedness is *not* transitive. In our imagined circumstance, Leonard's body in scene A would be connected with Leonard's body five years earlier, and his body five years earlier would be connected with his body ten years earlier. So if connectedness were identity, it would follow of necessity that Leonard's body in scene A is connected with Leonard's body of ten years ago. And that is false.

The solution is to move to a different relation: bodily *continuity*. Bodily continuity consists in overlapping chains of bodily connectedness. Consider L1 through L5 in Figure 5.1.

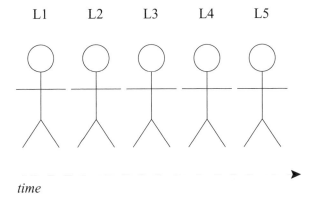

time

Figure 5.1 Bodily continuity

Suppose L1 and L5 are 10 years apart, and not bodily connected. But L1 is connected to L2, L3, and L4. L2 is connected to L3, L4, and L5, and so on. There is bodily continuity between all five, and so between L1 and L5.[5]

So far, so good, but the Body View isn't quite out of the woods yet. It turns out that there are two very different ways of allowing that persistence and change are compatible, because there are two very different ways of understanding persistence. They are called *perdurantism* and *endurantism*. Perdurantism, which I favor, is closer to Reid's view, agreeing with Reid that the relation between, for instance, L1 and L2, is *not* identity.

But perdurantists disagree with Reid that the Soul View is required, and that's because they hold a four-dimensional conception of a person. None of L1 through L5 is a person, rather, they are different (relatively tiny) *parts* of the same person, called *person-stages*. Perdurantists think of time as enough like space that things can be extended in it. Just as Leonard's body is extended in space in virtue of having different spatial parts located at different places, so it is extended in time in virtue of having different *temporal* parts (different stages), located at different times. Leonard's body is a *space–time worm*, and change over time is nothing more than qualitative difference between distinct parts of a persistent thing.

Body View endurantists think Reid is wrong on both counts. They regard persistence as involving the *very same thing*, appearing at different times, sometimes with different properties. So on the endurantist view, L1 = L2 = L3 = L4 = L5. I like to put the contrast this way: On the perdurantist view, L1 puts in a single appearance in space–time. On the endurantist view, L1 is a repeatable thing, appearing over and over again in space–time, as L2, L3, and so on.

Although I favor perdurantism about bodies, a good number of philosophers are endurantists, so the issue is far from settled. But either way, Leonard seems to satisfy the criterion of bodily continuity. Let's next consider the Mind View.

View 2: Connectedness and continuity of mind

In his *Essay Concerning Human Understanding*, John Locke, a defender of the Mind View, postulated that personal identity consists in relations of memory (1689: bk. 2, ch. 27). Consider Leonard's flashbacks to incidents that occurred before his injury. He recalls opening the bathroom door and seeing the intruder leaning over his wife, for instance. Since he remembers being the person who opened the door, by Locke's criterion he *is* the person who opened the door.

Of course, a nutcase who thinks he is Napoleon is not thereby Napoleon, and Locke would agree. Memory is *factive*—you can't *remember* something that never happened. (So, strictly speaking, "false memory syndrome" is a misnomer.) The nutcase only *thinks* he remembers being Napoleon. And the memory has to be of the right sort, anyway. The nutcase can in one sense remember that Napoleon was at Waterloo, since that really happened, but that's not at all the same as remembering *being* Napoleon at Waterloo.

But Locke's criterion is flawed. The problem is that remembering being a person at an earlier time doesn't seem necessary (even if it is sufficient) for being that person. The aforementioned Thomas Reid showed this with his example of a valiant officer who recalls being beaten as a boy for robbing an orchard, and eventually becomes an old general, who remembers being valiant but doesn't remember being beaten (1785: 357–8). By Locke's criterion, the general is the officer, but isn't the boy, but the officer is the boy, and is the general, too. That can't be right. (Like the bodily connectedness criterion, Locke's psychological connectedness criterion violates the transitivity of identity.) Locke not only fails to give a good account of personal identity, he fails to give a good account of *psychological* identity. So the Mind View might be true, but not in Locke's rendering.

Leonard Shelby provides a different case of failure of transitivity, where the middle man isn't in the middle chronologically. Leonard in scene G doesn't remember being Leonard in scene F, in which he hits Natalie. But Leonard in scene G remembers being Leonard in the incident. And Leonard in scene F remembers it, too. So by Locke's criterion, Leonard in scene F is Leonard in the incident, and Leonard in scene G is Leonard in the incident, but Leonard in scene F is *not* Leonard in scene G! That can't be right.

Locke is perhaps vulnerable to a second objection. Even had Locke given an otherwise adequate account of personal identity, Joseph Butler objected that his analysis would be circular, presupposing the very thing it was supposed to explain. According to Butler, the concept of memory must in turn be analyzed in terms of personal identity, since *remembering being someone* presupposes that you *are* that person (1836: 361–3). So Butler thinks Locke has it backwards.

Parfit shows how to rescue the Lockean approach from both these objections. First, as with the case of bodily identity, we can block the non-transitivity objection by moving to psychological *continuity* rather than connectedness, defining psychological continuity as overlapping chains of psychological connectedness. Second, we can sidestep Butler's objection (avoiding altogether the question of whether Butler's claim is true), by defining *quasi*-memory as a notion that definitely doesn't presuppose identity. Q-memory (for short) is otherwise just like memory—indeed, all memories (even assuming Butler is right) are also q-memories.

An example might help. Suppose Natalie is somehow *replicated* (for instance, in the manner invented by Tesla in Christopher Nolan's movie *The Prestige* (2006)), but in Australia. When Natalie's duplicate emerges from the replicator, she will think she is Natalie, even though she's not (Natalie hasn't gone anywhere). If Butler is right, then Natalie's duplicate doesn't *remember* being Natalie, she only *q-remembers* it.

Q-memory, like memory, is factive. (So the nutcase doesn't remember or q-remember being Napoleon.) And when a duplicate q-remembers what you had for breakfast this morning, they q-remember it for the same sort of reason you remember it: It happened, and its happening caused your q-memory and their q-memory, in the same sort of way.

So does Leonard follow the advice of his tattoo, and *remember Sammy Jankis*? On one interpretation of the story, Leonard has confabulated false "memories" about Sammy (especially concerning his non-existent wife). But other things he seems to remember happened all right, just to Leonard himself rather than Sammy.

This is compatible with Leonard's really remembering these things (and so, q-remembering them). Consider scene 21, in which we see Sammy in the mental institution, tantalizingly replaced for an instant with Leonard (1:29:56). Suppose it's true in the story that this scene really happened to Leonard, but he thinks it happened to Sammy (and the flash of Leonard is not part of his recollection, but there for dramatic purposes).

Then Leonard is, in his memory, seeing what happened (to Leonard himself) as though from the perspective of someone else. This is an entirely normal phenomenon. We often package memories of ourselves in this third-person way, and hardly notice. We just need to take care in

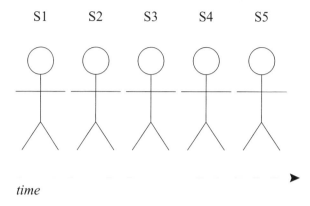

time

Figure 5.2 Psychological continuity

what memories we attribute to Leonard. He doesn't remember (or q-remember) *being* Sammy Jankis, any more than the nutcase remembers being *that* didn't actually happen.

So does Leonard q-remember enough? Because of his condition, he lacks all sorts of psychological connections that hold in normal persons, but thanks to his ability to remember what happened before the incident, the relation of psychological continuity holds.

In Figure 5.2., S1 is Leonard waking upon hearing a noise from the bathroom. S2 is Leonard opening the door to the bathroom. S3 is Leonard in scene C, being served a beer with some added bodily fluids. S4 is Leonard in scene D, sipping the beer. S5 is Leonard in scene F, hitting Natalie. S2 q-remembers being S1. S3 q-remembers being S1 and S2. S4 q-remembers being S1 and S2, but not S3. S5 q-remembers being S1 and S2, but not S3 or S4. There are overlapping chains of q-memory, so there seems to be psychological continuity from S1 through S5.

Parfit might disagree. Parfit defines psychological continuity more narrowly than we have so far, as "the holding of overlapping chains of *strong* connectedness," where strong connectedness is "enough" (1984: 206). It is difficult to say what counts as *enough*, and Parfit does not try. But he does tell us that the measure is both quantitative *and* qualitative. Quantitative first: He says that there is definitely strong day-to-day connectedness if there is at least half the number of direct connections as in the normal day-to-day case. The implication is that over any time period, there is strong connectedness if there is at least half the number of direct connections in a normal person over that period.

As for the quality of connections, Parfit writes that "more weight should be given to those connections which are distinctive, or different in different people. All English speakers, for example, share many undistinctive memories of how to speak English." (1984: 515 n.6). So Parfit would give more weight to Leonard's memory of the incident, and less weight to Leonard's memories involved in speaking English or other common practices, such as driving a car, shaving, and so forth.

Parfit also allows for connectedness of states besides memory, such as desires and intentions, or q-desires and q-intentions (1984: 205). This lets us identify all sorts of extra connectedness from S3 through S5. For instance, from S3 through S5 Leonard seems to retain the powerful intention to exact revenge upon his wife's killer. Qualitatively, this is likely to carry a lot of weight for Parfit, more so than Leonard's apparent intention to shower when the opportunity presents itself. But as long as Leonard has enough qualitatively weighty intentions and other states to compensate for memory loss, he might satisfy the criterion of strong psychological connectedness.[6]

Parfit can reach the same conclusion by adding a further consideration —Leonard's mementos—thanks to his account of Relation R as admitting psychological continuity "with any cause" (1984: 207–9, 215). The normal cause of psychological continuity in us is just our bodies, especially our brains, persisting and functioning. If you are replicated, then the psychological continuity between your pre-scan self and your replica does not have its normal cause, but so what, as long as it works? And the replication could work even if it's unreliable. So Parfit rejects the view that survival requires psychological continuity with either its normal cause, or a reliable cause. This leaves him with the "widest" view that it can have any cause.

If qualitative similarity by any cause will do, then Leonard's use of his mementos does provide genuine psychological connectedness, and so, arguably, continuity. In scene B, Leonard gets Fact 6 tattooed on his thigh: Car License SG13 7IU. So in scene B, he (probably) believes John G's car license number is SG13 7IU. In scene T, he believes the same thing, not via a normal cause, but via the tattooed memento.

This "widest-ness" is puzzling, though, because it seems thereby to permit connectedness between any two persons with any qualitatively identical mental states. That's *too much* connectedness, and needs to be mitigated. One mitigation will be that the number of such connections is usually relatively small. The other is that many of the widely shared states will be "undistinctive" ones.

Suppose Leonard had another tattoo that reads "The gas pedal is on the right." Even though Leonard in scene B might thereby be connected with Leonard in scene T, in virtue of them both believing that the gas pedal is on the right (and believing it only because of the tattoo), the belief is undistinctive. The belief that John G's car license number is SG13 7IU, by contrast, is distinctive. Hence it gets more weight in Parfit's calculus.

But it seems to me there's a better way of avoiding the "too much connectedness" problem that arises from the "any cause" condition. Consider first an ordinary case, such as S2 remembering being S1 awakened by a noise. Both S1 and S2 believe that a noise came from the bathroom when Leonard was sleeping. But the *reason* that S2 believes it is that S1 believed it: If S1 hadn't believed it, S2 wouldn't believe it, either. Similarly for S5's having the intention to exact revenge upon John G: S5 has it because S4 had it, and S4 had it because S3 had it.

What Parfit gets right is that such causal dependence does not depend upon a normal or even a reliable cause. In that sense, any old cause will do. So even if Leonard has states that are transmitted from one time to another only via mementos, that can be good enough for connectedness, and (if there's enough connectedness) continuity. What Parfit misses, though, is that whatever the cause of my memories, they must depend on the psychology of an earlier person stage. But this is much narrower than the "widest" notion.

To sum up this section, then, Leonard is Leonard throughout on the Mind View, suitably understood. He seems to have enough q-memories, q-beliefs, q-desires, q-intentions, and mementos to satisfy even a relatively strict criterion of psychological continuity.

View 4: Relation R

So there's one sort of answer Leonard can give to Teddy's challenge in scene S. Teddy wants to know what the point of exacting revenge upon "John G" is, if Leonard won't remember it afterwards anyway. Leonard no doubt would like to have his revenge *and* remember it, but since that choice is not on the table, having his revenge even though he won't remember can still matter. He wants it to be him that exacts revenge, and he can have that whether the Body View or the Mind View of personal identity is correct.

How can we choose between the Body and Mind Views? Can we hear anything but the dull thud of conflicting intuitions? Leonard's case suggests one sort of test to distinguish them. If we break enough psychological connections in one and the same persisting body, then psychological continuity is lost. Then, if personal identity is lost, that favors the Mind View, and if personal identity is not lost, that favors the Body View.

Locke proposed another sort of test. He imagined a case where a person with the outward appearance of a certain cobbler started behaving like, and claiming to be, a certain prince, and vice versa. (Think of any of the plethora of movies where this sort of thing occurs.) Of course, at first no one would believe their respective stories, but imagine (as happens in such movies) that they reveal personal information, and so on, until it becomes plausible that we have the cobbler's body occupied by the prince's psychology, and vice versa. Now we have a choice of description. We can say that the cobbler and the prince have swapped psychologies (the Body View), or swapped bodies (the Mind View). Locke himself thought that the correct description is that they have swapped bodies, and indeed that is the one that is favored in the movies.

The danger remains that these thought experiments only preach to the choir, revealing what you already believe. So let's try something else. Consider the replication case again, only this time, suppose that the scan kills Natalie immediately. Isn't she just dead? Her replica in Australia thinks she's Natalie, but isn't she just as mistaken as she would be if Natalie were still around? Her replica's q-memories are not memories, it seems. And this seems to favor the Body View.

But does it really? Consider Robert Nozick's "closest continuer" schema, described in *Philosophical Explanations* (1981: 29–47). When no death-by-scanning occurs, Natalie-still-here enjoys both bodily and psychological continuity with the scanned subject, whereas the Australian replica has psychological but not bodily continuity with them. So Natalie-still-here wins the contest to be the scanned subject. In the death-by-scanning case, on the other hand, the Australian replica wins, having no remotely close competitors. (Natalie's lifeless body might be a candidate, so imagine that the scanner cremates it, if you like.) This suggests that the Mind View is correct after all.

If bodily continuity can count into the closest continuer schema even given the Mind View, then that is more good news for Leonard's persistence. But the schema raises more puzzles. Suppose the scanner cremates Natalie, and we send two signals, so that two qualitatively identical replicas emerge, one in Australia and one in New Zealand. (Call this *Double Replication*, and the replicas OZ and NZ.) Now we have a tie for closest continuer. They cannot both be Natalie, since that would require them to be each other. So neither of them is Natalie!

Parfit's diagnosis of Double Replication is that psychological continuity is, like psychological connectedness, non-transitive. OZ is psychologically continuous with Natalie, and so is NZ, but they are not psychologically continuous with each other. He argues further that Double Replication is about as good as ordinary survival, and much better than ordinary death. So, in Double Replication, Natalie *survives*, even though she ceases to exist. So your survival is *not* your persistence—rather it is having someone in the future psychologically continuous with you now, whether or not they *are* you! Hence, View 4. (We can then analyze personal persistence as non-branching psychological continuity, to avoid the non-transitivity problem.)

Other diagnoses are possible. David Lewis argues that a case like Double Replication (assuming no other exotic processes occur in it), involves exactly two persons, not three as Parfit would have it (Lewis 1976). It's true that OZ is not NZ, but it's not true that there's some third person (the pre-scan Natalie that Parfit believes in). Lewis is a perdurantist, holding that a person is a four-dimensional space–time worm with body stages united by psychological continuity, and the pre-scan Natalie is really part of OZ *and* part of NZ. The two happen to overlap for part of the duration of their existence, by *sharing* person stages, the way two interstate highways can overlap for part of their spatial extension by sharing the same road surface. So Lewis defends the Mind View, suitably understood, *and* View 4. He thinks Parfit has it backwards in holding the two views to be incompatible.

I have focused on psychological continuity as Relation R, but Parfit actually claims (and Lewis concurs) that Relation R is psychological connectedness *and* continuity (Parfit 1984: 301–2). Again, the case of Leonard provides some obvious motivation. Both Natalie and Teddy ponder the point of Leonard's life, given that he won't remember much of what happens or his part in it.

But perhaps this only shows that it's *better* to have certain sorts of connectedness than not. I tend to think that Parfit and Lewis have this backwards, and that our preferences about connectedness show what properly matters *to us in* our survival, not what matters to our survival *itself*. They're preferences to survive with more rather than with less, not preferences to survive rather than not survive. Of course, they're very strong preferences, but so are others we have that aren't remotely connected to personal survival. Many of us very strongly prefer to have children rather than not, and to be remembered rather than not. But having children, or being remembered, are not ways of *surviving*.

This ends our survey of the main competing views on personal persistence. My purpose here has not been to decide between them, but rather to elucidate them using *Memento* as a case in point. I'd like to end by considering one more set of metaphysical concerns.

Memento, Relation R, and time travel

I have often used *Memento* in my time-travel class, and I'll explain why. The movie not only begins at the end, it begins *moving backwards*. Imagine for a moment what it would have been like had it continued in the same fashion. Visually, it's fairly easy to imagine, accustomed as we are to, for instance, VCRs that we can reverse while in "play" mode, watching the action in reverse. The other main aspect of a talking picture is the talking, the sound, and this is not so easy to understand in reverse.[7]

Time travel tends to be conceived of in three very different ways. One is *instantaneous*: One instant you're in 2008, say, the next instant you're in 2018. Second is an *insulated journey*: You experience a journey of, say 10 minutes to go from 2008 to 2018, but you travel via a wormhole or some other conduit, effectively insulated from the events in the rest of the world. Third is an *interactive journey*: This is the sort we see in the two movie versions of *The Time Machine* (1960 and 2002), where you are aware of events in the outside world as you journey. You push forward into the future, and the effect is like fast search on the VCR. The hands on the clock on the wall start to whiz around, while the watch on your wrist behaves normally. The sun races across the sky, flowers quickly open and close, and so on.

Ponder for a moment how you must look to the outside world, assuming they can see you. You would seem to be hardly moving at all. The metaphor of a moving body of water like a river is helpful here. Some parts of the river move faster than others, and if some move much faster, the rest will seem almost stationary from that perspective. If you could be heard, your speech would sound like a low-pitched drone, while the outsiders' speech would sound to you like a high pitched squeal. Slow down enough, and they might sound like the Chipmunks.

Leonard's mementos save him from an experience like that of repeated instantaneous time travel. They allow him to track the passage of time. If he really can lay down no new memories, then the incident in the bathroom would, without mementos, seem as though it had just happened each time Leonard "wakes up." (Indeed, if I were Leonard, I hope I'd go a lot further, and at least have a calendar or something where I entered the date of important events as they happened.)

Now imagine going backwards in time, on a journey from 2008 to 1998. On the instantaneous or insulated journey conceptions, the experience will not differ much from a journey into the future. But on the interactive journey conception, when you push backwards into the past, the hands on the wall clock will appear to go backwards. Flowers will come to life, get smaller and disappear into buds, and so on. It would be like watching the beginning of *Memento*. And how will you, the time traveler, look to outsiders? To *them*, *you* will appear to be the one going backwards because, inside your semi-permeable time bubble, you are aging normally, talking normally, moving normally, and so on.

By the way, this should allay a common misconception about backwards time travel. It's often claimed that you would get *younger* as you go into the past. I think folk make this mistake because in interactive time travel, you would *appear* to be getting younger as you journeyed backwards, if outsiders could see you for long enough.

Once again, the metaphor of a river helps. An eddy might form where some of the water is flowing backwards—in a direction opposite to that of the main body of water. (At the boundary, things are messy, so don't stick your hand through the surface of your time bubble!) From the perspective of each, the other is the one flowing backwards.

Now, finally, suppose that you get stuck this way—journeying past-wards in your semi-permeable time bubble. What sort of interaction could you have with the outside world? I hope you can see that it would be troublesome. Speech slowed down, or speeded up, and backwards would likely be unintelligible. You could use mementos: writing on a blackboard, perhaps, as could they. Each would appear to be removing the chalk from the board, but it could be read at least. And it could communicate information that is in the future of the message's recipient. But how do you have a conversation back and forth?

It would be more like the case of Leonard if you could get out every so often and interact normally with the world. Each time you got out, you would not remember what others remember, so in that respect they have an advantage over you. And that, fundamentally, is Leonard's problem —he has to rely on others for information that we normally rely on ourselves for. And that's the point of his mementos—to circumvent having to trust others.

This sort of time travel would be like the telling of Memento itself, in the color scenes. We see the scenes in reverse order, but with the exception of the very beginning, the scenes themselves are not reversed. We, the audience, are in an as-if time machine, traveling instantaneously into the past, and we get out every now and again to look around. We have our movie mementos, like Leonard's tattoos and photographs. Each time we see a photograph, it is later in our experience, but earlier in the story, so it is as if writing has been erased from it. Each time we see a scene, it is as if some of history has been erased. And we piece together the past in part from our memory of the future.

I could have used a time machine recently myself, when I lost an earlier version of this essay. As it was, I had the opposite problem to Leonard. I lost my memento—my e-copy of the draft—and so had to reconstruct what I could from memory. It was as if a part of the past was erased, and reconstructing it involved retracing my steps, working backwards from my current memories of what I had written.

A lot of Memento is backwards. One of Leonard's tattoos is spatially backwards—in mirror writing. To think meaningfully about time travel one has to imagine time and space to be alike, and alike reversible. (Indeed, one of the puzzles we examine in my time-travel course is why mirrors are apparently left-right reversed, but apparently not up-down reversed. Think about that one!)

On the face of it, time travel doesn't pose any special problems for survival on any of the views we've considered. On either the Body View or the Mind View (or the Parfitian View, for that matter), you can have

Figure 5.3 Something Leonard has backwards (T, 0:15:43)

personal identity backwards. But maybe that's because it's not *really* backwards—it's only backwards from the point of view of others. But then, from the time traveler's point of view, it's the others who are backwards.

So I'll suggest an even more bizarre hypothesis, and it was *Memento* that got me thinking about it again. Time travel gives us one way of remembering the future, but here's another. Suppose there was someone whose body and so on was aging normally (so the states of their body in 2009 depend counterfactually upon the states of their body in 2008, for instance), but whose *psychology* was (or was *as if*) temporally reversed (so the states of their psychology in 2008 depend counterfactually upon the states of their psychology in 2009).

This person not only would *remember* the future, but they'd *anticipate* the past. Take a moment to imagine what that would be like. It's mightily tempting, of course, to think it would be very useful to remember the future. But in this circumstance (a) you can't really *do* anything about it yourself, because your intentions and desires are mostly directed towards the past, and (b) there's not much anyone else can do about it, either, thanks to the communication problems we saw a moment ago. Also, though you definitely remember *their* future, do you remember your own?

The answer to this depends once again upon whether the Body View or the Mind View (or alternatively the Parfitian View) is correct. What's the best description of this strange existence? Is it a person whose psychology is reversed (the Body View)? Or a person whose bodily development is reversed (the Mind View, or the Parfitian View)?

So is such a person really possible—can you have personal identity really backwards? Perhaps. (It rather depends upon the analysis of *causation*, a topic way too deep to go into here.) What would it be like to be such a person? Weird, of course! In order to meaningfully interact with the outside world, you'd need to employ mementos, and even then you'd be at horrible risk of all sorts of miscommunication and loss of information. Even if you had information, action would be very difficult, since there's a good sense in which your body won't obey you, anyway. From your point of view, your body is living backwards, so even bodily mementos like tattoos may be no use to you!

If there's one impression, one *memento* to take away from this entire discussion, it might be gratitude that you have your memories—even the bad ones.

Notes

1   This way of putting it may be too strong. It seems commonsensical enough to desire to *survive*, so perhaps Parfit's thesis can just as well be read as the view that we are mistaken in our beliefs about what we *really* want when we want to survive. The difference will not matter to us here.

2   I have stated the Body View a little imprecisely to avoid a discussion that is not relevant to our concerns here. To be more precise, stipulate that bodies are concrete, and that what matters is that the body or some concrete proper part of it (such as the brain) persists.

3   To explain "intrinsic": Consider a man who is an uncle. Being an uncle is a matter of his relations to other things, whereas being a man is a matter of how he is independent of his relations to other things. So being a man is an intrinsic property, and being an uncle is not.

4   By the way, believing in a soul doesn't by itself get you to the Soul View, since you might identify the soul with the mind, and allow that the mind changes.

5   A wrinkle for the Body View concerns death. Is it *you* that we bury, or not? Different versions of the Body View can give different answers. For instance, you might think that only a *functioning* human body can be a person, in which case you would hold that the corpse is a "continuer" of you, but not you. Or you might take a simple composition view, and if your corpse is composed of enough of what composes you before death, then it is you.

6   There are doubtless other sorts of connectedness that we don't see, but can infer. Leonard obviously works out *a lot* to stay in such superb shape, for instance. This likely involves all sorts of robust intentions.

7   For this reason, the sound actually *plays forwards* in the opening scene of
    Memento, as Nolan reports (Mottram 2002: 132). (Thanks to Andrew Kania
    for pointing this out.)

References

Butler, J. (1836) "Of Personal Identity," in S. Halifax (ed.) *The Works of the Right
    Reverend Father in God Joseph Butler*, new edn, vol. 1, Oxford: Oxford University
    Press.
Lewis, D. (1976) "Survival and Identity," in A.O. Rorty (ed.) *The Identities of Persons*,
    Berkeley, CA: University of California Press.
Locke, J. (1689) *Essay Concerning Human Understanding*, J.W. Yolton (ed.) (1961),
    London: Penguin.
Mottram, J. (2002) *The Making of* Memento, London: Faber and Faber.
Nozick, R. (1981) *Philosophical Explanations*, Cambridge, MA: Harvard University
    Press.
Parfit, D. (1984) *Reasons and Persons*, Oxford: Clarendon Press.
Reid, T. (1785) *Essays on the Intellectual Powers of Man*, B. Brody (ed.) (1969),
    Cambridge, MA: MIT Press.

Further reading

Amis, M. (1991) *Time's Arrow, or, The Nature of the Offence*, New York, NY: Harmony
    Books. (A novel whose narrator seems to have a 'backwards' psychology, as
    described at the end of this essay.)
Olson, E.T. (2002) "Personal Identity," in E.N. Zalta (ed.) *The Stanford Encyclopedia
    of Philosophy*, Fall 2008 edn, online. Available at: http://plato.stanford.edu/
    archives/fall2008/entries/identity-personal/ (accessed 1 October 2008).
    (An excellent introduction to the issues, written by an advocate of the Body
    View, with a helpful bibliography.)
Parfit, D. (1984) *Reasons and Persons*, Oxford: Clarendon Press. (Anyone interested
    in these issues must read this book, which is one of the great contributions to
    philosophy in the late twentieth century. Parfit of course defends the Parfitian
    View.)

Chapter 6

Noël Carroll

MEMENTO AND THE PHENOMENOLOGY OF COMPREHENDING MOTION PICTURE NARRATION

Introduction

A S IS BECOMING INCREASINGLY apparent in the literature, Christopher Nolan's film *Memento* is replete with philosophical themes, including such topics as personal identity, truth, memory, knowledge (both of the self and of the external world), objectivity, free will versus determinism, retributive justice, and existential commitment.[1] Consequently, the film may be thought to broach questions of metaphysics, epistemology, and ethics. In this essay, I would also like to consider the philosophical contribution that *Memento* makes to aesthetics. For, although Andrew Kania has maintained that *Memento* does not address the ontology of art (Kania 2008) *and*, though this may be true under a very strict interpretation of that phrase, nevertheless, *Memento* does disclose to the thoughtful viewer certain insights about the dynamics of following a motion picture narrative. Thus, it may be construed as an instance of the philosophy of art, specifically the philosophy of motion pictures.

Nowadays, the issue of whether a motion picture can be said truly to do philosophy is a matter of pitched debate. Therefore, before dealing in detail with *Memento*, I will devote a section to explaining the sense in which I am claiming that *Memento* does philosophy, especially in terms of situating my conception of the way *Memento* does philosophy with respect to various skeptical arguments against the very possibility of movie-made philosophy. Next, I will attempt to locate *Memento* in a tradition of motion-picture production that attempts to meld popular genres with philosophical meditations. And then I will turn directly to *Memento* in order to show how it turns the film noir genre upside down in order to initiate the viewer into a phenomenological or introspective exploration of the experience of self-consciously constructing or co-constructing a narrative, thereby revealing to the viewer's reflective awareness a general aspect of the motion-picture experience that typically goes unnoticed and unacknowledged.

On the possibility of movie-made philosophy

During the last decade—undoubtedly prefigured and encouraged by the work of Stanley Cavell—Anglophone philosophers have become keenly interested in the philosophical potential of the moving image. Anthologies abound in which rank-and-file philosophers attempt to distill the philosophical message to be found in this or that movie. Indeed, the very book you hold in your hands right now is an example of this genre. And many of the articles in the journal *Film and Philosophy* are also in this vein.

Although many philosophers are interested in the relation between movies and philosophy, there is not a converging consensus about the nature of that relation. Some philosophers maintain that it is within the reach of the moving image to make contributions to philosophy that stand on all fours with the contributions made by card-carrying philosophers in journal articles and at academic conferences. Others argue that this is beyond the capability of the moving image. Such skeptics may concede that movies can illustrate philosophical ideas, motivate philosophical problems, suggest philosophical solutions, reframe problems, and possibly even present counterexamples to extant philosophical views. Nevertheless, the skeptics draw a line in the sand when it comes to the possibility of movies making philosophy—that is, of movies acting as vehicles for the creation and substantiation of original, positive philosophical theses. Since in this article I wish to claim that *Memento* has a positive philosophical contribution to offer, I must, therefore, first disarm the criticisms that are apt to be launched against a project like mine even before I get started.

Three recent arguments against movie-made philosophy have been advanced by Paisley Livingston (2006), Murray Smith (2006), and Bruce Russell (2005, 2008a,b).[2] Livingston begins by introducing two conditions that he maintains must be met in order for any example to count as an instance of movie-made philosophy. The first condition requires that x is a specimen of movie-made philosophy only if it is a historically innovative philosophical proposal, rather than simply an illustration of a pre-existing position. It must not be parasitic on previous philosophical discourse; it must be independent. Thus, Rossellini's *Blaise Pascal* (1972) does not count as movie-made philosophy, since the actor playing Pascal is only repeating what Pascal already said. Ditto Derek Jarman's *Wittgenstein* (1993).

In addition to this independence requirement, Livingston also demands that a candidate for the title of movie-made philosophy be articulated exclusively by cinematic means. Consequently, a cinematic recording of a contemporary philosopher, such as Bob Solomon, sharing his thoughts with the camera on the philosophy of the emotions—as he does in one of The Great Courses, produced by The Teaching Company —falls short of movie-made philosophy just because the mode of presentation does not really exploit features, like montage, that are putatively exclusive to the moving image. Rather Solomon basically communicates his philosophy to listeners in the conventional way by lecturing.

With these two criteria in hand, Livingston presents the proponent of movie-made philosophy with what he regards as the dilemma of paraphrase. It goes like this: Either the motion picture articulates a philosophical thesis that can be put into words—that can be paraphrased— or it doesn't. If it doesn't, then there is no call to suppose that it has propounded philosophy, either innovative or otherwise; the possibility of movie-made philosophy cannot be based upon something ineffable. On the other hand, if it can be put into words, Livingston maintains that this will run afoul of both the independence requirement and the demand for cinematic exclusivity. It will conflict with the cinematic exclusivity condition because, if it requires a paraphrase in order to be identified as a piece of philosophy, then this particular piece of philosophy has not been forged exclusively by cinematic means alone. It needs language to finish the job. Moreover, if the case in question requires, as it undoubtedly will, a paraphrase that must make reference to existing philosophical debates, then the candidate will not be altogether epistemically innovative. Thus, it will violate the independence requirement.

Murray Smith does not argue that there are things philosophy can do but movies can't. Both can, for instance, concoct thought experiments. However, the two practices fashion their thought experiments for different purposes. The philosopher hatches his in order to motivate a distinction or to pose a counterexample. The movie maker presents hers, first and foremost, for the sake of art. These differing purposes—that we might call, roughly and only provisionally, the *cognitive* and the *artistic*— shape the design of the thought experiments, issued from these different precincts. Ostensibly the philosophical thought experiment will aspire to clarity, whereas the artistic thought experiment will aim for ambiguity, insofar as ambiguity is a value of art. Moreover, this commitment to ambiguity will cashier the candidate movie from the order of philosophy, since however virtuous ambiguity is in the realm of art, it is a disqualifying factor when it comes to philosophy.

Bruce Russell explicitly identifies doing philosophy with explicit argumentation and explanation. Like Livingston, he would deny that a motion picture containing explicit argumentation and explanation would count as *movie-made* philosophy, since, he surmises, if a movie has a philosopher, or actor playing a philosopher, reciting an argument or an explanation outright, then it is not the movie making the philosophy, but the monologue. That is, language and not cinema gets the credit here.

I do not find the meta-philosophical assumptions upon which the preceding skeptical arguments rest to be ultimately decisive. Livingston's requirement that movie-made philosophy be created solely through cinematic means is not finally compelling. One problem here is isolating exclusively cinematic means. A feature of film, like montage, is shared with video, photography, and even the novel, as in the case of John Dos Passos. With respect to *Memento*, I will be arguing that it affords the reflective viewer insight into the processes of narrative comprehension through the way in which the film manipulates its narrative structure. Narrative structure, of course, is not exclusive to cinema. But I see no reason to deny that *Memento* makes a contribution to the thoughtful viewer's understanding of the way in which the structure of the movie narrative recruits her in the co-construction of the story.

Moreover, if I understand Livingston's worries about why paraphrasing the view of the movie compromises its status as independent philosophy, then I think that Livingston has set the bar for original philosophizing way too high.[3] He seems to think that if the paraphrase draws on pre-existing philosophical discussions, which it is indeed highly likely to do, then that shows that the movie is not truly independent. But I think that a standard this draconian would disallow most of what we are ordinarily ready to call philosophy. There aren't that many brand new positions. There are generally new arguments, new examples, and nuanced qualifications of already existing positions. Indeed, an absolutely independent philosophical thesis—one detached from pre-existing philosophical discourse—might just be too independent for any of us to grasp.[4]

Smith's argument on the basis of ambiguity is not conclusive because at best he is dealing with tendencies. Perhaps much philosophy, or, more accurately, most philosophy in a certain tradition, goes in for clarity. But sometimes a philosopher, especially one like Nietzsche, Kierkegaard, or Philip Kapleau, from a non-analytic tradition (or Wittgenstein from the analytic tradition), may have a motive for shrouding their thought experiments in ambiguity, while the thought experiments of some artists, such as George Orwell, serve his artistic purposes by being blazingly clear.

Bruce Russell maintains that philosophy requires explicit argumentation and/or explanation. If a thought experiment is presented, for example, its author has to accompany it with an explanation of how it works. I find it strange that Russell holds this position on thought experiments, since he agrees that motion pictures can provide counterexamples without auxiliary explanation, and, of course, many thought experiments are counterexamples.[5] Moreover, I am not convinced that movie-made thought experiments must always be attached to explicit explanations, because I'm not persuaded that the thought experiments union-certified philosophers bandy about always need to be explained. The context in which the example is offered may be enough to drive the point home, as may happen in the discussion period after the presentation of a philosophical lecture to informed listeners. The context may be so pregnant and the thought experiment so deft that everyone gets it on contact.

Since I am not swayed by any of the preceding skeptical considerations against the prospects of movie-made philosophy, I will outline, without embarrassment, what philosophy I believe can be found in *Memento*. However, even if these arguments had hit their target more accurately, I still believe that I could make the case for movie-made philosophy in *Memento*. For it seems that the preceding arguments against movie-made philosophy presuppose, either directly or indirectly, that the primary vehicle of philosophy must be language. But perhaps that presumption is up for grabs. Maybe audiences can be led to philosophical insights by having their experiences shaped and directed in certain ways.[6] They may come to a philosophical conclusion on the basis of their acquaintance with the phenomenon in question through their own experience, as that experience has been molded in order to facilitate the recognition of the processes upon which the experience rests.

Call this appeal to the audience's experience of an artwork for the purposes of casting reflection upon how the artwork works on the audience a matter of *phenomenological address*. It is my contention that *Memento* offers philosophical insight to reflective viewers by means of its phenomenological address to the audience. Moreover, since the structures of phenomenological address need not be strictly linguistic and may remain inexplicit, the movie-made philosophy that comes by way of phenomenological address is not threatened by the kinds of skeptical concerns rehearsed in this section.

Memento and the Art Cinema

Memento belongs to the popular cinema. It is an example of the well-entrenched genre of the film noir. Thus, it may seem strange to assert that it possesses a philosophical dimension. Motion pictures with philosophical pretensions, it might be thought, are native to the avant-garde and the "Art Cinema," not the mainstream, commercial cinema.[7]

However, it is a mistake to suppose that the popular cinema, the avant-garde cinema, and the Art Cinema are utterly insulated from each other. Since the days of the silent film, the avant-garde has poached popular forms for its own purposes. Sergei Eisenstein not only used circus techniques in his early masterpieces, but the style of editing that he perfected—along with Kuleshov, Pudovkin, and others—was rooted in the editing techniques of the American popular film, especially as those had been popularized by D.W. Griffith. And the found-footage films of cineastes such as Bruce Conner, Ken Jacobs, and Jim Hoberman often employ clips from popular movies.

Nor is the connection between popular film and the avant-garde a one-way street. Lewis Milestone re-appropriated Soviet montage in his *All Quiet on the Western Front* (1930), Walt Disney adapted Igor Stravinsky's *Rite of Spring* for *Fantasia* (1940), and Alfred Hitchcock hired Salvador Dali to do the dream scenes in *Spellbound* (1945). Moreover, further examples of these crossovers can be multiplied in both directions. For example, French New Wave directors, such as Jean-Luc Godard, enlisted American genre motifs for his modernist agenda in works from *Breathless* to *Alphaville*. Interestingly, for our purposes, many of these references to Hollywood movies were often allusions to American crime films, including films noirs. Perhaps emboldened by the example of Godard, some directors in the mainstream cinema began to help themselves to the techniques of the emerging Art Cinema of the sixties. In a number of cases, mainstream cinema began to be "Europeanized" in terms of the use of complex, nonlinear narrative structures and editing.

Richard Lester is an early example of this tendency, his experiments culminating with *Petulia* (1968). Other examples include Nicholas Roeg's *Don't Look Now* (1973) and *Bad Timing* (1980), John Boorman's *Point Blank* (1967), and some of the films of Arthur Penn and Mike Nichols. These movies, and others, imported some of the more venturesome narrative and editing experiments of the Art Cinema into popular genres, such as the crime movie (*Point Blank*) and the horror film (*Don't Look Now*). *Memento* is in the lineage of this tendency—that is, by now, a tradition—in popular cinema, a tradition that seeks to assimilate avant-garde developments into the mainstream.

However, in *Memento*, Christopher Nolan has not only dragooned the sort of experimental narrative structure more common to the Art Cinema and the avant-garde. He has also made one of the great projects of the avant-garde and the Art Cinema his own. The project, broadly speaking, is that of reflexive critique—the recurring modernist commitment to disclosing the conditions of possibility of the various art forms by reflecting upon exemplary instances thereof (for example, to reflect upon the conditions of painting by means of paintings, upon sculpture by means of sculpture, and so forth).[8] Moreover, the specific critique that *Memento* initiates involves an exploration of the way in which audiences follow and comprehend movie narratives and render said structures intelligible to themselves.

Memento pursues this theme by addressing audiences phenomeno-logically, that is, by problematizing their *experience* of the movie in ways that reveal something *essential* about following a movie narrative in general. *Memento* presents viewers with a work from a familiar genre, the film noir, but in an unfamiliar (or de-familiarized) way. This puts pressure on the audience to negotiate the film with a heightened consciousness of what they are doing. The audience, in other words, is encouraged, even nudged, toward adopting an apperceptive stance toward their own sense-making activities with respect to the narrative structure of *Memento*. And this, in turn, enables the thoughtful spectator to notice what is common between his or her experience of *Memento* and his or her less reflective encounters with the general run of movie narratives.[9]

In this regard, *Memento* recalls a classic film of the European Art Cinema, namely Alain Resnais's *Last Year at Marienbad* (1961).[10] In the course of that motion picture, the elusive, repetitive, inconclusive narrative structure constantly frustrates our desire to understand what is going on in the storyworld of the film. In this, it manages to make us aware of the degree to which our comprehension of narratives is organized around formulating tacit questions that we then expect the story to go on to answer. *Marienbad* provokes this insight by generating a plethora of questions—for example, did the couple meet the year before at Marienbad?—but then refrains from answering any of them. Likewise, in the tradition of Resnais's film, the narrative structure of *Memento* challenges spectators to make sense of it and, in the process, to observe introspectively the way in which they manage to accomplish this feat.

Memento and narrative comprehension

Memento is the story of Leonard Shelby, a one-time insurance investigator, who, in the course of a burglary of his home, is battered on the head by a thief with the result that Leonard is stricken by anterograde amnesia, a condition involving chronic memory loss. Leonard's memory can only hold onto things for ten to fifteen minutes. One of the most intriguing aspects of the film involves the ways in which Leonard attempts to make up for this deficit by tattooing vital information on his own body, writing notes and post-its to himself, and taking and annotating Polaroid photographs of the people and places that are important to his ongoing concerns.[11]

Foremost among those concerns is revenge. Leonard believes that during the burglary, his wife was murdered by a thief who escaped the scene of the crime and in whom the police are not interested, since they are not convinced this thief ever existed. It is even suggested that Leonard may have invented this thief in order to cover up his own skullduggery. Nevertheless, Leonard is certain of the thief's existence and is committed to tracking this man down and inflicting retribution. This quest is what gives meaning to Leonard's life. In this, he is aided by a former policeman, John "Teddy" Gammell, who, while assisting Leonard, also appears to use him for his own purposes involving drug-trafficking, as does the major female character in the story—a barmaid called Natalie.

Throughout the main story—the story of Leonard's revenge quest—there are flashbacks to Leonard's life with his wife, to the burglary, and to a parallel story of another case of anterograde amnesia—the story, told by Leonard, of one Sammy Jankis. This story sheds light on Leonard's condition and, it is suggested, may even be Leonard's own story projected upon the imaginary Sammy.

The action in Memento begins as the credits roll. We see a Polaroid photo of a blood-spattered wall. Gradually the Polaroid fades out of focus, alerting us to the fact that the scene is being shown in reverse, thus introducing the viewer to the signature stylistic variation in the movie—that the story is being told backwards. The opening scene of Memento is the last episode in the chain of events that comprise the particular segment of Leonard's life that is being recounted.

What we come to realize is that Leonard has just killed John "Teddy" Gammell (or "Teddy," for short). Ostensibly, Leonard has come to believe that Teddy is the person who killed his wife, although Teddy has just told Leonard that he, Leonard, killed the man who did that long ago. Indeed, Teddy has given Leonard a Polaroid showing an exultant, bloodied Leonard, which Teddy says was taken when Leonard nailed his wife's murderer.

But that does not deter Leonard from starting up the search again and again, this time concluding with the execution of Teddy. Does this happen because Leonard has simply forgotten that he has already exacted his retribution, or is it because Leonard realizes that it is only in virtue of an ongoing revenge quest that he has something to organize his life around and, in that way, to give it meaning?

Actually, by the end of the chain of events the story recounts, it seems to be a bit of both. It appears that Leonard, exploiting his own memory deficits and his memory prompts, is able to leave enough phony "clues" to himself to frame Teddy as his wife's murderer. That is, Leonard stage-manages his own situation in such a way that he is able to deceive himself, while simultaneously remaining unaware of what he's done. He sets Teddy up for the kill, thus removing the only person who, if he is telling the truth, can bring Leonard's quest to a halt. Yet with Teddy out of the way, Leonard is free to embark upon his mission of vengeance once more—killing one victim after another and then forgetting about it— thereby bringing unity and meaning to his existence.[12]

Memento was not the first story to be told backwards. Precedents include Harold Pinter's play *Betrayal* (1983), Martin Amis's novel *Time's Arrow* (1991), and an episode of *Seinfeld*. And subsequent to *Memento*, the French film, *Irreversible* (2002), another revenge quest, hit the screen. Although these works all employ backwards narration, each appears to do so for its own purposes. For example, *Betrayal* deploys the structure to underscore the reversal of fortune recounted in the play; the narration begins at the end of a love affair that it traces back to the beginning, where, ironically enough, the play itself ends happily. *Seinfeld* plays the structure for laughs, whereas *Irreversible* uses it to conjure up an aura of utter implacability.

In *Memento*, the backwards narration has more than one function. The one most commented upon is that it puts the viewer in a position some-what like Leonard's. Due to his condition, Leonard has no memory of what has immediately preceded the present moment on screen. Similarly, the audience does know what has just happened prior to the moment before us, since we haven't seen it yet. So we are being dropped into situations in *medias res*, which is, of course, the condition of Leonard's life.[13]

Of course, our experience is not exactly Leonard's plight, since at some point we are able to gain a semblance of a whole story, which will always lie beyond Leonard's ken. Nevertheless, the backwards narration is a very effective expressive device for communicating to viewers a taste of what Leonard is experiencing.

Again, our relation to the chain of events does not precisely mirror Leonard's insofar as he will never be able to reconstruct the big picture out of the puzzling fragments, whereas, since we are still in possession of our short-term memories and can convert them into long-term memories, we will be able, by the end of the film, to assemble a coherent story out of the pieces. And this is connected to a second function of the backwards narrative—what we might call its "meta-narrative function" in contrast to its function as an expressive means for conveying so effectively Leonard's bewilderment.

By telling the story backwards, Memento forces the audience to make sense of the narrative with heightened self-awareness.[14] The process of following the story becomes conscious and deliberate. We have to think overtly about what we are doing. We have to construct the story and, while we are putting it together, we need to stand back, figuratively speaking, to make sure we are tying up the loose ends. That is, we have to observe ourselves assembling the events of Leonard's life into a coherent story. And in the course of self-consciously configuring the narrative in this way, the reflective viewer ideally will arrive at certain discoveries *about* narration and narrative comprehension.

Of course, it is not the case that the spectator only constructs or co-constructs a movie narrative when the story is told backwards. The audience is always involved in constructing what happened in the storyworld from the movie narration, even when the story is told forwards.[15] But by narrating events backwards, the makers of Memento have made the execution of this process difficult, thereby forcing us to take a close look at it or, as the Russian Formalists liked to say, smashing the glass armor that surrounds the narrative structure in a way that requires that we take notice of it. The meta-narrative function of the backwards storytelling in Memento is, in other words, to afford the opportunity for the thoughtful spectator to gain certain insights regarding narrative— both in terms of its structure and its comprehension.

The most basic of those insights, of course, is that there is a distinction between the order in which events are told or shown in a narrative and the order in which those events follow each other in the storyworld. The difference between these two event orders is drawn by means of distinctions such as *story* versus *discourse*, or *histoire* versus *récit*, or *fabula* versus *syuzhet*, where the second term in each couplet refers to the event-order of the telling of the tale and the first refers to the order of events as they transpired in the pertinent world, whether fictional, merely possible, or the one we inhabit. Admittedly, this is a very basic idea, but it is one of those things that "everybody knows," yet which, at the same time, is fundamental, indeed, essential to the nature of narrative, however easily forgotten, and, therefore, always worthy of a vivid reminder.

The second insight that is likely to dawn on the thoughtful viewer has to do with the relationship between—to adopt one of the previous dichotomies—the story and the discourse. By means of the backwards narration in Memento, we realize by introspectively observing our experience and engagement with the film that we are involved in a constant process of constructing the story out of the discourse. This is part of what it is to follow any movie narrative. But with most movies this process flies, so to say, under the radar screen. That is, we are unaware with most movie narratives of our contribution to the narrative.

Memento not only makes us conscious of our participation in the co-construction of the narrative, however, it also alerts us to the way in which we follow the story by foregrounding—through its temporally reversed structure—the process by which we assemble a story out of the discourse. That is, the third insight that Memento affords the interested viewer is the opportunity to scrutinize the nature of the relationship between its story and its discourse—its storyworld and its telling—and Memento enables us to exploit that insight in order to reflect upon our commerce with more straightforwardly composed narratives.

But what exactly does this third insight come to? What precisely does the spectator do as she watches Memento progress—or, perhaps more aptly, regress? Primarily, I submit that we ask questions. The most obvious questions are: Who, and even more importantly, why was the man killed in the opening sequence? These are what we may call the movie's "presiding macro-questions." Moreover, a moment's reflection will reveal to the self-conscious viewer that most movies have presiding macro-questions and that we use them to unify our experiences of them. For example, we surmise that the movie is over when its presiding macro-question or questions have been answered; when the featured lovers kiss and make up, we realize that the film is on the brink of declaring "The End."

Yet it is not only presiding macro-questions that spectators use to organize their experience of following the story. Smaller questions—what we may call micro-questions—glue our attention to the screen in the expectation that they will be answered. In fact, we employ these questions to modulate our attention—that is, we stay on the lookout for answers to them.

For example, an early scene of Memento finds Leonard in the restroom of a restaurant. When he exits, the maître d' hands him an envelope and tells Leonard that he left it on the table. "Why was Leonard in the restaurant?" we ask ourselves. In a subsequent scene, Leonard enters the same restaurant, where he meets Natalie, who gives him the envelope containing compromising information about Teddy. Everything falls into place. Our question has been answered.

Other questions include: Why is Leonard in the bathroom holding a bottle of scotch, although he doesn't feel drunk? Why is Leonard running through the trailer park? Why is Leonard in Natalie's bed? Why is Natalie so nasty to Leonard upon first meeting him?

When we follow most movie narratives, the questions that we deploy to organize and direct our attention and to render ongoing events intelligible remain tacit. But the backwards narration of Memento forces them out into the open. We formulate them explicitly in our minds. We become aware that there is something we want to know and we process the film with an eye to finding it.

If with most movies, our attention is driven by questions about what happens next, Memento bids us to ask, "What happened earlier?" Moreover, since this is an unfamiliar way of having the story served up, it brings to the fore what is generally tacit: the fact that we are tracking the narrative with certain questions in mind.

There is no doubt that Memento is a challenging film to follow, more challenging, in fact, than Irreversible, another revenge quest that is told backwards. Perhaps the reason for this is that Memento is not only narrated in reverse, but also because Leonard may be being deceived—being given false information—by other characters such as Teddy, Natalie, and the hotel clerk, as well as himself. This, plus the manner in which the story is conveyed temporally, makes the movie difficult to cognize, and that provocation compels the viewer to reconstruct the story self-consciously, thereby, in the process, acquiring phenomenological access to one's response to the vast majority of movie narratives.[16]

Of course, it is no accident that our approach to most movie narratives involves question formation. For it is a long-known principle of plot engineering that this is one of the most effective ways of holding onto the audience's attention. With reference to playwriting, David Hume wrote, "Had you any intention to move a person extremely by the narration of an event, the best method of encreasing its effect would be artfully to delay informing him of it, and first to excite his curiosity and impatience before you let him into the secret" (Hume 1985: 221). What Hume here labels "the secret," I am now calling an answer to a question.

The vast number of movie narratives are erotetic—they motivate our continued interest, and structure and guide our attention by a network of questions and answers (Carroll 2008). Curiosity, as Hume argues, keeps us in our seats. Although it is uncertain how many people in Hollywood are familiar with Hume's essay, there is no question that the town understands Hume's method. For example, several screenwriting manuals recommend that plots be built upon the question/answer model. Dona Cooper advises "To create eagerness in the audience, the screenwriter intentionally plants questions in the viewers' minds— almost like leaving a trail of bread crumbs in the forest," while Michael Hauge writes, "When you open your screenplay, you want to create a question in the mind of your reader so that he will stick around (emotionally) to find out the answer" (both quoted in Keating 2008).[17]

Moreover, though Christopher Nolan may not have read Hume, Hauge, Cooper, or any other commentator on plot structure, he designed Memento with an awareness of the importance of the question/answer format. He says of the screenplay, " . . . I think that it's very important that we have answers to those questions. And that's how it's always been constructed. [The screenplay] is not deliberately contradictory. We were very deliberate in the plotting, and the answers to those questions" (quoted in Mottram 2002: 179).[18]

Thus, Memento, by means of a structure that in some ways is not typical of Hollywood plotting, not only affords the conscientious viewer insights into the nature of our experience of typical movie narratives; it also, by way of illuminating the structure of that experience, makes it possible for the spectator to grasp the way in which such plots are generally designed—in terms of questions and answers—to facilitate our under-standing of the story and to hold onto our interest in it. It is no accident that we call such stories "gripping."

The meta-narrative function of Memento involves enabling viewers to reflect upon the ways in which they both experience and process movie narratives, which, in turn, abets insight into the fundamental structure of typical movie narratives. By engendering awareness of the operation of the erotetic design of Memento, the audience is able to extrapolate what it has learned from Memento, and apply it, on the basis of their own experience, to the sorts of movies it is more accustomed to consume. In this way *Memento*, in virtue of its phenomenological address to its audience, fosters the discovery of essential features of a certain type of movie narration and, thereby, makes a contribution to the philosophy of the motion picture.

Concluding remarks

In this essay, I have argued that *Memento* makes a contribution to the philosophy of art, specifically to the philosophy of motion pictures. By means of phenomenological address, it encourages thoughtful audience members to reflect upon their experience of the film in such a way that they are suggestively led to certain philosophical insights about the nature of a typical species of movie narrative and the comprehension thereof. That is, by manipulating our cognition of it, *Memento* sends the audience in a certain direction of thinking where one may derive a novel idea or, at least, the recognition of standardly neglected, essential features of movie narration and comprehension. *Memento*, in other words, is the occasion for an *apprise de conscience*, one that has been carefully guided by the structure of the motion picture. Through *Memento* the reflective viewer can acquire philosophical insight because of the way in which Nolan has modified and defamiliarized the moviegoer's experience.

By locating the philosophical work that *Memento* gets done, I have attempted to evade skeptical objections to movie-made philosophy that are rooted in the prejudice that philosophy must in all cases be linguistic. In addition, I contend, one might draw philosophy from others maieutically by orchestrating their experience in such a way that they are led to certain philosophical insights, especially about the experiences in question and the conditions that give rise to them.

Nevertheless, I suspect the skeptics will not be placated by this maneuver. On the one hand, they are likely to charge that the philosophical insights I attribute to *Memento* are not original to that field. Some are at least as old as Hume. So the philosophical insights allegedly available from *Memento* do not meet the criterion of originality, discussed earlier, which is put forth by Livingston and Russell. On the other hand, it may be argued that *Memento* does not literally offer us philosophical insights. That is, the alleged insights are not, strictly speaking, provided *inside* the movie.

With respect to the latter objection, I agree that the insights I have catalogued are not in the motion picture itself. They emerge from the experience of the interested spectator as he or she reflects upon their experience of the movie. But I see no reason here to discount *Memento*'s philosophical stature. Leading folks to come to a philosophical conclusion seems to me to deserve the title of doing philosophy. Aren't we doing philosophy when by asking carefully chosen questions or making pregnant observations we point our students and non-philosopher friends in the direction of an insight that they work through on their own? Consider such luminaries as Socrates and Wittgenstein.

Surely, we can advance a philosophical thesis by asking a series of rhetorical questions. The answer is not literally contained in the rhetorical question, but the rhetorical question may function as a philosophical argument nonetheless, even if it needs to be completed in the minds of our interlocutors.

Likewise, simply posing situations in a pointed manner may provoke philosophy from listeners or viewers. And that is exactly what I contend *Memento* does. Against the argument that the philosophy in *Memento* isn't original enough, it is important, as I mentioned earlier, not to go overboard on the requirement that the philosophical thesis in question be absolutely original, since most of what we regard as philosophy usually involves incremental variations that sit on a continuum with past philosophical inquiry. Certainly, it counts as doing philosophy if one is able to come up with a new way of framing an old question and/or substantiating one's answer to it. And, in this way, it seems that *Memento* merits being classified as a contribution to philosophy.

Of course, the skeptic may reply that the so-called "insights" that I've culled from *Memento* are too banal to deserve being labeled "philosophy." The problem here is not that these supposed insights fall short of absolute originality. Rather, they are such hackneyed commonplaces that they lack any claim to originality whatsoever. For instance, consider the claim that the viewer learns that she is involved in co-constructing the work. How trivial can you get? What narratologist doesn't know that?

I think that this objection overlooks the venue for which movie-made philosophy is intended. It is not primarily made for working philosophers. There aren't enough of us to support the production costs of even a modest motion picture, let alone to guarantee profits. Movie-made philosophizing, like the movies that house it, is directed at the mass of non-professionals. It reminds them of things that they might have forgotten or neglected or it leads them to insights that are novel for them. That movie plots are driven by a network of questions and answers may be old news to the philosopher of narrative, but it may crystallize a new and exciting idea in the mind of the plain movie-goer. That is, relative to its theater of operations, the insights delivered by Memento are original enough to its audience, rather than banal.

Furthermore, returning to our earlier observation, Memento would appear to have a legitimate claim to finding a new way to draw the pertinent philosophical insights out of thoughtful viewers, even if those insights are not totally new philosophically. For, once again, it is not the case that doing philosophy is something that only transpires between academics in accordance with the protocols of their journals. We also philosophize with our students and our friends, and we are engaged in philosophy if we are able to produce a compelling new example that will draw a new idea from them by prompting and guiding their reflection on the case at hand. And in this way, too, Memento is worthy of being regarded as a contribution to philosophy.[19]

Notes

1 For an excellent survey of the philosophical themes in Memento, see Kania (2008).

2 These skeptical arguments on the philosophical limitations on cinema have been addressed critically by Aaron Smuts (2008) and by Thomas Wartenberg (2008). I have profited immensely from their remarks on this issue.

3 Livingston emphasizes the kind of originality he does because he presupposes that if a movie can be said to do philosophy, the philosophy must be articulated by the movie maker. This overlooks the possibility that the philosophical insight may be located in the viewer's uptake of the motion picture, albeit under the guidance of the cineaste. This insight, in turn, may be original to the target audience, even if it is not something altogether novel in the established universe of philosophical discourse. Later I will be arguing that Christopher Nolan manages to impart philosophy through Memento by enabling reflective spectators to acquire theoretical insight as a result of the way in which he, Nolan, has structured his film.

4 Points in this paragraph have been made by Wartenberg (2008) and Smuts (2008).

5 This observation has also been made by Wartenberg (2008).

6 Furthermore, this seems highly likely since people are able to derive philosophical insight through experiences that haven't been designed to bring

these about. Think of all the philosophy that has sprung from the phenomena of visual illusions.

7   For an account of the Art Cinema, see David Bordwell (1985, 2008).

8   My point here is not that self-critique is the exclusive property of the Art Cinema and the avant-garde, but rather that Nolan belongs to a tradition within the mainstream cinema that also dabbles in reflexivity. Evidence that Nolan is trafficking in reflexivity can be found in the analogy he draws between Leonard and motion picture directors (Mottram 2002: 173).

9   *Memento* not only comments on movie narration in general, but also specifically on the genre of film noir. Films noirs are, of course, often about memory, a theme that *Memento* reworks in a most unexpected way. Often film noir uses memory in order to articulate themes of fatalism and/or guilt. In *Memento*, the theme of guilt emerges when the possibility of Leonard's guilt—on more counts than one—is raised.

10 The reflexive interrogation of the motion picture experience and/or the essence of the motion picture were often the explicit topics of the avant-garde cinema movements of the sixties and seventies, especially in the United States and Great Britain. In this regard, there is an interesting correspondence between *Memento* and *Zorn's Lemma* (1970) by Hollis Frampton. Both films can be thought of as confronting the audience with memory tests for the purpose of indicating the indispensable operation of memory for processing motion pictures.

11 Perhaps the title *Memento* can be interpreted as referring to these memento.

12 It may be thought that without Teddy, Leonard will be unable to function— that killing Teddy, in other words, will undermine his "quest." On the one hand, whether in fact this would be so in the world of the fiction is irrelevant to what Leonard appears to believe and act upon. But, on the other hand, Leonard may very well be able to get along without Teddy. After all, he is able to dispatch Teddy pretty effectively. And he has his dossier. Moreover, there may be more handlers where Teddy came from—for instance, maybe Natalie.

13 Another parallel between Leonard's condition and that of the audience member is that many of the sequences in the main line of the story (that is, the story excluding the embedded flashbacks) approximate the length of Leonard's ability to remember. Like Leonard, we are plunged into a present time slice of a certain unnaturally delimited duration with no memory of what preceded it.

14 Responding to *Memento* is not like responding to something like a crossword puzzle, where responding to a crossword puzzle does not typically force us to self-consciously reflect upon the way in which we solve the pertinent problem. For *Memento* is of a different order of difficulty. Usually a crossword puzzle tells you the question that you need to answer. With *Memento*, you need to figure out and formulate the questions relevant to tracking the story as well as the answers. The viewer has to review her hypotheses and her

strategies for picking out and putting together clues. Our false starts and revisions brings the process of our making sense out of the movie to the forefront of our consciousness. Sometimes something like this may occur with a crossword puzzle as when we realize that we're dealing with a trick clue. But *Memento* is tricked out thus through and through.

15 See Bordwell (1985: 48–62, 156–204).

16 It might be argued that *Memento* is so uncharacteristically difficult that it cannot reveal much about our ordinary experience of processing narrative movies. But, on the one hand, *Memento* is not *that* difficult to follow. Surely it's no *Finnegans Wake*. And, on the other hand, what we observe ourselves doing in response to *Memento*—framing questions, tracking answers—can be readily observed in response to more mundanely structured movies. Just stop a motion picture at what screenwriters call "the turning point" and the audience's tacit questions will well up and be voiced loudly.

17 Keating (2008) also quotes Dona Cooper advising: "You guide and focus your viewers' attention by the way you give and withhold information. Viewers can then experience a sense of satisfaction when they finally get the *answer* for which they've been searching" (emphasis added).

18 Actually, there may be some evidence that Nolan is familiar with the textbook theories of movie narration and that he intends to draw our attention to the principles behind them. As Mottram points out, *Memento* has the conventional Hollywood, three-act structure with what is called "the twist" occurring precisely where it should—namely, as the second act turns into the third (Mottram 2002: 173). There is also evidence from the rest of Nolan's oeuvre. The very title of Nolan's first feature, *Following* (1998), surely refers not only to the characters' voyeuristic pursuits, but also the viewer's attempt to reconstruct the fragmented story. *The Prestige* (2006) begins with Christian Bale's character inquiring slyly, "Are you watching closely?".

19 I would like to express my gratitude to Andrew Kania and the anonymous reviewer of this essay. They certainly helped sharpen my thinking, although responsibility for the remaining flaws herein is mine.

References

Bordwell, D. (1985) *Narration in the Fiction Film*, Madison, WI: University of Wisconsin Press.

——— (2008) *The Poetics of Cinema*, London: Routledge.

Carroll, N. (2008) "Narrative Closure," in P. Livingston and C. Plantinga (eds) *The Routledge Companion to Philosophy and Film*, London: Routledge, pp. 207–16.

Hume, D. (1985) "Of Tragedy," in *Collected Essays*, E.F. Miller (ed.), Indianapolis, IN: Liberty Classics, pp. 216–25.

Kania, A. (2008) "Memento," in P. Livingston and C. Plantinga (eds) *The Routledge Companion to Philosophy and Film*, London: Routledge, pp. 650–60.

Keating, P. (2008) "Plot Points, Macro-questions and Emotional Curves: Three Ways to Think about Screenplay Structure," presented at the annual conference of the Society for the Cognitive Study of the Moving Image, Madison, WI.

Livingston, P. (2006) "Theses on Cinema as Philosophy," *Journal of Aesthetics and Art Criticism* 64: 11–18.

Mottram, J. (2002) *The Making of* Memento, London: Faber and Faber.

Russell, B. (2005) "The Philosophical Limits of Film," in N. Carroll and J. Choi (eds) *Philosophy of Film and Motion Pictures: An Anthology*, Oxford: Blackwell.

—— (2008a) "Film's Limits: The Sequel," *Film and Philosophy* 12: 1–16.

—— (2008b) "Replies to Carroll and Wartenberg," *Film and Philosophy* 12: 35–40.

Smith, M. (2006) "Film Art, Argument, and Ambiguity," *Journal of Aesthetics and Art Criticism* 64: 33–42.

Smuts, A. (2008) "Film as Philosophy: The Bold Thesis," presented at the Eastern Division Meeting of the American Society for Aesthetics, Philadelphia, PA.

Wartenberg, T. (2008) "On the Possibility of Cinematic Philosophy," presented at the annual conference of the Society for the Cognitive Study of the Moving Image, Madison, WI.

Further reading

Livingston, P. (2005) "Narrative," in B. Gaut and D.M. Lopes (eds) *The Routledge Companion to Aesthetics*, 2nd edn, London: Routledge, pp. 359–69. (An accessible introduction to some central issues in narrative theory.)

Wartenberg, T. (2007) *Thinking on Screen: Film as Philosophy*, London: Routledge. (A defense of the idea that film can "do philosophy," including several case studies.)

Chapter 7

Deborah Knight and George McKnight

RECONFIGURING THE PAST: MEMENTO AND NEO-NOIR

"Now . . . where was I?"
—Leonard's final voice-over remark (A, 1:50:16)

MEMENTO IS A NEO-NOIR psychological thriller ostensibly centered around the investigation of a crime and the search for justice and revenge. Noir and neo-noir narratives are typically located in dystopic urban settings. Central protagonists are of uncertain moral virtue. The fictional worlds in which they operate are morally ambiguous at best, and characters are typically left to their own devices to sort out questions such as who can be trusted and what is true. Noir and neo-noir operate in the ironic mode, emphasizing discrepancies between what the audience and the film's central protagonists initially think is true, and what we later either learn or suspect to be the facts of the matter. These neo-noir features are at work in Memento, all of them complicated by the curious condition that prevents the film's protagonist, Leonard, from being able to create and sustain new memories.

The plot of Memento—with part of the story told backwards and the other forwards in fictional time—presents viewers with the challenge of trying to discover just how the two parts of the story connect with and inform each other.[1] Aristotle famously recommended that tragic narratives be told so that they develop over a comparatively short period of time to emphasize the causal nature of plot action (Telford 1961). A tragedy was also to have a clear beginning, middle, and end. In an anti-Aristotelian gesture, Jean-Luc Godard[2] created narratives that have a beginning, middle, and end, but not necessarily in that order. Memento fuses these two seemingly incompatible visions of narrative storytelling. As the film unfolds, moving back and forth between the forward-moving and backward-moving temporal arcs of the plot, we discover that Memento does have a beginning, middle, and end in fictional time, but they are not presented in that order. By the time viewers have managed to comprehend the relationship between the two temporal arcs of the film, we discover something almost Aristotelian in the tight causal structuring of narrative events. Unlike in Godard's films, where plot elements can appear quite arbitrary, the forward/backward structure of Memento's plot is not arbitrary. Indeed, the back and forth structure plays an important role in determining the causality of the film's storyline.

At the center of the narrative is Leonard, whose brain injury forces him to deal with unfolding events within a memory window of mere minutes. As he tells Burt at the Discount Inn, if he remains in a conversation for very long, he'll forget how it started (U, 0:08:34). Leonard's injury makes it impossible for him to form new memories. Nevertheless, he believes he has developed a system to help him keep track of his plans and actions. Key features of this system include a series of Polaroid photographs labeled with notes to himself, a number of tattoos recording information (e.g., the various "facts") as well as some directions to himself (e.g., "remember Sammy Jankis"), the police report concerning the assault on him and his wife (some of which has been scratched out), and a chart that, in conjunction with the Polaroids and tattoos, helps to orient Leonard as he conducts his business and goes about the task of trying to find his wife's killer. Given that this is a neo-noir film in the ironic mode, with a plot structure that challenges viewers to try to figure out for themselves what has happened, who is telling the truth, and who is responsible for the actions that occur, it should ultimately not surprise us that Leonard turns out to be quite unreliable as a narrator and as an agent.

In this chapter, we will first establish the stylistic and generic background of Memento by placing it in the context of film noir and neo-noir. We will then consider the way the film presents the noir themes of mystery and detection, and continue by considering the role of the femme fatale in relation to Leonard as putative detective and protagonist. The objective of our analysis is twofold. First, we will show how the significant philosophical questions raised by *Memento* arise necessarily through the general aesthetic features and narrative structure of the film. Second, we will argue that these features and structure ultimately position the viewer as the one who must determine what can be believed, who is responsible for which actions, and how praise and blame are to be allocated. Finally, we will suggest that any attempt to make these decisions is complicated by the very aesthetic features and narrative structure that make the film what it is. The film's narrative structure, once it is sorted out, reveals a startlingly tight causal chain of action. But given Leonard's condition, the ambiguity of the information about Leonard's past, and the self-interest of other central characters (notably Teddy and Natalie), it is not immediately clear how to go about making appropriate moral judgments, especially about Leonard.

Noir and neo-noir

The films produced in Hollywood between the early 1940s and the mid 1950s that fall under the category of film noir raise questions about basic issues of classification because they cut across a range of generic categories. We agree with Steve Neale that, "As a single phenomenon, noir . . . never existed. That is why no one has been able to define it, and why the contours of the larger noir canon in particular are so imprecise" (2000: 173–4). Yet the notion of film noir persists. It involves a range of designations such as: a cycle or even cycles of films within the crime film and within detective films generally; a diverse range of films that share a world view characterized by a dark mood or tone and by certain recurring features of theme and style; or a period in film history.

Neo-noir is an even more elusive concept than noir itself. Neo-noir refers to films ranging from those that employ familiar thematics, styles, period settings, story lines or figures generally identified with noir—such as the figure of the hard-boiled detective in *Chinatown* (1973)—through to films that combine these features with the use of self-conscious allusions and postmodern referentiality—such as we see in *L.A. Confidential* (1997) and *The Black Dahlia* (2006). What tends to distinguish neo-noir films, however, is the self-consciousness of the ironic perspective inherited from noir, a self-consciousness that is evident in the employment of conventionalized noir features, including:

> the use of voice-over and flashback, the use of high contrast lighting and other "expressionist" devices, the focus on mentally, emotionally, and physically vulnerable characters, the interest in psychology, the culture of distrust marking relations between male and female characters, and the downbeat emphasis on violence, anxiety, death, crime and compromised morality.
>
> (Neale 2000: 174).

Interestingly, the only item on Neale's list that is not an important feature of Memento is the high-contrast lighting originally derived from German expressionist filmmaking. Memento is unusual as a film noir because it takes place primarily in broad daylight. Leonard's voice-over narration frequently directs viewers as to how they should understand depicted events. While Memento does not use flashbacks in anything like a conventional sense, something very like flashback is part of its governing structure. Real-time events are depicted in reverse chronological order within the film's narrative, and within both "present" and "past" sequences there are episodes presented as flashbacks or recollections (for instance, the entire saga of Sammy Jankis). Leonard is both a mentally and emotionally vulnerable character, given his faulty memory and guilt about his wife's death. Except for the marital relationship between Leonard and his wife, distrust is what should conventionally mark Leonard's subsequent relationships with women, especially Natalie who initially appears sympathetic and supportive.

Knowing of Leonard's condition, characters exploit him to their own ends, whether in a seemingly benign way, for instance, when Burt rents him two rooms at the Discount Inn because "business is slow" and Leonard will never remember, or when, with greater calculation, Natalie sets him up to defend her from Dodd, who has been threatening her. But in a variation on the convention, Leonard does trust Natalie, largely because, given his condition, he is unable to understand enough about how she manipulates him to learn to distrust her. We eventually discover that one of Leonard's worst errors is to disregard the note on the back of his Polaroid snapshot of Natalie reminding himself not to trust her. Neale's last point, concerning "the downbeat emphasis on violence, anxiety, death, crime and compromised morality," nicely captures the tone of the film.

Vivian Sobchack's attempt to theorize film noir can be seen as a supplement to Neale's. Her approach is "to locate and ground that heterogeneous and ambiguous cinematic grouping called film noir in its contemporaneous social context" (Sobchack 1998: 129) by identifying recurring locations and spaces such as "night clubs, cocktail lounges, bars, anonymous hotel or motel rooms, boardinghouses, cheap roadhouses and diners" (Sobchack 1998: 148). Motifs such as the diner or the motel room, she argues, "emerge as threats to the traditional function, continuity, contiguity, and security of domestic space and time" (Sobchack 1998: 156–7). As Sobchack's analysis of film noir would lead us to expect, Memento features, broadly speaking, two quite different types of locations. Each type is developed around similar, although not wholly identical, spaces that serve as polarities in the narrative and establish distinct sets of values. On the one hand, we have public locations and spaces that suggest anonymity and where any form of occupancy is transient, and on the other hand we have private spaces, such as the home with its suggestions of intimate and ongoing personal relationships. The three locations inside homes include two we see through Leonard's recollections (his home with his wife Catherine and the home of Sammy Jankis and his wife) and one (Natalie's house) that we see in the film's present time. Significantly, both of the homes we see through Leonard's recollections feature brief scenes suggesting emotional intimacy, although the security of these domestic spaces is shattered by sexual assault, murder, and accidental death. While the home setting in the film's ongoing present time suggests sexual intimacy when we find that Leonard has spent the night in bed with Natalie, any possibility of emotional intimacy is quickly dispelled when we discover Natalie's manipulation of Leonard.

The majority of the narrative action in the present occurs in public and largely anonymous spaces: in motels, diners, a bar, a trailer park with its rows of mobile homes, a derelict building, two different locations in an abandoned industrial site, a tattoo parlor, and on the streets and highways of the city where the film's action takes place. Leonard comments twice, in voice-over, on the anonymity of the rooms in which he awakens, correctly concluding both times that he is in a motel. Thematically speaking, the point is that the fictional world of Memento is one of dislocation and transience. The two motel rooms that Leonard rents at the Discount Inn are interchangeable with each other and with the motel room he breaks into in order to attack Dodd. These locations are not accidental to the narrative. They serve as a trope for Leonard's psychological and moral state, his dislocated and impersonal relationship to the world as a result of his condition, and his estrangement from conventional social relations.

Memento takes advantage of the stylistic and generic features of noir and neo-noir and defines itself through the uniqueness and originality of its reconfiguration of typical noir elements as well as its non-Aristotelian plot structure. It reworks the plot of the mystery, the figure of the detective, the use of voice-over narration, the figure of the femme fatale, the use of locations and settings, and the thematics of revenge and trust. Additionally, the film deals originally and forcefully with the idea that actions in the past govern actions in the present, particularly in relation to the noir thematic of the detective figure setting out to ensure some form of justice. The film's governing trope—reversal—is also perfectly suited to neo-noir, where things typically turn out not to be the way they initially seem. Examples of reversal range from the literal to the metaphorical and include the tattoo Leonard has had put on his chest backwards so he can always read it in the mirror, the reversal of the conventional chronological narrative construction of the film's plot, and ultimately the reversal in our understanding of the film's central characters. For example, with his inability to form new memories, Leonard is unreliable both as a character and as a narrator, although it takes the viewer some time to discover this. Initially, viewers are cautiously inclined to believe Leonard, to trust Natalie when she provides him with the information he seeks concerning John G, and to distrust Teddy. During the course of the film we realize that neither Leonard nor Natalie is trustworthy (Leonard because of his faulty memory and Natalie because she is exploiting Leonard's condition), and that, presumably, Teddy is the one who actually knows what has been going on and why. Given that we are initially aligned with Leonard and understand much about the narrative action because of what he does and what his voice-over narration tells us, it comes as a surprise to viewers that Teddy, a creepy and obnoxious character who seems to be stalking Leonard, turns out to be potentially the only character who can shed light on what has really occurred in Leonard's past. The fact that Teddy is not a morally upstanding character—he is, after all, setting up a drug deal with Jimmy Grantz in order to steal Grantz's money—does not mean we should automatically conclude that he is lying when he explains Leonard's past to him.

The film's most important use of reversal concerns the convention of narrative closure. Typically, detective fictions conclude by resolving the crime and presenting an explanatory account of the mysteries that have been the focus of investigation. Again, typically, detective fictions allow us to understand a sequence of past actions so that we know how to distribute blame and praise. By contrast, the plot of Memento ends leaving viewers with a horrible sense of omniscience. Typical detective narratives begin in medias res, in the middle of things, and in fact Memento seems to as well. Uncharacteristically, the conclusion of Memento's plot is in medias res with respect to the film's story. Moreover, after figuring out the actual chronology of the depicted events, you realize that what you initially thought, watching the first scenes of the film, is a situation you come into in medias res is in fact the conclusion of a chronological sequence— even though you can't understand it as such until the end of the film. Because of its unique narrative structure, the film's conclusion, with Leonard about to go into a tattoo parlor, leaves us in the middle of the chronological action of the story. From this vantage point, we realize that we have most likely been wrong to trust Leonard's account of events, while simultaneously we know how the events of the story unfold up to Teddy's death—that is of course the apparent mystery with which the film begins. Unexpectedly, when the two arcs of the narrative meet— the forward-directed "past" narrative and the backward-directed "present" narrative—everything we thought we could rely on has changed, while at the same time we now know what will happen. In a startling reversal of standard detective narratives where, by the film's conclusion, we know what happened in the past, at the conclusion of Memento, we know what will happen in the future, and why.

Memento, detection, and mystery

Initially, and despite his condition, Leonard appears to function as the detective figure in Memento. One does not need to be a licensed detective to undertake the detective's role. Given that he used to be an insurance investigator, the transition seems, to him at least, to be seamless. Leonard believes that he is in pursuit of his wife's rapist and murderer. In Leonard we have a cognitively and emotionally challenged—indeed, impaired—central detective figure. By his own testimony, his memory is intact until the night of his wife's assault and murder, during which he suffers the injury that leads to his inability to form what he, mistakenly, calls "short-term" memories. His goal, explicitly, is revenge. The irony is that, given his condition, even if he is successful, he will very quickly forget that he has avenged his wife. It might initially sound persuasive that, even if Leonard will not remember it, his wife deserves to be avenged. But as the narrative unfolds, this claim will become increasingly dubious. Teddy, after all, explains that Leonard has already killed the John G he believed was responsible for what happened to his wife, and in fact Teddy appears to have a Polaroid to prove it.

Despite Leonard's cognitive impairment, the audience is aligned with him as both the *de facto* detective trying to discover the identity of his wife's killer, and as himself a figure at least metaphorically on the run from events in his past and the guilt associated with having been unable to prevent his wife's death. But as the film proceeds, discrepancies slowly emerge between past actions and Leonard's present construal of them. So while the viewer's alignment with Leonard remains unaltered, what might initially have been something like allegiance to him is tempered.[3] If Teddy is telling the truth that Leonard's wife actually survived the assault and that it is Leonard who killed her with an overdose of insulin, viewers have clear reasons to reassess their response to Leonard and his quest for revenge. Initially, we believe Leonard when he claims to accurately remember everything up until the night of his wife's rape and murder. But there is reason to suspect that Leonard has confabulated her murder and attributed it to someone who, while guilty of rape, did not kill her. While initially Leonard serves as our surrogate, during the unfolding of narrative events viewers must begin to piece together and test evidence to determine what actually occurred and who is telling the truth, and this is especially important with respect to both Leonard and Teddy. While the reassessment of what we know and what we thought we knew may occur in a variety of genres, it is especially characteristic of noir-influenced mysteries, particularly when they feature a figure involved in some form of detection. Reassessment invariably results in a reconfiguration of narrative events as well as a moral reassessment of characters and their actions.

Films that feature a detective, or a surrogate detective such as Leonard, invite explanatory accounts of the mystery, the motives of the characters, and the construction of the narrative and its fictional world.[4] Conventionally, the mystery plot has a structure that begins with some initial object of investigation that will lead to the central crime or crimes, and the investigation finally culminates in some form of confrontation, during which the criminal is revealed. At that time, the detective figure provides an explanatory account of the crime and the various circumstances that have remained unclear until that point. The beginning of *Memento* raises various possibilities that indicate there may be some difficulty determining just what the initial mystery is. Possibilities would include: Who is being shot, by whom, and why? Shortly afterwards we discover the mystery surrounding Leonard's inability to retain new experiences in memory. These questions might appear to culminate in the mystery surrounding what we initially assume is the central crime, namely the death of Leonard's wife, and the identity of John G, the man Leonard holds responsible for her murder. In the final confrontation— which we might call the "test scenario" that takes place between the detective figure and the criminal or possible suspects—the detective is conventionally in control, or at least pretends to be, and hopes to reveal the guilty party and obtain a confession. As the primary investigator, however, Leonard is in no position to conduct any test, let alone provide a final explanatory account. How can he possibly test, since he forgets things?

A confrontation does occur near the end of the film, although considerably earlier in the chronological sequence of story events. It is between Teddy and Leonard (scene A). Unconventionally, the detective's explanatory account is provided by Teddy, who appears to have been somehow or other assigned to investigate the assault on Leonard's wife. Teddy explains that he has already helped Leonard locate and kill John G. So Leonard has already revenged his wife's death. Teddy also explains that Sammy Jankis had no wife, that Leonard's wife survived the assault, and that it was Leonard's wife, not Sammy's, who was diabetic. During this account there is a shot of Leonard injecting his wife, Catherine, with insulin just as Leonard has previously described Sammy injecting his wife, leading us to at least consider that it is Leonard, not the rapist, who killed his wife, and that he has no memory of doing so. What is of particular interest here is that although it is Teddy who tells the story, the shot of

Leonard injecting his wife with insulin is framed by shots of Leonard's face, suggesting that these are brief snippets of memory. Earlier in the film, we see recollected shots of Leonard and Catherine in the same position on a bed, but in these there is no hint of a syringe (K, 0:55:00). One interpretation is that, left to himself, Leonard has blocked out the fact that he injected Catherine after receiving his head injury, and by extension that Teddy's story has led to a fleeting recollection of Leonard's role in his wife's death. Leonard decides not to believe Teddy's account after reading the note on the back of Teddy's photo, "Don't believe his lies," and so he continues to search for John G, whom he has now set himself to believe to be Teddy. Teddy's explanation will not prevent Leonard from killing him, since of course he has no recollection of the events Teddy describes. Unconventionally, what will turn out to be the conclusion of the film's action in chronological time occurs at the beginning of Memento when Leonard shoots and kills Teddy.

Memento, neo-noir, and the femme fatale

A pivotal figure in film noir and neo-noir is the central female, often described as the femme fatale. That the central male figure becomes romantically involved with her has become a conventionalized feature of many of these films. She is central to how the romantic plot line and the action plot line are interwoven in the narrative, and her fate is typically one of the problems the central male character must deal with at narrative closure. She is often an enigmatic character because of the uncertainty of her true feelings or even, at times, her true identity. While her physical beauty and allure may be one feature of this character, her relationship to the male protagonist raises questions of trust and betrayal, frequent themes in noir and neo-noir. In film noir, the central male figure risks being deceived, manipulated, framed, and possibly even killed by her.

Like most noir femmes fatales, Natalie initially appears to be sympathetic and innocent. We first see her in a diner where she provides Leonard with a photocopy of John Edward Gammell's (that is, Teddy's) driver's license and car registration (scene S). It turns out that Leonard already has the plate number of Teddy's car tattooed on his thigh as Fact 6.[5] Natalie encourages Leonard to remember his wife, saying, "don't just recite the words. Close your eyes, and remember her" (S, 0:19:40).

Leonard's fragments of memory suggest a sensitivity and an intimacy between himself and his wife, which enables us to develop an initial rapport with him, even though we have already watched him kill. Natalie then compares herself with Leonard, telling him they are both survivors. From that point onwards in the narrative, however, deception and what appears to be sexual intimacy are revealed as the means by which she has secured his trust and help.

Because Leonard is unable to form new memories, he is incapable of sustaining the question of trust as an ongoing, conscious concern, except when he can record what has happened either as tattoos or as notes scribbled on his various Polaroids. Natalie exploits this when she removes anything Leonard can write with and then, knowing he will not remember either her words or actions, angers him with accusations about his wife's sexual behavior. Finally, he strikes her. She leaves, returning minutes later to claim that she has been beaten up by Dodd. Leonard is deceived by her story and sets out to get rid of Dodd, although he has forgotten why he is in Dodd's motel bathroom by the time Dodd returns. Leonard ignores Teddy's warning: "When she offers to help it'll be for her own reasons. . . . Do not trust her" (H, 1:07:02). Instead, Leonard trusts the note to himself on the back of Teddy's photograph, "Do not believe his lies."

The ambiguity developed around the figure of Natalie concerns whether she deliberately uses Leonard to avenge the death of her boyfriend, the drug dealer Jimmy Grantz. While she is quite aware Leonard is wearing Grantz's suit and driving his car when he drives up to the diner, it is never wholly clear whether she realizes that Teddy, who has been setting up a drug deal with Grantz, is John Gammell. It is at least possible that she has figured out that the Teddy she has heard about is John Gammell. Her motives for volunteering to get the background information about the car registration are unclear. Perhaps she simply wants to help Leonard, but perhaps she is advancing a scheme of her own. What we can be sure of is that what Natalie tells Leonard convinces him that Teddy is the John G he has been looking for. Natalie deceives Leonard about Dodd beating her and provides Leonard with the information that identifies John G's license plate; in both instances, Leonard acts as a direct consequence of her actions.

If our narrative understanding of the action is initially organized around Leonard's desire to seek revenge for the death of his wife, it could be reconfigured to think of the action as actually being driven by Natalie's desire to seek revenge. If so, we have another instance of reversal within *Memento*. It remains unclear whether Leonard has unknowingly become caught up in a scheme to revenge the death of Jimmy Grantz, just as he has been party to Natalie's earlier scheme concerning Dodd, Teddy's scheme to steal money from Grantz, and the schemes of others. If so, he unknowingly becomes party to his own victimization. We have been aware of incidents that cue us to Leonard's victimization, such as Burt's deception and Natalie serving him a glass of beer mixed with spit, but these had an almost comic element to them because at those moments the viewer had no reason to mistrust Leonard or necessarily question his justification for shooting Teddy. But if Natalie has a scheme to avenge Jimmy Grantz's death, Leonard is unaware of it, just as he was unaware of Teddy's scheme to steal money from Jimmy. The viewer is aware of Teddy's scheme, Natalie's lies, and her manipulation of Leonard. The viewer also realizes that Leonard is largely oblivious to these things.

One of the features of any mystery, particularly a noir-influenced mystery, is that the detective must determine which chain of events or line of action he or she is part of, and thus who can be trusted. Leonard is incapable of arriving reliably at such a determination. In the scene where he is running through a trailer park with a gun, he initially concludes that he must be chasing Dodd, only to realize that Dodd is actually chasing him. Leonard's comprehension of events comes into question at many points in the film, especially with regard to his dealings with Natalie. If Leonard should not trust Natalie but does anyway, then the viewer should no longer trust Leonard. Towards *Memento*'s narrative closure, the viewer's reassessment of characters and actions will become increasingly focused around Leonard's actions and the killing of Teddy. Unconventionally, however, once Natalie has provided Leonard with information about John Gammell, she is no longer part of the action and, in fact, in another reversal of a noir narrative featuring a central female figure, narrative closure does not resolve her fate. If providing Leonard with information that resulted in Teddy's death was part of her desire for revenge, then she has used Leonard successfully, let alone ironically, to get her revenge. More important, however, is that the figure of Natalie serves a central narrative function: to raise questions for the viewer about Leonard's comprehension of ongoing events and his own actions.

Neo-noir, detection, and narrative comprehension

While watching *Memento*, it becomes increasingly evident that it is the viewer who must finally serve as the detective. If there is a single, plausible narrative account of the characters and their actions, it falls to the viewer to try to sort out what it is and thus to resolve whatever mysteries remain. Central to the explanatory account we offer here of the central mysteries of the film is a single shot that occurs so briefly it might be missed. It occurs during Leonard's recollection of Sammy Jankis' time in what appears to be a medical or psychiatric institution (21, 1:29:56; see Figure 7). Sammy sits in a chair in the foreground of the shot with other patients and staff in the background. A figure passes behind Sammy, after which there is a cut to a shot of Leonard in the film's present time, clearly indicating this is Leonard's reconstruction of a past event. Next, there is an identical shot of Sammy in the chair with an unidentified figure passing in front of him. Just as that figure passes Sammy, concealing his face and body, there is a very brief shot of Leonard in the chair Sammy occupied, followed by another shot of Sammy in the chair. Blink and you will miss the shot of Leonard as an institutionalized patient. The shot raises the question whether anything Leonard says about the past is true.

The connection between Sammy Jankis and Leonard is so important to him that Leonard wears a tattoo that reads, "remember Sammy Jankis." This is, in effect, an order to himself. But, arguably, the story of Sammy is not what it initially seems to be, namely a memory of actual past events

Figure 7 Leonard remembers (being?) Sammy Jankis (21, 1:29:56)

concerning Sammy. Rather, on reflection it appears to be a story that has displaced Leonard's memory of the events concerning his role in his wife's death. If Teddy is right, Leonard is responsible for his wife's death—and as mentioned there is a brief shot of Leonard giving Catherine an insulin injection after the blow to his head that prevents him from forming new memories. It is possible that Leonard has displaced his own responsibility for his wife's death by creating the story of Sammy Jankis, the man he exposed as a fraud. His search for John G is an ongoing attempt to externalize whatever guilt he may have, consciously or unconsciously, with regard to Catherine's death. What Leonard putatively remembers, namely his wife's rape and murder, is arguably a false memory that he reinforces by hiring an escort to reenact his version of the night that Catherine was attacked. It is a displacement necessary to confirm Leonard's memory of his wife's death, just as it is necessary for him to recall this memory in a recurring way by externalizing it through his tattoo and his frequent retelling of the story about Sammy Jankis, his own surrogate. And in the film's most graphic form of displacement, Leonard serially finds and kills men he thinks are his wife's murderer even though, arguably, he is the one who killed her.

As we come to recognize Leonard's unreliability, his misrepresentation of the past, his displacement of responsibility for his own actions onto others, and his obsession with a task that in a very real sense he does not properly understand, it becomes clear that Leonard is not, after all, the detective figure in *Memento* but rather the film's central mystery. Teddy tries to get Leonard to grasp this very point when he says, "You wander around playing detective. . . . Well, maybe you should start investigating yourself"—although when Teddy originally says this, we have not yet discovered that he can be trusted (H, 1:08:10). Indeed, Teddy—who at one point identifies himself as a "snitch" and then later as a detective working undercover—turns out to be the character on whom audiences must rely if they are to have any hope of correctly understanding the events of the film.

Assessing Leonard

The two things that a typical noir or neo-noir detection film requires are that the protagonist sort out who is trustworthy and who is not, and that the protagonist finally be able to provide an explanatory account of the events of the narrative, ultimately determining who is responsible for which crimes. Because of his condition, Leonard is unable to perform either role. Indeed, his condition means that he cannot reliably discriminate between those he should trust and those he should not. A good point of comparison would be *The Maltese Falcon* (1941), where Sam Spade must finally decide whether or not to trust that film's femme fatale, who goes by various names including Brigid O'Shaughnessy. At the film's conclusion, Spade hands O'Shaughnessy over to the police, despite his very strong protective and amorous feelings for her, because he knows he cannot trust her. As Sam says, he will not be her sap. Leonard, by contrast, is incapable of reliably figuring out whom he can and cannot trust. This problem is exacerbated because the notes he writes down on the back of his Polaroids—notes about who is and is not trustworthy— are themselves unreliable. The focal example of this is the scene at the abandoned building after he has killed Jimmy Grantz, when he changes his recorded instructions to himself so as not to trust Teddy, despite the fact that Teddy has just told him about his condition, his role in his wife's death, and the fact that he has already killed the John G who assaulted her. Even during the short window when he can remember what has just happened, he cannot be relied upon to arrive at sound judgments.

The notes on his Polaroids and his tattoos are key parts of the system Leonard relies on to preserve whatever memory he has. In time, we discover that these records are not reliable. In particular, the direction to himself to "remember Sammy Jankis" is, we have argued, part of an elaborate confabulation. Another tattoo directs him to kill John G. We are not sure that anyone other than Leonard killed Catherine, so the objective to kill John G is misconceived and morally blameworthy. In any case, despite the fact that he thinks he is pursuing a clear and logical train of facts, Leonard is wrong to kill Teddy as John G, since there is no reason to believe that Teddy had any role in Leonard's wife's death. Given that Teddy is the one person in this narrative who has an overall understanding of Leonard and his actions, it can only be seen as lamentable and ironic that Leonard finally kills him. Of course, because Leonard's memories are unreliable (although he doesn't realize this), Leonard cannot appreciate the mistake he has made in killing Teddy. Given the unreliability of his memory, as well as the unreliability of the tattooed records of what count for him as legitimate memories, it eventually dawns on viewers that Leonard completely lacks the moral orientation that we initially thought he had.

One of the most familiar ideas in philosophy is that knowledge is *justified true belief*. Since at least Plato, a clear distinction has been drawn between what one knows and what one merely believes. Knowledge is thought to connect to what is true, whereas belief lacks this sort of warrant. A child might believe in Santa, but of course there is no Santa. Leonard might believe that his wife was raped and murdered, but the belief is no guarantee that this was her fate. Leonard is adamant about many things concerning his memory, for instance, that what he remembers up to the moment of his wife's murder is reliable. What becomes increasingly apparent is that many of Leonard's beliefs are neither justified nor true. Because of his condition, it would be virtually impossible for his beliefs to have any sort of justification that he could rely on, since he is unable to remember what would count as the appropriate justification. Initially we might think that his notes on the backs of his Polaroids, or his tattoos, track the truth and therefore should count as justified true beliefs—despite the fact that they are externalized records. But we soon learn that these are just markings that are not necessarily connected to what is true. Whatever else is going on in *Memento*, it is certainly a cautionary tale about what can go wrong when someone deliberately pursues a course of action while being unable to keep a reliable track in memory of what has actually gone on. It is also a vivid illustration of the problem of false belief. Except in extremely aberrant situations, no one can properly claim both that p is false and that they believe that p. This is a manifest contradiction. The problem of false beliefs is that we don't know they are false as long as we believe them. Leonard's condition makes it the case that he bases most of his actions on a set of quite false beliefs—of course, not knowing them to be false. Thus doubting Teddy, trusting Natalie, thinking that he has yet to kill the man who assaulted his wife, remembering the story of Sammy Jankis, and failing to acknowledge that he might be responsible for killing his wife, combine to produce the circumstances in which Leonard tries to carry out his misguided plan for revenge.

All this of course leads up to the obvious problem of deciding how to determine responsibility for the actions that Leonard is engaged in. What might seem to a viewer watching the film for the first time to be an unusual but perhaps laudatory search for justice turns out to be a sequence of events that are completely removed from the real crime because Leonard has no ability to keep in mind what the real crime he thinks he is avenging was. Leonard's problem is, precisely, that he cannot remember accurately. What we find in *Memento* is a narrative in which our central protagonist recklessly and wrongfully kills Teddy, and yet there is no obvious way to hold Leonard responsible for this wanton act. Leonard's problem, of course, is that his memory is completely unreliable, but he continues to cling to self-narratives (for instance, that he witnessed his wife's murder after a sexual assault) that are false. Teddy is the only character in *Memento* who understands Leonard's situation and his past. By killing Teddy, Leonard ends any possibility of self-understanding because he kills the one person who might challenge his own self-narratives about his past.

Concluding observations

To conclude, we want to return to the question about how to understand the narrative structure of *Memento* with respect to the paradigm offered to us by Aristotle in the *Poetics*. There, Aristotle was primarily concerned with dramatic tragedy. A paradigmatic Aristotelian tragedy has a beginning, a middle, and an end, and in that order. The duration of narrative action is fairly clearly circumscribed, with a governing arc to the depicted actions. That is, the plot of a paradigmatic Aristotelian tragedy would display this sort of order. Furthermore, it would feature a protagonist who is superior to us in moral terms but who suffers from a flaw preventing him from fully appreciating the consequences of his actions. The tragic protagonist will, however, undergo a reversal of fortune, face up to a serious failure of moral judgment, and accept the consequences. Oedipus didn't set out to murder his father and marry his mother. Rather, he killed the old man on the road and later married the beautiful Jocasta. The pivotal moment of tragic drama occurs when the protagonist recognizes an aspect of his actions that he had not understood when the actions took place. Oedipus comes to understand that the old man was his father and that the beautiful Jocasta is his mother. The linear-causal structure of tragic drama emphasizes the inevitability of the otherwise apparently contingent sequence of events.

The plot of *Memento*—that is to say, the order of presentation of the narrative events by the film—is clearly non-Aristotelian. But if our job as viewers is to extract the *story* from the presented *plot* of the film, then something curiously Aristotelian happens. The story of *Memento* is a nearly perfectly Aristotelian one. Once the audience has sorted out how to tell a linear-causal narrative of the events that *Memento* depicts in its two contradictory plot trajectories, what we recover is an Aristotelian story in the ironic, rather than the tragic, mode. Ironic because, unlike the tragic protagonist, Leonard's condition means that he is not morally superior to us as viewers. Ironic also because, again unlike the tragic protagonist, Leonard is incapable of that moment of self-recognition that is the narrative centerpiece of Aristotelian tragedy. *Memento* begins and ends with sequences developed around the killing of a John G— beginning around the death of John Gammell and concluding around the killing of Jimmy Grantz. Ironically, Teddy pays for using Leonard to kill Jimmy Grantz when Leonard kills Teddy, believing he is the John G he has been searching for. Whether she is aware of it or not, and whether she has engineered it or not, Natalie is avenged for the loss of Jimmy. And in the final irony, Leonard continues to pursue what we might now think of as an obsession to kill John G. While the story of *Memento* is Aristotelian, Leonard is the antithesis of an Aristotelian protagonist, given that he is unable to experience the moment of self-realization characteristic of the tragic protagonist who in a moment of shocking clarity understands what harms he has caused.

The final words spoken in the so-called "present" of the film could not better illustrate the irony of the film's perspective. Driving away from the deserted building where he has just killed Jimmy Grantz, Leonard brakes when he sees a tattoo parlor. Clearly, within the limitations of his short-term memory, he plans to have information recorded on his body—information that by this point we anticipate will either be false or liable to misinterpretation. Leonard says to himself, "Now . . . where was I?" This seemingly innocent remark perfectly captures his incapacity to track his own past actions or situate himself properly within a reliable self-narrative. The sad irony is that Leonard does not really know where he was, but must continue to act as if he does. This perspective is what will ultimately lead to the death of Teddy.

Notes

1   A word about key terms here. By "plot," we mean all the events presented directly by the film in the order in which they are presented. By "story," we

mean the causal, chronological sequence of events as they would occur in real time. The story includes information inferred from but not directly presented by the material of the film's plot. *Memento* is a textbook example of the need to infer the story of the film from its plot. What makes *Memento* such a challenging film is that its first plot element, the shooting of Teddy, is the last element of the film's story. On the relationship between plot and story, see Bordwell and Thompson (2004) and Bordwell (1985). By "narrative," we mean the conceptual arrangement of all the actions and events presented by the film's plot. We will use the term "narrative structure" to indicate the organization and frequency of actions and events in the film. For example, the narrative is structured around two murders, at the beginning and at the end of *Memento*.

2   French New Wave film director (b. 1930) best known for such works as *À bout de souffle* (*Breathless*) (1959), *Weekend* (1967), and *Tout va bien* (1972).

3   For an analysis of the notions of alignment and allegiance, see Smith (1995).

4   For a more complete account of how detection mysteries are constructed, see Knight and McKnight (1997).

5   As an example of the complex relationship between the plot of *Memento* and its story, recall that at this early stage, the so-called "Fact 6" has been tattooed on Leonard's body, while the conclusion of the film finds him outside a tattoo parlor, about to have "Fact 6" inscribed.

References

Bordwell, D. (1985) *Narration in the Fiction Film*, Madison, WI: University of Wisconsin Press.

Bordwell, D. and Thompson, K. (2004) *Film Art: An Introduction*, 7th edn, New York, NY: McGraw-Hill.

Knight, D. and McKnight, G. (1997) "The Case of the Disappearing Enigma," *Philosophy and Literature* 21: 123–38.

Neale, S. (2000) *Genre and Hollywood*, New York, NY: Routledge.

Smith, M. (1995) *Engaging Characters: Fiction, Emotion, and the Cinema.* New York, NY: Oxford University Press.

Sobchack, V. (1998) "Lounge Time: Postwar Crises and the Chronotope of Film Noir," in N. Browne (ed.) *Refiguring American Film Genres*, Berkeley, CA: University of California Press.

Telford, K. (1961) *Aristotle's Poetics: Translation and Analysis*, Chicago, IL: Gateway.

Further reading

Conard, M.T. (ed.) (2006) *The Philosophy of Film Noir*, Lexington, KY: University Press of Kentucky. (A collection of essays on philosophical aspects of many classic films noirs.)

—— (ed.) (2007) *The Philosophy of Neo-noir*, Lexington, KY: University Press of Kentucky. (A collection of essays on philosophical aspects of many neo-noir films, including personal identity in *Memento*.)

Silver, A. and Ursini, J. (eds) (1996) *Film Noir Reader*, New York, NY: Limelight Editions. (A collection of classic essays on film noir.)

Chapter 8

Andrew Kania

WHAT IS *MEMENTO*? ONTOLOGY AND INTERPRETATION IN MAINSTREAM FILM

A T THE END OF THE FLASHBACK, quite late in Memento, when we finally get to see what Leonard remembers of the incident that led to his memory impairment, the camera pans slowly away from a close-up of Leonard's head, oozing blood onto the tiles of his bathroom floor (E, 1:19:27).[1] Just before the flashback fades out, and we return to the present in which Leonard is recounting this memory to Natalie, the frame includes only the bathroom floor, tiled entirely in white with the exception of two black tiles in opposite corners of the screen, like dots begging to be connected. Here we have a small metaphor for one of the reasons for Memento's success. Audiences went straight from the theater to the coffeehouse in order not only to discuss the deeper issues raised by the film, such as the nature of memory and the self, but also to connect the narrative dots and figure out what actually happens in the film.

It is no mean feat just to reconstruct the chronology of the film's present; it is difficult to keep clear in one's mind even such unambiguous facts as which events occur before or after which other events. The most obvious reason for this difficulty is that the color scenes are presented in reverse chronological order, but the parallels between certain events (for example, Leonard's killings of Jimmy and Teddy), and the subtle transition in the final scene from the straightforward chronology of the black and white scenes to the reverse chronology of the color scenes, add to the viewer's confusion. In my experience, first-time viewers seriously overestimate even the time covered in the film's present (about 48 hours).[2] Then there are the more complicated implications of what happens on screen. To what extent are Natalie and Teddy using Leonard for their own ends, and to what extent are they genuinely interested in helping him? The question about *Memento*'s plot that exercises viewers most, however, is what really happened to Leonard and his wife, Catherine, during and after "the incident" when they were attacked in their home.

In this essay, I begin by considering the evidence within the film that suggests different answers to this question. I then briefly introduce some popular theories of interpretation, and discuss their implications for how to approach the film. There is an additional interpretive puzzle that *Memento* raises, however. There is fictional material *external to* the film that looks like it might have significant implications for the interpretation of *Memento*. After a brief discussion of this material, I turn to the question of whether we should take this material into account as part of *Memento*, that is, whether *Memento* is really a film, or something more complicated.

Two theories of what happens in *Memento*

Two main interpretations of what happens in *Memento* are presented within the film. One, which I will call "Leonard's view," is suggested by what Leonard tells various other characters throughout the course of the film. The other, which I will call "Teddy's view," is suggested by Teddy in the final scene (A).[3]

According to Leonard's view, Catherine was raped and killed during a home invasion, while Leonard was hit on the head and left for dead. As a result, Leonard is unable to form new long-term memories, though he retains his memories of events that occurred before he sustained his injury. In this respect, Leonard is like Sammy Jankis—the subject of one of Leonard's investigations before the incident, in his life as an insurance investigator. Sammy was involved in a car accident, and became unable to form new long-term memories, just like Leonard. However, Leonard's condition differs from Sammy's in one important respect: Leonard is able to learn through "conditioning." That is, he can learn to do some things *automatically* that he cannot *remember* to do. For instance, he seems to check his pockets more often than most people would for clues about the situation in which he finds himself; presumably he has been conditioned to do this.[4] This difference is tied to Leonard's claim that his condition is "physical," while Sammy's is "psychological." The distinction seems to be between brute trauma to the physical "hardware" of the brain, such as the removal of some grey matter, and the malfunctioning of the psychological "software" of the brain, such as a systematic repression of certain memories. (See Kania (2008: 655–6) and McKenna (this volume) for more on this distinction.)

According to Teddy's view, Leonard and Catherine alike were left for dead by their assailants, but both survived the assault. The story that Leonard repeatedly tells himself and others about Sammy Jankis is really a story about himself; his constant recounting of it as a story about Sammy is a method (and result) of "conditioning" himself to believe it is so. In fact, Leonard's wife was diabetic, she had difficulty dealing with Leonard's condition, and it was she who administered Leonard's "final test," deceiving him into giving her a lethal overdose of insulin. Leonard's subsequent search for Catherine's supposed killer is a radical strategy for avoiding the awful truth that he is responsible for her death.

Teddy's interpretation can initially be very compelling. It is presented at the climax of the movie, when we might expect just such a twist to resolve the multiple unanswered questions of the plot. Even the use of music in this scene suggests that Teddy's putative revelations are indeed the dénouement.[5] Moreover, Teddy's account seems to seriously worry Leonard, who, while being very defensive about Teddy's accusations ("You think I don't know my own wife?") has conflicting "flashbacks" of pinching Catherine's thigh (Leonard's view) and injecting insulin into her thigh (Teddy's view) (A, 1:43:30).[6]

On the other hand, there are strong reasons, on reflection, to reject Teddy's account. For one thing, throughout the film Teddy lies to or otherwise misleads Leonard in attempts to manipulate him. For instance, the phone conversation that occurs throughout most of the black and white scenes seems to be an effort on Teddy's part to convince Leonard that John G is a drug dealer—Jimmy Grantz—and to get him out of his hotel room so that he will go and kill Jimmy. Throughout the color scenes, Teddy spends much of his time trying to get into the trunk of the Jaguar Leonard took from Jimmy after killing him, to retrieve the $200,000 that was a major, if not the sole, reason for having Leonard kill Jimmy in the first place. The most convincing reason for rejecting

Teddy's view, however, is that the events in the story of Sammy Jankis all occur before the incident, and thus should be immune to Leonard's condition. His memory of these events should be as good as any ordinary memory of an extraordinary chain of events a few years in the past. Similarly, as Leonard implies, whether or not Catherine was diabetic is something he should remember from before the incident.

But things may be more complicated than I have suggested so far. At the beginning of his supposed revelations, Teddy says that Leonard's account of Sammy Jankis is a "[g]reat story. Gets better every time you tell it. So you lie to yourself to be happy. There's nothing wrong with that—we all do it. Who cares if there's a few little details you'd rather not remember?" (A, 1:42:24). A little later, checking Jimmy's shoes for size,[7] Teddy says "I guess they can only make you remember the things you want to be true" (A, 1:43:52). Though this might be taken as just one more apothegm about the nature of memory in general, it could also be taken to refer to Leonard in particular. That is, it may be that Leonard's condition is not as he describes it throughout the film. Rather than a "physical" condition, it may be that Leonard's condition is "psychological." If this is so, the question of what Leonard can and can't remember no longer turns on when the event occurred (before or after the incident), but on the complex economy of Leonard's dysfunctional mental life, in which he seems to be keeping his guilt down to manageable levels by repressing or altering certain details of memories of his life both before and after the incident, while also attempting to maintain a coherent and relatively stable overall account of that life. If this is the case, then all bets are off regarding what Leonard can and can't remember, given his condition.

Thus far, you might think that Leonard's view is still to be preferred on the grounds of simplicity. For instance, an additional question to be answered by a defender of Teddy's view is what Leonard's condition was immediately following the assault. Even if Leonard is repressing memories as a result of unintentionally killing his wife with an insulin overdose, he must have had some memory problem already, to explain the accidental killing. But then it's not clear how he could feel guilty enough about killing his wife to trigger his radical repression, since he would not realize he had done it, nor remember it for long if someone told him.

However, there are many features of the film that seem explicable on the basis of Teddy's view, but inexplicable if Leonard's view is correct.

One is the nature of Leonard's memories of Catherine. He always describes Catherine in positive terms, but the images that accompany his recollections belie these descriptions.[8] Catherine is almost never depicted as smiling; rather, she seems sad, or even lost—much like Sammy's wife after his accident.[9] This suggests, at least, that Leonard is misremembering the nature of his marriage, and perhaps that these memories are from *after* the incident, when Catherine was having trouble dealing with Leonard's condition.[10] The most extended memory of Leonard's married life is a bedtime scene, presented in flashback, in which Leonard taunts Catherine for re-reading her favorite book when she already knows "what happens next," and she responds by calling him a prick (K, 0:55:22). While this is partly a comment on the peculiarity of *Memento*'s narrative structure, it is hardly representative of a happy marriage. Leonard twice asks Natalie not to call him "Lenny," saying that his wife called him that and he hated it (S, 0:17:43; G, 1:11:37), and says of his memories of Catherine that "[y]ou can feel these extreme moments, even if you don't want to" (S, 0:20:12). Finally, and arguably most troublingly for Leonard's view, there is a lightning-fast color flashback of a syringe being flicked when Leonard glances at his "remember Sammy Jankis" tattoo at Natalie's place (E, 1:21:26). That this is Leonard's genuine memory of using a syringe is implied by the same shot's reoccurrence during the climax, as Leonard considers Teddy's view (A, 1:42:54).[11]

In addition to these narrative inconsistencies, there are non-narrative hints that the fictional world presented in *Memento* may not be as it seems. The distinction between narrative and non-narrative material is the distinction between those aspects of the film that affect its fictional truths (such as whether Leonard's marriage was a happy one) and those that do not (Levinson 1996: 256–60). For instance, there are several examples of what would be continuity errors, were they not clearly intended. In different shots, Teddy's license plate is shown to be "SG13 7IU" (A, 1:46:54) and "SG13 71U" (O, 0:44:13). Similarly, in the photo of herself and Jimmy that Natalie shows Leonard, first Jimmy has a moustache, then he does not, and then does once more! (P, 0:35:42–0:39:02) These shots are clearly not indications that *Memento* is a kind of "metaphysics fiction" film, wherein objects spontaneously change their properties from time to time. Nor are they subjective shots displaying the fallibility of memory, as we might interpret some of the flashbacks depicting Leonard's memories to be. These are relatively objective shots showing us the film's present. Thus, I suggest, they are non-narrative. They do not make it the case that we should suppose there are two similar but distinct photos of Jimmy in Natalie's house; rather, they are hints from the film-maker that we should watch closely for inconsistencies, since things may not be as they first appear.[12]

Perhaps the most suggestive evidence that Leonard is Sammy, in some sense, is the moment when we see Leonard replace Sammy in his chair in the institution where he has been committed after killing his wife (21, 1:29:56). Again, this is obviously not an attempt at "metaphysics fiction"; we are not supposed to think that at some point in time Sammy's body was magically replaced by Leonard's. But this shot is highly ambiguous. It might be taken as evidence for Teddy's view, that is, as an indication that Leonard is Sammy in some sense. But it might just as plausibly be interpreted along the lines of Leonard's view. After all, explicit parallels are constantly being drawn between Sammy and Leonard throughout the film. There is good reason for this, even on Leonard's view, since Sammy's and Leonard's conditions are so similar. In fact, these shots occur while Leonard is drawing an explicit parallel between himself and Sammy. In the end, then, this shot fits either interpretation, and thus is not decisive between them.

There are several other narrative issues that, like the ambiguous shot of Leonard as Sammy, seem to turn on which interpretation is correct, and yet do not provide any evidence for one view over the other. Is there really a John G, that is, a second assailant in the incident whom the police do not believe exists? If so, has Leonard really killed him already? Why is Leonard's copy of the police file about the incident incomplete, with some material deleted, and whole pages missing? If Teddy's view is correct, and Leonard is "lying to himself to be happy," then it seems more likely that Leonard has "created a puzzle he could never solve" by inventing John G, and expunging material from the police file. If Leonard's view is correct, it seems more likely that there was a second assailant, and that Teddy has doctored the police file, though it is hard to believe that Teddy was motivated by justice or compassion to help Leonard find John G. The point here is that these issues are red herrings in terms of figuring out whether Leonard's or Teddy's view is more plausible. The reliability of the evidence for whether or not there was a second assailant, for example, (e.g., that Leonard remembers there being one) turns on which view is correct (e.g., whether Leonard's pre-incident memories can be trusted), and thus this evidence cannot be used to decide between the two views.

In sum, the evidence in the film arguably supports Leonard's and Teddy's views about equally; there is no good reason to prefer one of their interpretations over the other.

Theories of interpretation

When people think about interpreting works of art, such as paintings, novels, or films, they often have in mind what we might call "deep" interpretation, that is, the excavation of what the work has to say about some important topic, whether a contemporary political issue or an abiding human concern. But, in general, interpretation is just an attempt to make sense of something the significance of which is not obvious. The question of "what really happened" in Memento is a nice example to think about because most people who see the film are easily drawn to the narrative puzzles in the film and engage naturally in debate over their correct solution. We might say that each of the views discussed above is an interpretation that attributes a different "story meaning" to Memento (Currie 1993: 94).

The notion of a *correct* interpretation is sometimes met with skepticism (heated debates over Memento's story-meaning notwithstanding), since one of the features we value most in artworks is their ability to be interpreted in many different ways. To a large extent, this skepticism rests on confusion or false assumptions. One thing to note is that the idea of a correct interpretation does not imply that there is one, uniquely best interpretation. Sometimes this point is made more explicit by referring to "acceptable" or "admissible" interpretations, rather than "correct" ones. Alternatively, it might be that there is a single correct interpretation of a work, but that it imputes ambiguity to the work. For example, it might be that the best interpretation of Memento's story-meaning is that it is ambiguous between the two views I consider above.

Another source of confusion is the mistaken idea that there is a single goal of all art interpretation. Rather, when we interpret an artwork, we might do so for quite different purposes, and a particular interpretation may be good with respect to one goal but unsatisfying with respect to another. For instance, a Marxist critic may be primarily interested in representations of class in Memento and the extent to which the film implicitly endorses or subverts contemporary American social ideology. It may be unhelpful to criticize such an interpretation as narrow, ignoring much that is of interest in the film, if the critic is not trying to give a broad account of the film's meaning.[13] Nonetheless, there is some consensus that one central interpretive project is the attempt to uncover the whole of the work's meaning. While no actual piece of criticism is likely to do this, we can see much actual criticism as aimed at contributing a part of the total meaning of the work, much as we might see individual articles by various psychologists as each contributing a part to our understanding of the mind as a whole. Thus, while *Memento* may have "deep" meanings about the nature of memory and the self, as attested by several essays in this volume, such meanings rely on claims about the story-meaning of the film, which is thus just as much a part of the film's total meaning as these deeper claims.

Three theories of what determines the meaning of an artwork have recently received much attention from philosophers: (1) actual intentionalism, (2) hypothetical intentionalism, and (3) conventionalism. Despite their differences, which I shall come to shortly, those who support these theories tend to share a conception of what an artwork is. They agree that an artwork derives its identity in part from its context of creation. For instance, it is a fact that *Memento* is a neo-noir film in English in part because of when and how it was produced. In a sense, we could interpret *Memento* as if it were a film in a different language, where the words characters speak mean something different from their actual meanings. Or we could interpret *Memento* as a postmodern romantic comedy. Or we could close our eyes and try to experience the soundtrack as if it were a kind of musical work, composed of pure sounds. But to do any of these things would be to treat *Memento* as something other than the artwork it actually is, just as to praise Shakespeare's collected works as very good for kindling a fire is to treat them as something other than the works of art they actually are. Such interpretations, then, are not interpretations of the work under consideration.

Another thing these theorists agree on is that an artwork has some determinate nature. At the very least, not every aspect of a work is open to interpretation; some things are "beneath interpretation" (Shusterman 1990). You might think that *everything* about *Memento* is open to interpretation. But some things are not. Perhaps it is open to interpretation that Leonard is a human being. Maybe a cunning interpreter could find some clues that he is an alien in disguise. Or maybe the entire film is Leonard's hallucination as he sits in the mental institution. These interpretations are wildly implausible, but let us allow that such matters are not, at least in principle, beneath interpretation. Still, it cannot be disputed that the first scene of Memento consists of color images of a certain sort that represent beings that *appear* human, at least, and that *appear* to be behaving in a backwards fashion. This much is not open to interpretation, and any complete interpretation of the film will have to make sense of these facts.

Now let me introduce the three theories of interpretation mentioned above. Actual intentionalism is the theory that the artist's actual intentions determine the meaning of the work. An extreme version of this theory would hold that if Christopher Nolan intended Memento to be the story of a Martian invasion, then that is its true story-meaning, and any other interpretation is incorrect. The most plausible versions of actual intentionalism are more modest, claiming that, for instance, the artist's intentions determine the meaning of the work only if they are compatible with what she has produced.

Suppose that the two interpretations I considered in the previous section are equally well supported by the film, but also that Nolan intended Teddy's view to be the story-meaning of the film. Since Teddy's view is compatible with the film, the actual intentionalist must acknowledge that it is the correct interpretation of the action, and that alternative interpretations, such as Leonard's view, or the view that the film is ambiguous, are incorrect. Opponents of actual intentionalism argue that this is an unacceptable consequence of actual intentionalism. It does not match our actual interpretive practices, nor would such a practice be preferable to our current practices, given the value we place on the multiple interpretability of many of our richest artworks.

Another objection is that actual intentionalism is incomplete. A moderate actual intentionalist grants that there could be (and probably are) cases where the artist fails to realize his intentions in his work, in which case the artist's intentions *do not* determine the meaning of the work. In such cases, however, the work does not fail to have a meaning. Thus the actual intentionalist must give some account of how meaning is determined in these cases, that is, he must appeal to a different theory of interpretation. But then it seems reasonable to ask why we should not adopt this alternative approach in *all* our interpretive engagements with artworks.

Both hypothetical intentionalism and conventionalism can be seen as just such alternatives. The hypothetical intentionalist agrees that what we properly do when interpreting an artwork is to make hypotheses about what the artist's intentions must have been, given the artwork before us and knowledge of the work's context of creation. The main difference between actual and hypothetical intentionalism is that certain evidence is ruled out of court by the latter. For instance, hypothetical intentionalists rule out "private" evidence of the artist's intentions, such as her diaries. Also, the hypothetical intentionalist may exclude public evidence from after the completion of the work. Thus, some of Christopher Nolan's commentary on the DVD editions of *Memento* is presumably good evidence of his actual intentions in making the film, but the hypothetical intentionalist might rule this evidence out on the grounds that it was not available to the audience when the film was released. According to hypothetical intentionalism, the *best hypothesis* of an *ideal audience* obeying these restrictions determines the meaning of the work, regardless of whether it matches the actual intentions of the artist. Hypothetical intentionalism thus attempts to tread a middle way between actual intentionalism and non-intentional views, such as conventionalism. The hypotheses that determine the meaning of the work are about the actual artist's intentions, yet the work is granted a degree of autonomy from those intentions.

Conventionalism is the view that we ought not to be concerned with the artist's intentions concerning the work's meaning at all. Rather, there are certain conventions that govern our interpretation of artworks. These conventions are doubtless quite complex, but central to them is the idea that in interpreting artworks, we aim at maximizing their value. That is, we prefer interpretations that make an artwork more expressive, thought-provoking, unified, and so on, to interpretations that make the same work less so. For example, we might prefer the interpretation of *Memento*'s action as ambiguous to either Leonard's or Teddy's view alone, since such an interpretation makes the work richer, regardless of what Nolan intended, or even what an ideal audience would infer he must have intended (on the basis of his previous work, say). Although, like actual and hypothetical intentionalists, the conventionalist takes note of the social and art-historical context in which the work was created, she may consider this context more broadly. Rather than think of *Memento* as having been produced by Christopher Nolan in particular, the conventionalist may treat it merely as having been produced in Hollywood at the turn of the twenty-first century. As a consequence, the conventionalist has the most freedom in interpretation, since she is unfettered by any of the particular facts about the actual creator of the work before her.

As we move down the line, then, from actual to hypothetical intentionalism and finally to conventionalism, the artist becomes less central to the evidence we use to arbitrate between interpretations. Thus, although hypothetical intentionalism and conventionalism are more unified theories, applying to all artworks regardless of the success of their creators' intentions, we will be drawn back to actual intentionalism to the extent that we think of the artist as the creator of her work's meaning.

The website material

I have already mentioned the disputed relevance of the director's commentary tracks on the DVD editions of Memento, but there is other material on the DVD that seems relevant to interpreting the film. There are images of (i) newspaper articles about the incident and Leonard's actions during the film's "present," (ii) official psychological reports from two different medical institutions where Leonard seems to have been treated in the time between the incident and the film's present, (iii) notes Leonard wrote to himself during this time, and (iv) fragments of a diary he kept during this time. This material is notable for several reasons.

First, unlike the director's commentary,[14] it is fictional material. That is, the extra material does not comprise actual newspaper articles and psychological reports; rather, we are supposed to imagine that these documents were produced by people in the fictional world of Memento. Second, this is the only material that unambiguously represents events from the period between the incident and the film's present. Third, the material has been connected with the film from the very beginning. It was not added after the production of the film, but first appeared on a website that went up before the release of the film.[15] Nor was the website a pure marketing ploy on the part of the producers. Jonathan Nolan, the director's brother (upon whose idea Memento is based), was in charge of the production of the website, but Christopher had "authorial" oversight, insisting on certain changes. The material has also been reproduced on DVD editions of the film.

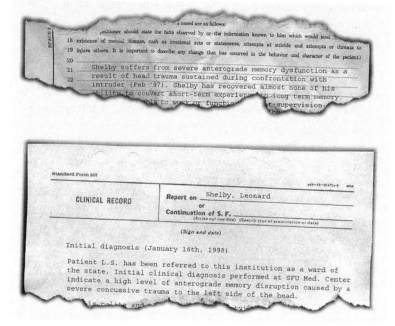

Figure 8 Some website material

Most interestingly for our purposes, however, two clear implications of this material are that (1) Leonard was committed to an institution, and (2) eleven months elapsed between the incident and Leonard's committal. The first implication is clear from the very nature of some of the material—they are obviously official psychological reports, and they make reference to Leonard's committal. It is worth noting that if we consider only the film, it is not obvious that Leonard spent any time in an institution. It is possible that Teddy began helping him search for "the second assailant" shortly after the incident, since the other police investigating the incident were never convinced there was such an assailant. There is, of course, the highly suggestive cut wherein Leonard replaces Sammy in the institution, but as noted above, this cut is inconclusive. The second implication is clear due to the fact that much of the material is quite literally *dated*. The incident is placed at around 1:30 a.m. on February 24, 1997; Leonard is committed at some point in early to mid January 1998; and he goes missing from the institution at some point in September 1998.

The less obvious, but strong implication of all this is that *Leonard's wife survived the assault*, and thus that she was killed by Leonard's administering an overdose of insulin; in other words, Teddy's view is correct. This is implied by the fact that Leonard was *not* committed until eleven months after the incident, which would be inexplicable if his wife were dead, since Leonard could not possibly have functioned by himself, at least when he first had his condition. (Some of the website material shows that it was during his time in the institution that Leonard learned to train himself by conditioning.)

What is Memento?

Finally, then, we come to the central question of this essay: What is *Memento*? Few people would hesitate to answer that *Memento* is a film, and yet, if the material I have just been discussing is part of *Memento*, *Memento* is not a film. Rather, it is a kind of hybrid artwork: a film-plus-website-material.[16] This is an "ontological" conclusion—one about the kind of thing *Memento* is—and a relatively radical one. One of its implications is that anyone who has seen only the film has experienced only part of *Memento*. The film is undoubtedly an important part of this hybrid work, yet the website material is also important, especially if one is concerned, as most audiences are, with the story-meaning of the work. If the website material is part of *Memento*, the consequences for interpretation of the action are so considerable that ignoring it would be comparable to trying to understand a detective novel without having read the last chapter, in which whodunit is revealed.

I will argue that the website material is *not* part of *Memento*. *Memento* is "just" a film, not a hybrid work. Even if this is correct, you might think that we should take the website material in account in interpreting the film, since it is part of the art-historical context surrounding the film, and according to all three theories of interpretation we have considered, we should take such context into account. However, none of these theories allows artists to *stipulate* the meaning of their works. Unless the website material is literally part of *Memento*, it would seem to constitute such a stipulation. Thus, if we are to take the website material into account, it must be as part of the single artwork we call *Memento*.

There are different ways of combining art works and media. Think of a ballet, or the director's cut of a film, or an illustrated novel. In each of these cases we have two closely related items—the music and dance of the ballet, the original and director's cuts of a film, and the text and illustrations of the novel. Does any of these serve as a good model for the relation between Memento's film and website material?[17]

The music of a ballet might be appreciated by itself or with the accompanying dance, but the central features of the music will not change with the addition of the dance, whereas the central features of Memento (e.g., its story meaning) are radically altered by the addition of the website material. This suggests that the website material is not just an optional part of Memento; it is either part of the work or it is not. The film-plus-website-material is not like a director's cut of a film, either. For one thing, it is not simply a film, but a hybrid entity. For another, the website material was released at the same time as the film; it is not part of a later version of the work, as with directors' cuts. Again, this encourages us to consider the material either as part of the film or not from its initial release. Finally, ordinary illustrations of novels do not affect their interpretation. Though a picture of Jason Compton in an illustrated edition of The Sound and the Fury (1929) might encourage you to imagine him looking a certain way, it is not constitutive of the fiction that his appearance is just so. These illustrations do not make Faulkner's work a hybrid. However, there are novels that include pictures—even moving images—as constitutive parts (for instance, Jonathan Safran Foer's Extremely Loud and Incredibly Close (2005)). If Memento is a hybrid work, it is more like this—an integration of different artistic media.

There are two main reasons to consider Memento such a hybrid. First, Christopher Nolan had creative control over the website material, in the same sense in which he had creative control over the film. For instance, he seems to have removed some references to the date of Leonard's wife's death from earlier versions of the website (Andy Klein, quoted in Zhu 2001). Second, Nolan sometimes implies that he intended Memento to be a hybrid work. For instance, he says that

> [w]hat the Blair Witch people got absolutely right . . . was if you really looked at the website before you went to see the film, you actually got a lot more out of the film. It creates a larger experience than film-makers . . . do. . . . If you can do it yourself, and not just hand

it to a PR department which doesn't add anything creative, you
can increase people's understanding of the film, allowing them to
re-experience it again.

(Quoted in Mottram 2002: 72–3)

On the other hand, Nolan also says things that indicate Memento is just a
film:

If you watch the film, and abandon your conventional desire for
absolute truth—and the confirmation of absolute truth that most
films provide you with—then you can find all the answers you're
looking for. As far as I'm concerned, my view is very much in the
film—the answers are all there for the attentive viewer, but the terms
of the storytelling prevent me from being able to give the audience
absolute confirmation. And that's the point.

(Quoted in Mottram 2002: 26)

This is enigmatic in terms of the actual story-meaning of the film, as
Nolan intends, but it is pretty clear in terms of what Nolan takes Memento
to be—a film—particularly when it comes to evidence for its story-
meaning. I am not sure how to resolve this tension in Nolan's expressed
intentions regarding the website material, but since the case is arguably
more interesting if we take his intentions to be that the website material
is part of Memento, I will assume that this is the case for the remainder of
this essay.

This assumption might seem to settle the question once and for all.
After all, if an artist does not get to determine where the boundaries of
his work lie, who does? However, our brief discussion of theories of
interpretation gives us reason to consider this rhetorical question literally.
For one might similarly think, at first, that no one but the artist could
determine the meaning of an artwork. The arguments against actual
intentionalism, though, and those for hypothetical intentionalism and
conventionalism, show that things are not so simple. Nonetheless, the
latter theories are usually presented as theories about only meaning of
artworks, not about the kinds of things artworks are. Hypothetical
intentionalists and conventionalists can be actual intentionalists about
such matters. For instance, Jerrold Levinson claims that an artist's
intentions about a work's meaning

do *not* determine meaning, but categorial intentions, such as concern a literature maker's basic conception of what is made [e.g. a poem rather than a short story], *do* in general determine how a text is to be conceptualized and approached on a fundamental level. . . .

(Levinson 1990: 188–9, original emphases)[18]

Why does Levinson fall back on the actual intentions of the artist when it comes to categorizing the work in question? The main reason seems to be that *someone* has to decide what it is we should engage with when we want to engage with a particular work. We *could* engage with just the film, or the film-plus-website-material, or the film-plus-our-favorite-painting, or only the color scenes of the film, or whatever we choose. The question is what we *ought* to engage with if we want to engage with *Memento*, and Christopher Nolan seems well placed to decide that, since he created *Memento*. As Levinson puts it,

[w]ithout a basic grasp of a work's categorial identity—its genre, medium, or artform—interpretation is wholly unlikely to arrive at what a work is saying, expressing, or conveying. That is why categorial intentions and semantic intentions with respect to a work of art cannot be thought of as on a par or equally negotiable.

(Levinson 2007: 305)

One problem with this line of thought is the main problem with actual intentionalism about meaning, namely, that actual intentions can fail. This means that something other than just intentions are involved in the determination of the basic nature of an artwork. Levinson is aware of this, which is why he says that categorial intentions determine the nature of the work "in general." His actual intentionalism about a work's categorization is "modest" in the same sense as more plausible actual intentionalist theories of interpretation. That is, the intentions of the artist only determine the basic nature of the work "so long as the [item] in question at least allows of being taken, among other things, as [the author intends]" (Levinson 1990: 188). But, as with actual intentionalism about interpretation, this raises the question of what is produced when an artist's categorial intentions fail. Consider, for example, a book-length work of literature that could be taken either as a series of interlocking short stories or as a novel.[19] Such a work is in the middle of a spectrum between clear examples of short story collections and clear examples of novels. It seems possible for the author to have seriously intended the work to be a novel, and yet for everyone to agree that she has failed to realize these intentions, producing only a set of interrelated short stories. What makes it the case that, despite her intentions, the author has produced a short-story collection? Presumably it is the fact that the relevant audience for the work takes it to be a short-story collection, rather than a novel. This is simply a move to hypothetical intentionalism or conventionalism about the nature of the work, however. And, as with theories of interpretation, if we ought to subscribe to such a theory in cases where the artist's intentions fail, there seems to be no reason to hold on to actual intentionalism in cases where such intentions succeed. For in such cases, the rival theories will deliver the same results as actual intentionalism.

It might seem, though, that *Memento* is a more difficult case than the one we've just considered. After all, in the novel/short-story-collection case, we have a text that we are attempting to categorize correctly. But in the case of *Memento*, we're unsure even what the "text" is. It is more like a case where we discovered that the author of a novel also made a series of drawings that portrayed some of the same characters and events in her novel, but in different situations that could be interpretively relevant to the novel, and then suggested that the drawings and novel were all part of a single hybrid artwork. Again, though this would be a strange case, our first thought might be that the artist gets to decide what her artwork is. For one thing, there appear to be no rules governing what artists can do. All manner of strange things have been successfully put forward as artworks since the early years of the twentieth century, including much stranger congeries than a novel yoked to a series of paintings or a film conjoined with a website.

Nevertheless, I believe that Christopher Nolan has not succeeded in producing a hybrid artwork with *Memento*, even if that is what he intended to do. It seems to me that it makes a difference that Nolan was working within the mainstream film world, and that he did not clearly and explicitly indicate that the website material was part of the work. Part of the reason it is so easy for contemporary artists working in the "high art" or "avant-garde" artworld to put anything forward as an artwork is that there is a history in that tradition of presenting all manner of things as art. Thus the audience for such art is alert to a huge range of possibilities for what constitutes any work they encounter. For just this reason, creators, exhibitors, and curators of contemporary art attempt to make it quite clear what exactly is being put forward for appreciation. This explicitness is something quite new in the history of art, and is bound up with the avant-garde artworld's theoretical turn in the twentieth century. Prior to the twentieth century, artists worked almost exclusively within fairly robust traditions, governed by conventions that were well understood, though rarely made explicit. If you encountered an object made of stretched canvas covered in oil paint hanging on a wall, you could be sure that what was relevant to appreciating the object was (roughly) the appearance of the distribution of paint. You could be equally sure that the wallpaper behind the painting, the means by which it was attached to the wall, and what was on the back of the canvas, were all irrelevant to appreciation of the work. In contemporary art, by contrast, none of this can be taken for granted. I am not suggesting that there are no conventions in contemporary art, but it seems obvious that the conventions are much more permissive than at any time in the past.

"Popular," "mass," or "mainstream" art is more traditional than avant-garde art in this respect, for somewhat obvious reasons. Such art is supposed to be accessible to large numbers of people (Carroll 1998: 196). At a bare minimum, then, large numbers of people must be able to figure out pretty quickly the kind of thing they are engaging with. One easy way to ensure this is to work within a well-known tradition of such things. That is, if you produce a sit-com, or a romance novel, or a pop single, huge numbers of people will immediately understand what it is they're supposed to be attending to. One "cost" of working within such a tradition is that you are restricted by its conventions. An eighteenth-century painter arguably could not have splashed some paint on his bed and offered it up as a visual artwork, since the eighteenth-century conventions for visual artworks did not allow for such things. I am suggesting that Christopher Nolan is in just such a position with regard to the tradition of mainstream film within which he is working.

You might wonder whether this argument begs the question by assuming that Nolan is working within the tradition of mainstream film, rather than that of avant-garde art. What someone produces is surely a major indicator of the tradition within which she is working. That is why we take someone to be speaking non-literally when she presents us with a chunk of carved marble and calls it her "latest symphony." Such a person is working within the tradition of carved sculpture, not music. Shouldn't we similarly take Nolan to have produced a hybrid work if that is what he intended and he produced things that could be taken in this way?

This objection ignores the complexity of the context of artistic creation. What someone produces is indeed a major indicator of the tradition within which she is working, but note that "what someone produces" is precisely what is under discussion. When we engage with an artwork (as when we engage with any person's intentional action), we take all sorts of factors into account. If some of these factors contradict others, as in the case of the sculptor's actions and words, we must seek a kind of "reflective equilibrium," figuring out the best overall interpretation of what the person is doing. The best overall interpretation of Christopher Nolan's actions, I suggest, taking into consideration the context in which he performed them, is that he has produced a film in the tradition of mainstream cinema, not a hybrid work comprising a film and the website material.

I should note, finally, that conventions change. It might be that, in the future, more and more "film-makers" will do the kind of thing that Nolan did, and that audiences will come to expect to have to take such additional material into account if they are to fully understand the works that such artists produce. But we are not at that stage yet. Almost no film websites or DVD extras contribute to the fictional content of the films they accompany in the radical way that *Memento*'s website material would, were it part of the work. Nor do audience members expect to have to acquire information from such sources in order to engage with the entire work. If such hybrid works become standard in the future, *Memento* and its website material may come to be seen as an important precursor of such works, but *Memento* is, and will remain, simply a film.

Conclusion

One of the most intriguing aspects of *Memento* is its apparent narrative ambiguity, which is of interest not only as an intellectual puzzle, but for its relation to the deeper themes of the film. The website material that has accompanied the film from its creation threatens to reduce this rich ambiguity. However, since *Memento* was created in the context of mainstream film at the turn of the twenty-first century, and little effort was made to communicate to its audience that the work was anything but a film, the website material is not part of the work, even if that was the intention of its creator. *Memento* is, in fact, the narratively ambiguous film its audiences usually take it to be.[20]

Notes

1 I refer to parts of the film by scene and time (in minutes:hours:seconds). The system of scene numbering is explained in the introduction to this volume.

2 Christopher Nolan notes this same phenomenon in an interview included on the regular edition DVD. Perhaps this is the appropriate place to thank all the students at the University of Maryland and Trinity University who have enthusiastically discussed *Memento* with me.

3 These labels are not meant to imply that either of these characters actually believes the view he espouses, though I leave that possibility open.

4 You might wonder how someone in Leonard's condition could engage in the systematic behavior required for conditioning. But there are several ways this could happen. He could have been trained to look in his pockets by someone else, or conditioned by his success in finding things in his pockets over time. Perhaps, despite his affliction, he could have recorded and followed instructions to condition himself.

5 The "spooky" music begins just as Teddy begins to imply that Sammy's story is really Leonard's, and dramatically cuts out when he claims Sammy didn't have a wife, that Leonard's wife was diabetic.

6 There is also an ambiguous shot of Catherine blinking immediately after the incident, which might indicate her surviving the assault. Leonard's memory of Catherine waking next to him in bed (S, 0:20:33) seems to be a counterpart to this shot.

7 A nice dramatic irony, given that Teddy is about to step into those shoes, metaphorically speaking.

8 Nolan acknowledges his debt to Terrence Malick for these brief shots (Mottram 2002: 121–2). Compare the shots representing Private Witt's and Private Bell's memories of civilian life in *The Thin Red Line* (1998), particularly Bell's memories of his wife—who devastatingly betrays him. For more on these scenes, see Davies (2009).

9 Apart from the ambiguous extended flashback discussed below, the one smile Catherine gives quickly vanishes, as if she had been in a temporary reverie, and then come back to reality (S, 0:20:29).

10 In particular, there is one brief shot where Catherine seems to be despairing over some bills (S, 0:20:13), echoing part of Leonard's story about Sammy's wife: "The medical bills pile up, his wife calls the insurance company, and I get sent in" (6, 0:27:09).

11 Thanks to Berys Gaut for bringing this shot to my attention and compellingly arguing for its significance.

12 Throughout this essay, I ignore complications about the complex authorship of films, and talk of "the film-maker" as if there were a single controlling intelligence responsible for all *Memento*'s features. For an entrée into the debate over film authorship, see Gaut (1997) and Livingston (1997).

13 We might, of course, criticize particular kinds of interpretive projects on various grounds. For instance, in the last twenty years there has been much

criticism of psychoanalytic approaches to film, largely on the grounds that the Freudian theory underpinning such approaches is simply false. See, for example, many of the essays in Bordwell and Carroll (1996).

14 Perhaps. There are actually four different directorial commentary tracks accompanying scene 22/A on the Limited Edition DVD, one of which is selected randomly each time the disc is played. The different commentaries are inconsistent. Thus, it appears that Nolan is teasing the audience, rather than actually asserting these interpretations, and might be offering an implicit critique of actual intentionalism, by mocking the audience's desire for the artist's authoritative interpretation. (For a guide to accessing these tracks, go to http://world.std.com/~trystero/Memento_LE.html.)

15 The website is still available at www.otnemem.com/index.html.

16 I use the phrase "website material" advisedly. It is not the website *per se* that may or may not be part of *Memento*, but the material that is included both on the website and DVD editions of the film. The generic label for such material is "extras," but in this case that would come close to begging the question of whether the material is part of the work.

17 Thanks to Curtis Brown for making me think harder about these possibilities.

18 I ignore, throughout, the distinction between categorial and ontological intuitions. Ontological intuitions are even more basic than categorial ones. If, by inscribing some text on a flat surface, you intend to produce a literary work admitting of multiple, equally authentic copies, rather than a unique drawing, then your intention is ontological. If you further intend this text to be a poem, rather than a short story, your intention is categorial. Levinson does not discuss ontological intentions, but I presume he would defend the same sort of actual intentionalism about them as he does about categorial intentions.

19 Some real examples that come close are James Joyce's *Dubliners* (1914) (which I was once assigned to read in an undergraduate course on the twentieth-century novel), Sherwood Anderson's *Winesburg, Ohio* (1919), and Alice Munro's *Lives of Girls and Women* (1971).

20 Thanks to Berys Gaut and Paisley Livingston for some very helpful comments on early versions of this essay.

References

Bordwell, D. and Carroll, N. (eds) (1996) *Post-Theory: Reconstructing Film Studies*, Madison, WI: University of Wisconsin Press.

Carroll, N. (1998) *A Philosophy of Mass Art*, Oxford: Oxford University Press.

Currie, G. (1993) "The Long Goodbye: The Imaginary Language of Film," reprinted in N. Carroll and J. Choi (eds) (2006) *Philosophy of Film and Motion Pictures: An Anthology*, Malden, MA: Blackwell, pp. 91–9.

Davies, D. (2009) "Vision, Touch, and Embodiment in *The Thin Red Line*," in D. Davies (ed.) *The Thin Red Line*, London: Routledge, pp. 45–64.

Gaut, B. (1997) "Film Authorship and Collaboration," in R. Allen and M. Smith (eds) *Film Theory and Philosophy*, Oxford: Oxford University Press, pp. 149–72.

Kania, A. (2008) "Memento," in P. Livingston and C. Plantinga (eds) *The Routledge Companion to Philosophy and Film*, London: Routledge, pp. 650–60.

Levinson, J. (1990) "Intention and Interpretation in Literature," in *The Pleasures of Aesthetics*, Ithaca, NY: Cornell University Press, pp. 175–213.

—— (1996) "Film Music and Narrative Agency," in D. Bordwell and N. Carroll (eds) *Post-Theory: Reconstructing Film Studies*, Madison, WI: University of Wisconsin Press, pp. 248–82.

—— (2007) "Artful Intentions: Paisley Livingston, *Art and Intention: A Philosophical Study*," *Journal of Aesthetics and Art Criticism* 65: 299–305.

Livingston, P. (1997) "Cinematic Authorship," in R. Allen and M. Smith (eds) *Film Theory and Philosophy*, Oxford: Oxford University Press, pp. 132–48.

Mottram, J. (2002) *The Making of Memento*, London: Faber and Faber.

Shusterman, R. (1990) "Beneath Interpretation: Against Hermeneutic Holism," *Monist*, 73: 181–204.

Zhu, D. (2001) *Memento FAQ*, online. Available at: www.designpattern.org/wp/?page_id=13 (accessed 17 October 2008).

Further reading

Davies, S. (2006) "Authors' Intentions, Literary Interpretation, and Literary Value," *British Journal of Aesthetics* 46: 223–47. (Davies defends a contextualism he calls the "value-maximization theory," and argues that hypothetical intentionalism is ultimately equivalent to it.)

Gaut, B. (1993) "Interpreting the Arts: The Patchwork Theory," *Journal of Aesthetics and Art Criticism* 51: 597–609. (Gaut argues that any unified theory of interpretation must be inadequate, and that we should instead use a "patchwork" of different interpretive techniques.)

Levinson, J. (1984) "Hybrid Art Forms," *Journal of Aesthetic Education* 18: 5–13. (A discussion of artforms that combine pre-existing media.)

—— (2002) "Hypothetical Intentionalism: Statement, Objections, and Replies," in M. Krausz (ed.) *Is There a Single Right Interpretation?*, University Park, PA: Pennsylvania State University Press, pp. 309–18. (A clear statement and defense of hypothetical intentionalism.)

Livingston, P. (2005) *Art and Intention: A Philosophical Study*, Oxford: Clarendon Press. (An overview of the roles intention plays in art, including a defense of a modest actual intentionalism.)

Index

Scene index